Betting on China

Betting on China

Chinese Stocks, American Stock Markets, and the Wagers on a New Dynamic in Global Capitalism

Robert W. Koepp

WILEY

John Wiley & Sons Singapore Pte. Ltd.

Other Wiley Editorial Offices

John Wiley & Sons, 111 River Street, Hoboken, NJ 07030, USA
John Wiley & Sons, The Atrium, Southern Gate, Chichester, West Sussex, P019 8SQ, United Kingdom
John Wiley & Sons (Canada) Ltd., 5353 Dundas Street West, Suite 400, Toronto, Ontario, M9B 6HB, Canada
John Wiley & Sons Australia Ltd., 42 McDougall Street, Milton, Queensland 4064, Australia
Wiley-VCH, Boschstrasse 12, D-69469 Weinheim, Germany

ISBN 978−1−118−08714−5 (Cloth)
ISBN 978−1−118−08716−9 (ePDF)
ISBN 978−1−118−08715−2 (Mobi)
ISBN 978−1−118−08717−6 (ePub)

Typeset in 11.5/14pt, BemboAR Rmn by MPS Limited, Chennai, India.
Printed in Singapore by Markono Print Media Pte Ltd

10 9 8 7 6 5 4 3 2 1

To Michelle and Robbie

Contents

Acknowledgments

There are many people to thank for their support of my efforts to bring *Betting on China* to fruition. Sufficiently acknowledging all of them is not feasible, so I hope that all those who have been of help in so many different ways will not mind indulging me to limit recognition here to those who played the most direct roles in the book's realization.

First, I equally acknowledge (in alphabetical order) Ian Lewis, partner at Mayer Brown JSM in Beijing, and Jerry Wu, the founder and CEO of Draco Natural Products, a San Jose, California–headquartered, Shanghai-based manufacturer of pharmaceutical-grade herbal ingredients. Both Ian and Jerry were instrumental in providing deeply appreciated logistical support for the research and writing of the book. Ian also provided extremely useful comments on the manuscript. Additional facilitation of the research effort was provided by David Kuo, principal at Los Angeles, California–based boutique investment bank NewCap Partners, whose international focus is on the Greater China region.

I am especially grateful to Nick Melchior, senior publishing editor at Wiley, for taking an interest in the book and accepting—in ways that I know repeatedly tried his patience—my frequent changes with content and scheduling. Emilie Herman, senior editorial manager, and Judy Howarth, senior development editor, were instrumental in the formulation of the final product, as was Stefan Skeen, senior production editor.

The unflappable James Barth, senior finance fellow (and a former colleague and mentor) at the Milken Institute, proved once again to be an enlightening and intellectually challenging discussion partner as we reviewed core ideas in the book via long-distance communications and during his occasional visits to Beijing. Jim also provided thoughtful commentary on the written contents that were especially helpful in adding perspective to my thinking on the subjects covered.

A longtime friend and business associate, John Carlson (whose interest in and dedication to constructive U.S.–China dialogue goes back to his days as assistant press secretary to President Richard Nixon and then deputy press secretary to President Gerald Ford), as usual showed himself to be unflinchingly morally supportive of an undertaking like *Betting on China*. John is literally a gung ho ex–U.S. military Special Forces officer who, while always the consummate gentleman, likewise never hesitated to call me out when he thought my thinking ran astray.

Carrie Wang, the epitome of a multitasking, transcontinental Chinese media entrepreneur who has more affiliations than can be easily mentioned here, was phenomenal in her willingness to listen to my evolving thoughts for the book and to encourage me through to its finalization. She furthermore offered invaluable feedback from her experiences as a been-there, done-that former officer of a NASDAQ-listed Chinese corporation.

Zach Fanders, a young and rising member of Beijing's expatriate financial community, proved to be a great person for exchanging ideas with in between weight-lifting sets at the health club where we both are members. Zach also helpfully fed back his written thoughts on the disjointed early version of the manuscript I sent him, a body of written work whose condition was about as out of shape as my own body became while I sacrificed gym time for trips to restaurants, cafes, and bars to complete the book.

Special thanks also to Tom DiVivo, managing director and group manager for Asia/Pacific Depositary Receipts in New York at BNY Mellon. Tom was great for suggestions of parts of the manuscript and off-the-record sharing or experiences and perceptions of the inner workings of the American Depository Receipts system.

A great number of others among colleagues, clients, associates, and friends have also contributed less directly to the development of this work. To avoid possible offense at unintentionally leaving anyone out or—considering some of the book's controversial subject matter—unintentionally leaving anyone in, I do not mention them here by name but thank them nonetheless.

It should go without saying that despite the wonderful, collective support I have received in taking *Betting on China* from concept to completion, the responsibility for any errors or omissions in the manuscript is mine alone.

Finally, I want to acknowledge my children, Michelle and Robbie, to whom this book is dedicated. Their importance to me is beyond description. They have been constant sources of inspiration. Mentioning as much and dedicating this book to them are but small tokens of my gratitude for them simply being just who they are.

Preface

Getting It and Betting It

China is easily the least understood of the world's major economies. Given the mystery that perpetually enshrouded the China of older times to the world outside, this is hardly a new phenomenon. But it is one whose implications grow increasingly consequential with each day that the People's Republic of China (PRC) rises in importance as a modern economic superpower.

Not "getting" China did not matter much for the people beyond its borders during the nearly two millennia in which trade with the lands of the Celestial Empire was conducted by caravans lumbering along the trails of the Silk Road; or when newly industrialized foreign powers could unilaterally dictate terms of commerce with the weakened Chinese states of the late Qing dynasty and warlord-dominated Republican era. After a fiercely independent Communist-led "New China" of the current PRC arose in 1949, its governing ideology pushed the country to recuse itself from international commerce until market-oriented reforms began three decades later.

Since China's pivotal reopening to the outside in 1979, both it and the world beyond have been dramatically changing. China has gone from avoiding foreign trade to becoming the epicenter of a worldwide, integrated manufacturing system. Along the way, it has emerged as a leader in key global industries such as mobile telecommunications, automobiles, and alternative energy. China's demand today for and supply of commodities and natural resources moves world prices. An apocryphal story that used to circulate in the World Beyond China (WBC) not so long ago related that *if all the people in China jumped at the same time, the Earth would be knocked off its axis.* Turned out that the teeming masses of China never needed to jump; they just needed to start producing and consuming enough to genuinely reorient the world in its material economic existence.

In response to this reorientation of our planet's economy, companies from the WBC have beat a path to China to invest their euros, dollars, and yen in order to hitch a ride on what appears to be the unstoppable steamrollering of China's economic juggernaut. People from every corner of the WBC flock to Chinese cities for study or employment, or to strike deals in order to maintain competitiveness in a global market system that effectively revolves around the machinations of a country whose modern existence bears truth to the Chinese name for China: "*zhong guo*" (中国), which literally means "the central nation." This state of affairs has stood out in stark relief throughout the dismal months and years during and after the global financial crisis of 2008–2009, when China's unhesitating economic expansion hummed along as the only major engine for worldwide economic growth.

The WBC has been betting on China, and betting *big*. Because of the sheer size of these wagers—the money, resources, talent, planning, and ambitions at stake—"getting" China in a way that is both meaningful and practically useful has become more important than ever before.

As with any hot topic, the world (both inside and outside of the PRC) lacks not for experts, regardless of whether they can legitimately claim true insights or expertise. Complicating matters, China engenders a plethora of extremes in opposing viewpoints about its true nature, unlike almost any other topic of mainstream business and economics discourse. China bulls see solid fundamentals that point to long-term growth, offering attractive returns for those who buy into the China story. Bears see a country riddled by contradictions and unsustainable drivers that point to a hard landing or a collapse—some predict another version of the implosion that occurred with Japan just as that nation's hard-charging economy seemed poised to take over the world in the early 1990s.

A Prism that Cuts Through the Fog

This book differs from others by suggesting a new prism through which to view key aspects of China's rise, present-day workings, and future prospects in the global economy: stocks. More specifically, it focuses on the stocks of China-operating companies that are listed on the major U.S. stock markets of NASDAQ and the New York Stock Exchange (NYSE).

The reasons for this approach are many. Fundamentally, from an analytical point of view, an enormous advantage lies in the way that detailed and vetted information about Chinese enterprises and the industries in which they operate is available from firms that are listed on U.S. stock markets.

This is partially because of regulatory requirements and stock exchange listing rules concerning timely and robust disclosure. There are market-based inducements for transparency as well. Prevailing financial market sentiment, "the Street," tends to reward with higher valuations those companies that practice high standards of corporate governance. Companies that work to communicate to the public about what management is up to generally benefit from this market tendency. As with any U.S. equity market–traded enterprise, there are multiple incentives for Chinese companies publicly listed in the United States to tell investors and the world at large about what is really happening with these enterprises and, by extension, with China's economy.

The mechanism of interactivity that occurs with Chinese companies trading on U.S. stock exchanges offers diverse benefits. It strengthens Chinese enterprises by providing them with capital investment while exposing them to the discipline and rigors of the U.S. financial system, by far the largest and most liquid in the world. It also allows the WBC to better understand what is actually happening within China and avail itself of opportunities to take stakes in the country's economic growth. Beyond the advantages offered to these market participants, in an intricately interlaced planetary economy whose efficiency depends heavily on robust flows of both information and capital (and in that order), the means by which shares in Chinese enterprises and international information consumers and investors can meet up in U.S. equity markets contributes to the functioning and development of the global market system.

The world's ongoing bet on China's reemergence—following a relatively brief period of comparative decline in that colossal nation's material development during the nineteenth and twentieth centuries after China economically flourished for millennia—as a major world economy finds a unique and influential transaction point in the American equity marketplace.

An Emerging Dynamic

The bet on China that is occurring via the platform of U.S. stock markets, although a fairly recent phenomenon, has been identifiably impacting China and the world beyond in numerous ways:

- The attractive forces of the dynamic are bringing together the world's two largest economies in a far more balanced and economically productive manner than occurs in other dimensions of the financial relationship between China and the United States.
- The watershed event that effectively opened the door for Chinese listings in the United States, the 1997 initial public offering (IPO) on the NYSE of shares in China Mobile (NYSE:CHL), not only proved to China and the outside world what was possible with such stock market listings but also helped underwrite the transformation of the worldwide mobile communications industry.
- Hundreds of China-operating companies have followed since China Mobile's watershed IPO in 1997 to issue shares in U.S. stock markets. Across a range of industries, they have broadened and deepened the PRC economy's exposure to the benefits and demands of what U.S. stock market listings entail.

- The rate of Chinese IPOs in the United States took off when the WBC plunged into a devastating worldwide financial crisis. Just as with China's unrelenting macroeconomic growth during that period, its IPO activity crucially helped stabilize and stimulate global markets as well.
- The deeper and longer-lasting effects of Chinese listings in the United States relate to the increased transparency and accountability that is being brought to Chinese issuers. This facilitates the get-bet transactions of the WBC while it similarly strengthens the Chinese issuers' knowledge of and responsiveness to global market forces.

The latter point is especially critical in what is already known about the dynamism of these listings. The process of building transparency was a lengthy and involved one at China Mobile and its affiliated companies—and not one lacking in extraordinary ironies.

As more and more private Chinese enterprises have gone to market, weaknesses in some of the methods for listing and auditing the firms have come to light. This has brought forward another set of challenges for foreign investors, Chinese issuers, and U.S. and Chinese regulators. The situation has also exposed how *getting things straight* amid all the *betting taking place* still remains a work in progress. Despite these limitations, U.S. stock market–driven information on Chinese companies remains an unrivaled source for publicly available, transparent, rapid, and insightful data about the workings of China Inc. The wagers riding on this new dynamic in global capitalism are not just about money, even if money remains the major motivating factor for placing the bets. The dynamism that propels all the betting is about *a new way of looking at China* and providing *a new way for China to look at the world*.

The Cards in This Deck

The main contents of this book fill seven chapters.

Chapter 1 explores the importance of the U.S.–China equity exchange dynamic from top-down and bottom-up perspectives. It considers the nature of shares that are traded and the companies and industries represented.

Chapter 2 starts off by examining the surge of Chinese IPOs on U.S. markets from 2009 to 2010 and what this has meant for Wall Street. It looks at the companies and industries that played a role in the wave of Chinese issuances along with the contradictory best and worst performances that these stock debuts turned in. It then reviews the sometimes-uneasy market détente that exists between two highly dissimilar economic systems, highlighting some of the populist antitrade tendencies that still resonate within China. Continuing on, it explains the new dimensions of the Sino-American financial relationship borne by Chinese stock issuances, putting the significance of this relationship in the context of selected economic theory and history.

Chapters 3 and 4 are full-length case studies. Chapter 3 discusses the story of China Mobile's birth, rise, and spillover effects as the first major Chinese IPO in America. This is not a typical company-centric case analysis; it is an examination of industrial upgrading and the creation of whole new product categories and marketplaces. If there is any one, singularly compelling illustration of the transcending benefits that come from the U.S.–China equity exchange mechanism, it is China Mobile.

Chapter 4 looks at the unwarranted fear and panic that had come to surround Chinese issuances in U.S. markets by mid-2011 from the example of NASDAQ-traded Spreadtrum Communications (NASDAQ:SPRD). China Mobile demonstrates the rewards that can accrue to those who go long on China; Spreadtrum demonstrates another aspect of this reality by portraying the perils to those who dare go short without good reason. While China Mobile is a major large-cap Chinese stock of around $200 billion in market capitalization, Spreadtrum is a small cap with a market value of approximately $1 billion. The differences in scale provide a degree of balance to the two chapters' side-by-side showcasing of company stories.

Chinese reverse mergers—a type of Chinese stock issuance that became so notorious as to be given its own CRM acronym by the U.S. Public Company Accounting Oversight Board (PCAOB)—are studied in detail throughout Chapter 5. CRMs represent a gray area of the China bet. Many legitimate China-operating enterprises have used the reverse merger process as a low-cost and efficient way to list on NASDAQ or the NYSE. Yet enough had ulterior motives, or suffered from exceedingly poor management, as to become sinkholes for investors. This chapter looks at a sampling of noteworthy CRMs from the role of accountants, short sellers, funds, regulators, commentators, and other market participants and influencers.

Chapter 6 peers into the stock market debacle known as Longtop Financial (PINK:LGFTY), the veritable *Titanic* of the U.S.–China public equity exchange relationship. It considers the extraordinarily negative consequences of Longtop's suspected fraudulent practices and subsequent NYSE delisting. The greatest damage caused by the company's failure has arisen from the way that U.S. and Chinese regulators have scrambled to control fallout without first securing good intergovernmental coordination. Chapter 7 concludes the book by considering the implications of these developments in historical context and how, if not properly managed, the regulatory impasse threatens the continuation of the Sino-American public equity dynamic as the world has come to know and benefit by it.

For those wanting to dig further into the details on those watershed frictions surrounding Chinese listings in the United States, an appendix presents the contents of the administrative subpoena issued by the U.S. Securities and Exchange Commission (SEC) to Longtop's auditor. The subpoena's contents reveal much about regulatory frustrations and differences of approach for how best to enforce transparency and accountability with Chinese listings in the United States.

As noted about the "getting" behind the "betting," the greater social value of U.S.-listed Chinese stocks is the information they convey about an extremely influential but poorly understood economic power. As information products, these stocks' perceived value can be highly subject to the forces of media writ large: company disclosures, government filings, analyst reports, journalist coverage, online blogs, and public sentiments generally.

With exactly this point in mind, while highly opinionated, an overriding objective of *Betting on China* is to present topics as objectively as possible, using transparent and easily verifiable information. Unless otherwise stated, all stock prices and related data have been sourced from information freely available at Google Finance (www.google.com/finance). Readers can just as easily reference other popular and readily accessible financial websites for such information, including Yahoo!

Finance (finance.yahoo.com) or China-based sites like 新浪财经 (Sina Finance, finance.sina.com.cn) and i美股 (imeigu.com, www .imeigu.com). References in the text that deserve citation or are in relation to statistics or other information not generally known are footnoted. Where appropriate, original verbal or textual commentary is extracted to give a fuller voice to varying points of view. This book is an attempt to present facts as much as possible in the original and let readers draw their own conclusions.

As with any iterative, evolving phenomenon, the characteristics of Chinese stocks traded on American stock markets are constantly in flux. This book analyzes the fundamentals of their market presence, the big-picture as well as ground-level factors that contribute to their performance, and the lessons that can be derived. However conditions inevitably change, readers will still be able to apply to the continuously unfolding scene of Chinese listings in America whatever insights they take away from this work.

Ultimately, *Betting on China* is about ways of perceiving the PRC of today and its impact on the world outside. The book's discussion focuses on interaction between China and the United States within the framework of financial economics, specifically equity finance. The implications of these topics stretch far, particularly into fields such as global management, corporate strategy, industrial development, international relations, corporate communications, and public policy. There is much here for anyone interested in China and global affairs, not just those who are active in the world of finance.

The Dealer's Hand

Here, the author lays his cards on the table.

First, to make unambiguously clear a statement of disclosure: During the research, writing, and until at least the initial period surrounding the planned publication of this book, the author did not directly own, nor harbor intention to directly own, any type of equity position—long, short, or otherwise—in the companies that this book discusses.

Betting on China and the sources it cites should by no stretch of the imagination possibly be construed as providing investment advice. *Caveat emptor* applies as much to interpretation of the contents of this book as it would to the purchase of any financial instrument.

As the author previously served as a research fellow at the Milken Institute—an economic think tank whose founder, Michael Milken, has in the past engaged in very high profile disagreements with the SEC and Department of Justice—this might conceivably be perceived as a source of bias by the author against these agencies of the U.S. government. This is certainly not the case. The positions of government organizations such as SEC and the PCAOB, which operates under the SEC's authority, are given ample voice throughout this book. Most of that voice is presented without accompanying criticism of any kind. What critiques the author does make of regulatory actions are offered as constructive remarks that take issue with tactics and strategies, not motives.

In any event, the last word in this book literally goes to the Commission, whose subpoena relating to Longtop Financial is extracted in full in the appendix. Readers—among whom it is hoped will include officials from the SEC and other branches of government in the United States and China—are free to, and in fact *encouraged to*, reach their own conclusions about the author's appraisal of the regulatory actions that are discussed. Those U.S.–China policy missteps and frictions, by the way, should always be thought of as part of the unfolding nature of the dynamic. They, by themselves, are neither "good" nor "bad" but, rather, integral dimensions of the iterative process of exchange. Hopefully, those involved with government policy making will resolve issues in the wake of Longtop and any other problems that might arise in the future so that market participants can stay active in generating gains of trade for themselves and society at large.

Under the auspices of the World Bank, the author has also served as a consultant to Chinese government agencies in the past and might well do so again in the future. This likewise could possibly be construed as biasing the author in another direction, namely, toward favoring Chinese government interests. This also is definitely not the case. The author raises questions about the actions of Chinese regulators, though these comments are more limited in scope. This is not done from a sense of pulling punches but, rather, is a reflection of the reality that in regard to regulating Chinese issuers in the United States, SEC and the PCAOB have (understandably) taken more prominent roles. The higher visibility and market impact of their positions offers up more substance for discussion.

In terms of current influences, after performing a variety of finance-related roles in China (including an earlier, long-since finished advisory position at a foreign fund that made a limited number of small investments into CRM companies), as of the submission of the book's manuscript, the author is consulting a number of NASDAQ- and NYSE-listed Chinese issuers on their investor relations strategies. Such past and present roles might also be viewed as causing the author to take sides with the position of Chinese issuers and insider investors at the expense of the perspective of outside investors. Again, the author does not see such background factors as affecting the balance and accuracy of the book's contents. Perusing the following pages, readers will have a chance to decide for themselves. In any event, none of the U.S.-listed Chinese companies that the author is advising (or has advised) are described in detail within the pages of *Betting on China*.

Summing Up

Concluding this preface with a bit of historical perspective to the frictions that have arisen between U.S. and Chinese officials who yield authority over the China–U.S. public equity pipeline, two Chinese idioms seem apt. The first comes from a classical treatise on Chinese economic and defense strategies, *Discourses on Salt and Iron*, a record and commentary on government policy debates that occurred in 81 BCE (making it a tad older than the contents that went into the New Testament of the Christian Bible). A tenet of governance proffered by *Discourses* is that public officials should "promote righteousness and deemphasize wealth" (*zhongyi qingcai*, 重义轻财).[1] The phrase articulates a traditional Confucian-influenced view that sees financial gain as less important than moral rectitude. Such age-old principles, while not always practiced, remain part of the ethical doctrine of contemporary

Chinese society. This kind of thinking coexists alongside the motto of China's present era: "to get rich is glorious" (*zhifu guangrong*, 致富光荣), a concept that seems similarly adopted by outsiders betting on China's economic growth prospects.

Finding ways to ensure that "getting rich" is still accomplished by "doing right" presents an ongoing challenge for China and its trading partners, one intensified by the interfacing of highly divergent national systems. Nevertheless, the challenge can be met. In the realm of public equity trading, mutually rewarding interactions require supportive markets matched by effective oversight. Winnings need to be justly earned—something that all responsible parties in authority can agree to. The author's greatest hope is that policy makers on both sides of the equation that administer the U.S.–China public exchange mechanism can resolve differences as they arise so that this vital relationship does not merely continue, but thrives.

Chapter 1

Wagers of the Dance

*China, America, and the Interplay
of Public Equity*

*Looking at China today, I see a whole lot of room for upward growth
in Chinese industry, including power and energy, tourism and media,
agriculture, infrastructure, high-tech . . . For those willing to put aside
old prejudices and put in the time, the future AT&Ts, Microsofts, and
General Motors are waiting to be discovered. No wonder I'm a bull
when it comes to this China shop.*

—Jim Rogers[1]

A Hierarchy of Financial Footwork

In the beginning years of the second decade of the twenty-first century, dynamic flows of financial supply and demand have been drawing
China and the United States ever more closely together. The dynamism of Sino-American financing has created an array of entwined
motions between the world's two economic superpowers—countries

1

basically on friendly terms with one another, yet often casting suspicious glances back and forth—as if they were engaged in a series of intricate dances.

Consider the capital flows driven by national account balances, for example. In this setting for financial interaction, we can imagine an opulent scene, as of a banquet held in a stately ballroom. Like someone who has eaten sparingly during a prolonged feast, China has resisted temptation to splurge its national wealth, leaving a large portion of its economic harvest untouched. The People's Republic of China (PRC) stashes away more than half of its rapidly expanding annual gross domestic product (GDP), which the International Monetary Fund estimates to amount to over $7 trillion in 2012. China's 54 percent gross national savings rate means that its "leftover" national wealth piles higher than that of any other major economy.[2]

Sitting next to the PRC at the head of this table of global economic powers is the United States. Although having more to consume from its plate of $16 trillion in GDP for 2012, the United States has been bingeing. This puts the country (with only about a 15 percent gross national savings rate) as the biggest feaster of its own national wealth among all the world's major economies.

To support its manufacturing industries, China, the lean consumer, wants Americans to keep buying Chinese made goods. Plus, it needs a reliable place to park some of that nearly $4 trillion in savings that it has accumulated through its thriftiness. So the PRC willingly, though not necessarily cheerfully, underwrites America's eating habit. The PRC held over $1 trillion in U.S. Treasury bills by 2011. By then, although the Chinese were tempering a once seemingly unshakable consent to finance American bingeing, the PRC remained the United States' biggest creditor. After variously partaking of their respective economic harvests, a still-lean China and an engorged America make for imbalanced, yet oddly well-matched, pair of dance partners. In a two-step waltz of national account balances, America spends and China lends. The two sides move around in this financial relationship in an awkward embrace.

In a different type of dance scene based on cross-border investment flows, the two commercial superpowers also move to the tunes of foreign direct investment (FDI). With FDI capital movements, money hits

its marks in smaller, brisk, tensely executed finance steps. The rhythm is more like a high-charged tango than a languid waltz. In the realm of FDI, American footwork leads, with $4.05 billion of investment poured into China by U.S. firms in 2010. China paces behind with $1.39 billion invested in the United States.[3] America murmurs happily to its partner that 85 percent of its companies operating in China are seeing increased profits—then sighs that things would be better still if what American businesses view as unnecessary Chinese bureaucratic procedures and unclear regulations were improved.[4]

The dance's direction reverses and China coos with satisfaction at its 81.4 percent growth rate for FDI placed into the United States but then frowns while relating the frustrations of Chinese companies in their efforts to invest in the United States. The travails of the Chinese telecommunications equipment giant Huawei—whose sales approximated renminbi (RMB) RMB200 billion ($30 billion) in 2010—is a ready-made example. Huawei, a private company but one that many in the United States suspect of having overly intimate connections to the Chinese central government, is the most prominent in a lengthening line of China-based firms whose investments into America have met with opposition from Washington. Contradicting the standard drumbeat from America for more open markets around the world, the U.S. Congress has prohibited a variety of Chinese FDI deals. In 2011 it opposed a purchase by Huawei that involved as little as $2 million to acquire technology from a bankrupt California company.[5]

So it goes. As with many aspects of Sino-American economic and financial relations, arguments for increased transparency and fairness can work both ways. While the two sides enjoy their FDI interactions (investment is only made, after all, with expectations of future gain), the partners remain on their guard. A Hollywood version of this FDI dance would be reminiscent of the tango scene in the action film *True Lies*. There characters played by actor and—in regard to Huawei, appropriately—the former governor of California, Arnold Schwarzenegger, and Asian actress Tia Carrere strut about with a physically charged zeal tempered by the thoughts that other side might well be up to something.

Further down in the hierarchy of capital flows are private equity (PE) transactions that pair the United States and China in ways that, though not always smooth, nevertheless move with less political tension and more fluidity than the other movements of monetary interaction. PE (traditional big-ticket, late-stage PE financing as well as PE's junior versions of earlier stage venture capital (VC) and angel financing) since the second half of the twentieth century has risen to prominence largely as an American-style financial art form. Within the current dance metaphor, PE would be analogous to contemporary pop music dance moves, as its deal-making mechanisms set and most closely follow investment fads. VC, the riskier form of PE that typically injects funding into a company at its seed and preliminary growth stages, has played a massively important role in the global economy. VC has fueled the rise of innovative, epoch-making firms such as Google, Apple, Intel, and Hewlett-Packard that are bred in industrial cluster locations like Silicon Valley and other hotbeds of creative enterprise.

American VC and PE funds led the charge of foreign risk investment into China beginning in the 1980s, after the PRC began its still-evolving economic transformation based on a policy of market "reform and openness" (*gaige kaifang*, 改革开放). Since the 2008 financial crisis, however, foreign dominance in VC and PE deals in China has slipped. By 2010, foreign VC/PE was participating in only about one-third of all Chinese deal flow. At the same time, foreign sources were investing over half of the total capital that went into those deals.[6] That means foreign private equity in China is facing less deal access combined with more concentrated deal exposure. The jury is still out on the results of this shift in investment positioning. In the meantime, the number of local Chinese PE and VC funds proliferates. Chinese investors are laying out less cash and exhibiting quicker moves that get them into more transactions. Owing to portfolios of less diversified, concentrated investments, American and other foreign private equity funders are potentially increasing their risks.

VC/PE typically garners greater attention because of the high stakes involved and the big payoffs—not to mention the more noble role that it plays in building up new companies and industries. Most private equity funders do not risk their money for sheer thrill and altruistic purposes, however. The *exit strategy* of a PE investment is the end game that drives deal valuation.

IPOs for Cash-out and Cash-in

By far the most preferred exit for private equity investors is to list the shares of an invested company on a public equity market. This is mainly accomplished through an IPO. For investors of a privately held company, an IPO generally provides the biggest bang for the buck. By and large, we can say that the ultimate goal of private equity *is* public equity.

An IPO transaction is also significant because it represents a hand-over of equity participation in a company. Private investors cash out their investment to allow public investors to cash in.

The markets in which company shares then trade, especially in the case of main board equity exchanges, can be especially stimulative to the economic health of a society. Public equity markets provide an imperfect yet comparatively open, transparent, efficient, information-rich, and fluid arena for conducting the push–pull interplay of capitalist finance. Stock markets represent ground level in a hierarchy where capital flows are channeled downward by governments (through national account balance transactions), corporations (through FDI), and funds (through PE and VC deals). Equity markets offer a venue where individual and institutional investors alike participate in financing and the sharing of its risks and wealth creation. They are a place where equity capital is effectively democratized.

Ever since the electronically operating NASDAQ stock market launched in 1971, leading stock exchanges around the world have been pressured to enhance technology and organizational structures to increase efficiencies, lower costs, and boost competitiveness. Modern, globally accessible stock markets have simultaneously responded to and spurred on the desire of stock issuers and stock investors to come together at those exchanges that best facilitate equity trades.

As home to the most highly capitalized equity markets in the world, U.S. stock market liquidity—principally found in the NYSE and NASDAQ markets—has been attracting waves of Chinese companies to list their shares. These listings are now largely conducted through sales of equity instruments known as American Depository Shares (ADSs). ADSs are stocks tradable in the United States because of the American Depository Receipt (ADR) system, which allows U.S.

intermediary banks to hold shares issued by foreign companies. A single ADS will equate to a specific number of originally issued shares in a foreign enterprise. For example, one ADS might represent four ordinary foreign company shares. Otherwise, an ADS functions in a U.S. market essentially in the same way as does typical equity stock of a domestic American company. Introduced back in 1927, ADR facilities are crucial building blocks in the global accessibility and competitiveness of U.S. stock markets.

The public equity of Chinese companies that makes its way across the trading arenas of U.S. exchanges brings together a cacophony of people and money, substance and hype, rationality and emotionality, and cultures possessing different world outlooks and business practices.

Although the venerable NYSE (traditionally known as the Big Board) still maintains a physical trading floor, the drama of stock transactions whether on the NYSE, NASDAQ, or other markets in reality plays out across electronic screens, not dissimilar in essence from the core work conducted to put out a streaming music video. Different company "performances" of various of industry "genres" are broadcast to an investment "audience" through a network of financial service providers who fulfill various roles in the performance's "production." "Critics"—ranging from professional analysts to commentators and bloggers of all stripes—rate corporate performances based on their opinions of how well management effectively "choreographs" a company's operations. The jagged peaks and valleys whose contours jerk back and forth across a company's stock chart trace out the intricately articulated dance steps arising from this massive interplay of forces.

Regardless of how one envisions the interplay of Chinese issued equity as it is publicly traded in America, the rhythm of these transactions moves in sync with the genuine heartbeat of U.S–China economic relations. In those trading venues that bustle with the exchanging of enterprise ownership, throb with profit-seeking animal spirits, and pulse with the instantaneous flow of electronic transactions, the commercial power of the two nations intermingles face-to-face in real time. Any investor from nearly every corner of the planet can take part, not just governments, corporations, or funds. In U.S. bourses, the financial energy of China and America comes together in ways like nowhere else. The dance of Chinese listings in American markets not only further entwines the world's two largest economies but also forms a new dynamo for the global economy.

A Ground-Level View

Stocks are a variable store of value. Their upward and downward price movements can inspire euphoria or panic. The profit motive being what it is, changes in a stock's price-based valuation are where investors and the public generally focus attention. Still, the passive, monetary worth stored in equity shares is relatively limited. The greater possibilities for enrichment reflected by those prices relate to information: the disclosures, explanations, analysis, and data-centric discourse that feeds into and off of stock movements and trends. When properly understood, the collective, interlacing forces that influence the issuance and pricing of corporate equities reveal more than just insights into individual companies. They are windows into the workings of industries, nations, and global interconnectedness.

The following chapters of this book delve into the specifics of a various Chinese listings in U.S. equity markets and their broader implications. Before taking that plunge, this chapter presents a base-level view for understanding some fundamental characteristics of Chinese issuances in American markets.

By the start of the fourth quarter (Q4) 2011, 272 Chinese issuers had ADR facilities for ADS trading on U.S. markets. Among those China-operating businesses that list equity shares on U.S. stock markets, the more substantial ones usually do so through a depository program. ADS issuances also frequently do not involve companies that list on U.S. markets through a process known as a *reverse merger* (RM) or *reverse takeover,* a kind of backdoor means of listing on an equity exchange that—though once common for smaller Chinese issuers— since 2010 has been heavily criticized because of the lack of oversight these reverse listings entail.

Accordingly, the universe of quoted ADSs on the over-the-counter (OTC), NYSE, and NASDAQ stock markets provide a fairly encompassing view of the presence of mainstream corporate economic actors from the PRC. Though this pool of stock issuers excludes many names because it does not count RM companies—only a minority of which, it deserves noting, have shown themselves to be fraudulent or negligently managed—the ADR pool is useful in providing a base-level, cross-section view of Chinese industries and companies active on U.S. securities markets.

Most of the global investment community's interest in Chinese stocks traded in the United States regards equity listed on the structured exchanges of the NASDAQ and NYSE. A far larger body of Chinese ADSs trade over the counter through middlemen dealers who as "market makers" literally constitute the OTC marketplace. Among domestic issuances, the OTC markets have a somewhat shady reputation as the home of thinly traded, low-value "penny stocks" of insufficient quality to list on an exchange. Leaving aside some of the misconceptions of that common interpretation, in the case of Chinese ADS issuances that trade on the OTC markets, the characterization can be extremely misleading. Many of China's leading corporations that trade on main board exchanges in mainland China and Hong Kong have issued ADSs via the OTC route. These high-quality "red chip" stocks share strange company with less reputable, and in some cases, discredited shares that lack the qualifications to list on an exchange or have been delisted because of past shortcomings.

Traded on the OTC Pink Sheets, for example, one can find ADSs issued by the Industrial & Commercial Bank of China (PINK:IDCBY), the PRC's most profitable bank and—since a $254 billion market capitalization generated by multiple share listings on the stock exchanges of Hong Kong and Shanghai in 2007—the biggest bank in the world based on total share valuation.[7] In the same general neighborhood of the OTC market, one could also find (at least for a short time before the OTC Markets Group discontinued quoting its share price) Longtop Financial, a financial software firm whose ADSs were delisted from the NYSE in August 2011. (The background and ramifications of the Longtop scandal, which earned the ignominy of being the single greatest instigating factor of frictions between U.S. and PRC officials concerning Chinese stock issuances in America, is explored in greater detail in Chapter 6.)

For a ground-level view of Chinese ADR issuers, a compilation based on data provided by BNY Mellon's *DR Directory* is shown in Table 1.1. The information is current as of October 1, 2011. (Updated data is available at www.adrbnymellon.com.)

Table 1.1 Chinese ADRs Trading on U.S. Markets (organized by industry)

No.	ADR Issuer	Symbol	Exchange	Industry	Effective Date
1	China Longyuan Power	CLPXY	OTC	Alternative Energy	Apr 22, 2010
2	China Ming Yang Wind Power	MY	NYSE	Alternative Energy	Oct 06, 2010
3	China Power International	CPWIY	OTC	Alternative Energy	Apr 02, 2009
4	China Shenhua Energy	CSUAY	OTC	Alternative Energy	Oct 20, 2008
5	China Sunergy	CSUN	NASDAQ	Alternative Energy	May 22, 2007
6	Daqo New Energy	DQ	NYSE	Alternative Energy	Oct 06, 2010
7	Gushan Environmental Energy	GU	NYSE	Alternative Energy	Dec 24, 2007
8	Hanwha SolarOne	HSOL	NASDAQ	Alternative Energy	Dec 26, 2006
9	JA Solar	JASO	NASDAQ	Alternative Energy	Feb 12, 2007
10	JinkoSolar	JKS	NYSE	Alternative Energy	May 19, 2010
11	LDK Solar	LDK	NYSE	Alternative Energy	Jun 06, 2007
12	ReneSola	SOL	NYSE	Alternative Energy	Feb 01, 2008
13	Suntech Power	STP	NYSE	Alternative Energy	Dec 13, 2005
14	Trina Solar	TSL	NYSE	Alternative Energy	Dec 21, 2006
15	Yingli Green Energy	YGE	NYSE	Alternative Energy	Jun 13, 2007
16	Bitauto	BITA	NYSE	Automobiles & Parts	Nov 17, 2010
17	Brilliance China Automotive	BCAUY	OTC	Automobiles & Parts	Feb 03, 2010
18	China Engine Group	CNYYY	OTC	Automobiles & Parts	Nov 12, 2010
19	China Zenix Auto International	ZX	NYSE	Automobiles & Parts	May 17, 2011
20	Dongfeng Motor Group	DNFGY	OTC	Automobiles & Parts	Jan 27, 2009
21	Double Coin	DCHLY	OTC	Automobiles & Parts	Oct 01, 1995
22	Lentuo International	LAS	NYSE	Automobiles & Parts	Dec 10, 2010
23	Weichai Power	WEICY	OTC	Automobiles & Parts	Jan 12, 2009
24	Agricultural Bank of China	ACGBY	OTC	Banks	Sep 17, 2010
25	Bank of China	BACHY	OTC	Banks	Oct 20, 2008

(continued)

Table 1.1 Continued

No.	ADR Issuer	Symbol	Exchange	Industry	Effective Date
26	China Construction Bank Corporation	CICHY	OTC	Banks	Oct 20, 2008
27	China Merchants Bank	CIHKY	OTC	Banks	Jul 07, 2010
28	China Minsheng Banking	CMAKY	OTC	Banks	Jan 21, 2010
29	Industrial and Commercial Bank of China	IDCBY	OTC	Banks	Oct 20, 2008
30	China Huiyuan Juice	CYUNY	OTC	Beverages	May 18, 2009
31	Tsingtao Brewery	TSGTY	OTC	Beverages	Nov 06, 2009
32	ChemSpec International	CPC	NYSE	Chemicals	Jun 23, 2009
33	China Bluechemical	CBLUY	OTC	Chemicals	Jan 12, 2009
34	Kingboard Chemical Holdings Limited	KBDCY	OTC	Chemicals	Nov 03, 2008
35	Shanghai Chlor-Alkali Chemical	SLLBY	OTC	Chemicals	Mar 01, 1994
36	Sinofert Holdings	SNFRY	OTC	Chemicals	Nov 05, 2008
37	Sinopec Shanghai Petrochemical	SHI	NYSE	Chemicals	Jul 23, 1993
38	Asia Cement China	AACEY	OTC	Construction & Materials	Jan 12, 2009
39	China International Marine Containers	CHAOY	OTC	Construction & Materials	Nov 03, 2008
40	China National Building	CBUMY	OTC	Construction & Materials	Oct 17, 2008
41	China National Materials Company	CASDY	OTC	Construction & Materials	Mar 06, 2009
42	China Overseas Land & Investment	CAOVY	OTC	Construction & Materials	Nov 03, 2008
43	China Railway	CRWOY	OTC	Construction & Materials	Nov 03, 2008
44	China Railway Construction	CWYCY	OTC	Construction & Materials	Nov 03, 2008
45	China State Construction	CCOHY	OTC	Construction & Materials	Apr 14, 2009
46	Hopewell Highway Infrastructure	HHILY	OTC	Construction & Materials	Apr 26, 2004
47	Metallurgical Corporation of China	MLLUY	OTC	Construction & Materials	Mar 03, 2010
48	Shenzhen Expressway	SHZNY	OTC	Construction & Materials	Jan 27, 2009
49	China Hydroelectric	CHC	NYSE	Electricity	Jan 28, 2010
50	Datang International Power Generation	DIPGY	OTC	Electricity	Sep 04, 2001

51	GOME Electrical Appliances	GMELY	OTC	Electricity	Nov 04, 2008
52	Huadian Power International	HPIFY	OTC	Electricity	Jan 12, 2009
53	Huaneng Power International	HNP	NYSE	Electricity	Aug 19, 2003
54	AAC Technologies Holdings Inc	AACAY	OTC	Electronics & Electric. Equip.	Nov 03, 2008
55	BCD Semiconductor Manufacturing	BCDS	NASDAQ	Electronics & Electric. Equip.	Feb 02, 2011
56	China Digital TV Holding	STV	NYSE	Electronics & Electric. Equip.	Oct 05, 2007
57	Bank of Communications	BCMXY	OTC	Financial Services	Apr 10, 2009
58	China Everbright	CEVIY	OTC	Financial Services	Nov 05, 2008
59	China Taiping Insurance Holdings Co	CTIHY	OTC	Financial Services	Nov 03, 2008
60	Hengan International Group	HEGIY	OTC	Financial Services	Nov 04, 2008
61	IFM Investments	CTC	NYSE	Financial Services	Jan 28, 2010
62	Noah Holdings	NOAH	NYSE	Financial Services	Nov 09, 2010
63	Shenzhen Investment	SZNTY	OTC	Financial Services	May 18, 2009
64	VODone	VODOY	OTC	Financial Services	Feb 16, 2010
65	Camelot Information Systems	CIS	NYSE	Fixed Line Telecomm	Jul 21, 2010
66	China Telecom	CHA	NYSE	Fixed Line Telecomm	Nov 06, 2002
67	Anhui Conch Cement Company	AHCHY	OTC	Food & Drug Retailers	Nov 03, 2008
68	China Nepstar Chain Drugstore	NPD	NYSE	Food & Drug Retailers	Nov 09, 2007
69	Fufeng	FFNGY	OTC	Food & Drug Retailers	Jun 19, 2009
70	Lianhua Supermarket Holdings	LHUAY	OTC	Food & Drug Retailers	Jan 12, 2009
71	Little Sheep Group	LSGLY	OTC	Food & Drug Retailers	Jan 12, 2009
72	Shandong Luoxin Pharmacy Stock	SLUXY	OTC	Food & Drug Retailers	Dec 09, 2009
73	Agria Corporation	GRO	NYSE	Food Producers	Nov 13, 2007
74	Ausnutria Dairy	ASNDY	OTC	Food Producers	Feb 23, 2010
75	Chaoda Modern Agriculture	CMGHY	OTC	Food Producers	Oct 15, 2008
76	China Agri-Industries Holding	CIDHY	OTC	Food Producers	Nov 03, 2008
77	China Foods	CHFHY	OTC	Food Producers	Oct 10, 2008

(*continued*)

Table 1.1 Continued

No.	ADR Issuer	Symbol	Exchange	Industry	Effective Date
78	China Mengniu Dairy	CIADY	OTC	Food Producers	Nov 03, 2008
79	China New Borun	BORN	NYSE	Food Producers	Jun 16, 2010
80	Country Style Cooking Restaurant	CCSC	NYSE	Food Producers	Oct 01, 2010
81	Le Gaga Holdings	GAGA	NASDAQ	Food Producers	Nov 03, 2010
82	Synear Food	SYNRY	OTC	Food Producers	Oct 10, 2008
83	Tingyi (Cayman Islands)	TCYMY	OTC	Food Producers	Jan 23, 2006
84	Uni-President China	UPCHY	OTC	Food Producers	Oct 14, 2008
85	Want Want China	WWNTY	OTC	Food Producers	Apr 28, 2009
86	Duoyuan Global Water	DGW	NYSE	Gas, Water & Multiutility	Jun 24, 2009
87	Sound Global	SGXXY	OTC	Gas, Water & Multiutility	May 05, 2011
88	Tianjin Capital Environmental Protection	TCEPY	OTC	Gas, Water & Multiutility	Dec 23, 2003
89	Yingde Gases	YINGY	OTC	Gas, Water & Multiutility	Sep 17, 2010
90	China XLX Fertiliser	CXLFY	OTC	General Industrials	Feb 24, 2010
91	Ossen Innovation	OSN	NASDAQ	General Industrials	Feb 10, 2011
92	Sinotruk (Hong Kong)	SHKLY	OTC	General Industrials	Nov 03, 2008
93	Weiqiao Textile	WQTEY	OTC	General Industrials	Jan 27, 2009
94	ZhongDe Waste Technology	ZHTYY	OTC	General Industrials	Aug 26, 2010
95	Acorn	ATV	NYSE	General Retailers	May 08, 2007
96	Alibaba.com	ALBIY	OTC	General Retailers	Apr 28, 2010
97	Anta Sports Products	ANPDY	OTC	General Retailers	Nov 03, 2008
98	ATA Inc	ATAI	NASDAQ	General Retailers	Jan 28, 2008
99	Belle International	BELLY	OTC	General Retailers	Oct 14, 2008
100	Bosideng International	BSDGY	OTC	General Retailers	May 18, 2009
101	C C Land	CCLHY	OTC	General Retailers	May 18, 2009
102	China Dongxiang	CDGXY	OTC	General Retailers	Jul 31, 2009

#	Company	Ticker	Exchange	Sector	Date
103	China Taisan Technology Group	CTTGY	OTC	General Retailers	Dec 29, 2009
104	China Xiniya Fashion	XNY	NYSE	General Retailers	Nov 29, 2010
105	ChinaEdu	CEDU	NASDAQ	General Retailers	Dec 14, 2007
106	Daphne International	DPNEY	OTC	General Retailers	Oct 14, 2008
107	E-Commerce China Dangdang	DANG	NYSE	General Retailers	Dec 13, 2010
108	Golden Eagle	GDNEY	OTC	General Retailers	Oct 14, 2008
109	Huabao International Holdings Limit	HUIHY	OTC	General Retailers	Nov 03, 2008
110	Mecox Lane	MCOX	NASDAQ	General Retailers	Oct 25, 2010
111	New Oriental Education & Technology	EDU	NYSE	General Retailers	Sep 07, 2006
112	Parkson Retail	PKSGY	OTC	General Retailers	Apr 02, 2009
113	Stella International	SLNLY	OTC	General Retailers	Oct 14, 2008
114	Wumart Stores	WUMSY	OTC	General Retailers	Jul 10, 2009
115	China Kanghui	KH	NYSE	Healthcare Equip. & Serv.	Aug 16, 2010
116	China Medical Technologies	CMED	NASDAQ	Healthcare Equip. & Serv.	Aug 15, 2005
117	Concord Medical Services	CCM	NYSE	Healthcare Equip. & Serv.	Dec 16, 2009
118	Golden Meditech	GMDTY	OTC	Healthcare Equip. & Serv.	Jan 12, 2009
119	Mindray Medical International	MR	NYSE	Healthcare Equip. & Serv.	Sep 29, 2006
120	Haier Electronics	HRELY	OTC	House Goods & Home Const.	Oct 10, 2008
121	Aluminum Corporation of China	ACH	NYSE	Industrial Metals & Mining	Dec 05, 2001
122	Angang Steel	ANGGY	OTC	Industrial Metals & Mining	Dec 06, 2002
123	China Rongsheng Heavy Industries	CGVYY	OTC	Industrial Engineering	May 09, 2011
124	Guangzhou Shipyard International	GSHIY	OTC	Industrial Engineering	Jul 13, 1995
125	Lonking Holdings	LKHLY	OTC	Industrial Engineering	Apr 29, 2009
126	Shanghai Electric	SIELY	OTC	Industrial Engineering	Jan 13, 2009
127	Shanghai Erfangji	SHFGY	OTC	Industrial Engineering	Dec 01, 1993
128	Anhui Expressway	AUHEY	OTC	Industrial Transportation	Jun 11, 2009
129	China Communications Construction	CCCGY	OTC	Industrial Transportation	Nov 10, 2008

(continued)

Table 1.1 Continued

No.	ADR Issuer	Symbol	Exchange	Industry	Effective Date
130	China COSCO Holdings	CICOY	OTC	Industrial Transportation	Oct 10, 2008
131	China High-Speed Transmission Equip	CHSTY	OTC	Industrial Transportation	Nov 03, 2008
132	China Merchants Holdings	CMHHY	OTC	Industrial Transportation	Oct 30, 2008
133	China Shipping Development	CSDXY	OTC	Industrial Transportation	Mar 01, 1996
134	Cosco Pacific	CSPKY	OTC	Industrial Transportation	Oct 20, 2008
135	CSR Corporation Limited	CSRGY	OTC	Industrial Transportation	Jan 12, 2009
136	Jiangsu Expressway	JEXYY	OTC	Industrial Transportation	Dec 23, 2002
137	Tianjin Port Development	TJIPY	OTC	Industrial Transportation	Jan 12, 2009
138	Zhejiang Expressway	ZHEXY	OTC	Industrial Transportation	Feb 14, 2002
139	Giant Interactive Group	GA	NYSE	Leisure Goods	Nov 01, 2007
140	Noah Education	NED	NYSE	Leisure Goods	Oct 24, 2007
141	Perfect World	PWRD	NASDAQ	Leisure Goods	Jul 30, 2007
142	Shanda Interactive Entertainment	SNDA	NASDAQ	Leisure Goods	May 17, 2004
143	Shanghai Jin Jiang Intl Hotel	SJJIY	OTC	Leisure Goods	Dec 15, 2006
144	The9	NCTY	NASDAQ	Leisure Goods	Dec 14, 2004
145	Zuoan Fashion	ZA	NYSE	Leisure Goods	Feb 18, 2011
146	China Life Insurance	LFC	NYSE	Life Insurance	Jan 04, 2010
147	Ping An Insurance Company of China	PNGAY	OTC	Life Insurance	Mar 28, 2005
148	Airmedia	AMCN	NASDAQ	Media	Nov 13, 2007
149	Bona Film Group	BONA	NASDAQ	Media	Dec 08, 2010
150	Charm Communications Inc.	CHRM	NASDAQ	Media	May 05, 2010
151	China Mass Media	CMM	NYSE	Media	Aug 07, 2008
152	Focus Media	FMCN	NASDAQ	Media	Jul 18, 2005
153	Phoenix New Media	FENG	NYSE	Media	May 11, 2011
154	Shanda Games	GAME	NASDAQ	Media	Sep 25, 2009

155	Tudou	TUDO	NASDAQ	Media	Aug 22, 2011
156	VisionChina Media	VISN	NASDAQ	Media	Dec 11, 2007
157	Xinhua Sports & Entertainment	XSELY	OTC	Media	Mar 14, 2007
158	China Coal Energy	CCOZY	OTC	Mining	Apr 02, 2009
159	China Molybdenum	CMCLY	OTC	Mining	Oct 21, 2008
160	China Resources Power	CRPJY	OTC	Mining	Nov 03, 2008
161	China Vanadium Titano–Magnetite	CVDMY	OTC	Mining	Feb 25, 2010
162	CITIC Resources Holdings	CTJHY	OTC	Mining	Nov 03, 2008
163	Hidili Industry International Devel	HIIDY	OTC	Mining	Nov 04, 2008
164	Jiangxi Copper	JIXAY	OTC	Mining	Oct 07, 2003
165	Mongolia Energy	MOAEY	OTC	Mining	Nov 12, 2008
166	Xinjiang Xinxin Mining	XJXNY	OTC	Mining	Aug 02, 2011
167	Yanzhou Coal Mining	YZC	NYSE	Mining	Mar 27, 1998
168	Zijin Mining Group	ZIJMY	OTC	Mining	Apr 10, 2009
169	China Mobile	CHL	NYSE	Mobile Telecomm	Oct 16, 1997
170	China Unicom (Hong Kong) Limited	CHU	NYSE	Mobile Telecomm	Jun 16, 2000
171	Kingtone Wirelessinfo Solution	KONE	NASDAQ	Mobile Telecomm	May 19, 2010
172	KongZhong	KONG	NASDAQ	Mobile Telecomm	Jul 14, 2004
173	Ku6 Media Co., Ltd	KUTV	NASDAQ	Mobile Telecomm	Feb 04, 2005
174	Linktone	LTON	NASDAQ	Mobile Telecomm	Apr 26, 2007
175	Rda Microelectronics	RDA	NASDAQ	Mobile Telecomm	Nov 09, 2010
176	Sinotel Technologies	SNOXY	OTC	Mobile Telecomm	Sep 14, 2009
177	Sky Mobi	MOBI	NASDAQ	Mobile Telecomm	Dec 15, 2010
178	Z–Obee	ZOBEY	OTC	Mobile Telecomm	Apr 16, 2010
179	ZTE	ZTCOY	OTC	Mobile Telecomm	Oct 10, 2008
180	CNInsure	CISG	NASDAQ	Nonlife Insurance	Oct 30, 2007
181	PICC Property and Casualty	PPCCY	OTC	Nonlife Insurance	Oct 31, 2008

(continued)

Table 1.1 Continued

No.	ADR Issuer	Symbol	Exchange	Industry	Effective Date
182	China National Offshore Oil-CNOOC	CEO	NYSE	Oil & Gas Producers	Feb 20, 2001
183	China Petroleum & Chemical	SNP	NYSE	Oil & Gas Producers	Oct 18, 2000
184	ENN Energy Holdings Limited	XNGSY	OTC	Oil & Gas Producers	Nov 03, 2008
185	Jutal Offshore Oil Services	JUTOY	OTC	Oil & Gas Producers	Jan 12, 2009
186	Kunlun Energy	KLYCY	OTC	Oil & Gas Producers	Nov 12, 2008
187	PetroChina	PTR	NYSE	Oil & Gas Producers	Mar 30, 2000
188	Anton Oilfield Services	ATONY	OTC	Oil Equip., Serv. & Dist.	Jan 12, 2009
189	China Oilfield Services	CHOLY	OTC	Oil Equip., Serv. & Dist.	Mar 26, 2004
190	Shandong Molong Petroleum Machinery	SHANY	OTC	Oil Equip., Serv. & Dist.	Jan 12, 2009
191	SinoTech Energy	CTE	NASDAQ	Oil Equip., Serv. & Dist.	Nov 08, 2010
192	Sinotrans Shipping Ltd	SSLYY	OTC	Oil Equip., Serv. & Dist.	Nov 04, 2008
193	WSP Holdings	WH	NYSE	Oil Equip., Serv. & Dist.	Dec 11, 2007
194	Li Ning	LNNGY	OTC	Personal Goods	Nov 05, 2008
195	Peak Sport Products	PSPRY	OTC	Personal Goods	Mar 04, 2010
196	3SBIO	SSRX	NASDAQ	Pharmaceuticals & Biotech	Feb 07, 2007
197	China Nuokang Bio-Pharmaceutical	NKBP	NASDAQ	Pharmaceuticals & Biotech	Dec 09, 2009
198	China Shineway Pharmaceutical	CSWYY	OTC	Pharmaceuticals & Biotech	Oct 10, 2008
199	Far East Pharmaceutical Technology	FEPTY	OTC	Pharmaceuticals & Biotech	Mar 02, 2004
200	Fosun International	FOSUY	OTC	Pharmaceuticals & Biotech	Nov 03, 2008
201	Guangzhou Pharmaceutical	GZPHY	OTC	Pharmaceuticals & Biotech	Jun 21, 2002
202	ShangPharma	SHP	NYSE	Pharmaceuticals & Biotech	Oct 18, 2010
203	Simcere Pharmaceutical	SCR	NYSE	Pharmaceuticals & Biotech	Apr 25, 2007
204	WuXi Pharmatech	WX	NYSE	Pharmaceuticals & Biotech	Aug 14, 2007
205	Agile Property	AGPYY	OTC	Real Estate Invest. & Serv.	Nov 04, 2008
206	China Real Estate Information	CRIC	NASDAQ	Real Estate Invest. & Serv.	Oct 21, 2009

207	China Resources Land	CRBJY	OTC	Real Estate Invest. & Serv.	Jan 27, 2009
208	China Vanke	CVKEY	OTC	Real Estate Invest. & Serv.	Nov 03, 2008
209	Country Garden	CTRYY	OTC	Real Estate Invest. & Serv.	May 18, 2009
210	E-House (China)	EJ	NYSE	Real Estate Invest. & Serv.	Aug 13, 2007
211	Guangdong Investment	GGDVY	OTC	Real Estate Invest. & Serv.	Nov 05, 2008
212	Guangzhou R&F Properties	GZUHY	OTC	Real Estate Invest. & Serv.	Nov 03, 2008
213	Shanghai Forte Land	SGFTY	OTC	Real Estate Invest. & Serv.	Jan 27, 2009
214	Shanghai Jinqiao Processing Development	SJQIY	OTC	Real Estate Invest. & Serv.	Jul 01, 1996
215	Shanghai Lujiazui Finance & Trade Zone Development	SLUJY	OTC	Real Estate Invest. & Serv.	Jul 01, 1996
216	Shanghai Waigaoqiao Free Trade Zone	SGOTY	OTC	Real Estate Invest. & Serv.	May 01, 1995
217	Shenzhen S.E.Z. Real Estate and Properties	SZPRY	OTC	Real Estate Invest. & Serv.	Aug 01, 1994
218	Sino-Ocean Land	SIOLY	OTC	Real Estate Invest. & Serv.	Apr 02, 2009
219	SouFun Holdings	SFUN	NYSE	Real Estate Invest. & Serv.	Sep 22, 2010
220	Syswin	SYSW	NYSE	Real Estate Invest. & Serv.	Nov 23, 2010
221	Xinyuan Real Estate	XIN	NYSE	Real Estate Invest. & Serv.	Dec 17, 2007
222	Yuexiu Property Company Limited	GUAZY	OTC	Real Estate Invest. & Serv.	Dec 09, 1999
223	Baidu	BIDU	NASDAQ	Software & Computer Serv.	Aug 04, 2005
224	Beijing Beida Jade Bird Universal Sci-Tech	BJBJY	OTC	Software & Computer Serv.	Dec 20, 2005
225	Changyou.com	CYOU	NASDAQ	Software & Computer Serv.	Apr 07, 2009
226	China Finance Online	JRJC	NASDAQ	Software & Computer Serv.	Oct 20, 2004
227	HiSoft Technology International	HSFT	NASDAQ	Software & Computer Serv.	Jun 29, 2010
228	Kingdee International Software Group	KGDEY	OTC	Software & Computer Serv.	Nov 10, 2008
229	Longtop Financial Technologies	LGFTY	OTC	Software & Computer Serv.	Oct 24, 2007
230	Netease.com	NTES	NASDAQ	Software & Computer Serv.	Jun 29, 2000
231	Ninetowns Internet Technology	NINE	NASDAQ	Software & Computer Serv.	Dec 08, 2004
232	Qihoo 360 Technology	QIHU	NYSE	Software & Computer Serv.	Apr 04, 2011

(continued)

Table 1.1 Continued

No.	ADR Issuer	Symbol	Exchange	Industry	Effective Date
233	Tencent Holdings Limited	TCEHY	OTC	Software & Computer Serv.	Oct 20, 2008
234	TravelSky Technology	TSYHY	OTC	Software & Computer Serv.	Dec 27, 2002
235	VanceInfo Technologies	VIT	NYSE	Software & Computer Serv.	Dec 17, 2007
236	Youku.com	YOKU	NYSE	Software & Computer Serv.	Dec 13, 2010
237	21Vianet	VNET	NASDAQ	Support Services	Apr 27, 2011
238	51job	JOBS	NASDAQ	Support Services	Oct 04, 2004
239	Ajisen	AJSCY	OTC	Support Services	Oct 21, 2008
240	Ambow	AMBO	NYSE	Support Services	Aug 10, 2010
241	AutoNavi	AMAP	NASDAQ	Support Services	Jun 30, 2010
242	China Distance Education	DL	NYSE	Support Services	Aug 04, 2008
243	China Shipping Container Lines	CITAY	OTC	Support Services	Jun 25, 2008
244	ChinaCache	CCIH	NASDAQ	Support Services	Oct 06, 2010
245	Global Education & Technology	GEDU	NASDAQ	Support Services	Oct 14, 2010
246	iSoftStone	ISS	NYSE	Support Services	Dec 13, 2010
247	Jiayuan.com	DATE	NASDAQ	Support Services	May 16, 2011
248	NetQin Mobile	NQ	NYSE	Support Services	May 04, 2011
249	NWS	NWSZY	OTC	Support Services	Oct 09, 2009
250	Renren	RENN	NYSE	Support Services	May 09, 2011
251	TAL Education	XRS	NYSE	Support Services	Oct 25, 2010
252	Taomee Holdings	TAOM	NYSE	Support Services	Jun 08, 2011

253	Xueda Education	XUE	NYSE	Support Services	Nov 05, 2010
254	Actions Semiconductor	ACTS	NASDAQ	Tech. Hardware & Equip.	Dec 05, 2005
255	BYD	BYDDY	OTC	Tech. Hardware & Equip.	Oct 10, 2008
256	BYD Electronic	N/A	OTC	Tech. Hardware & Equip.	Oct 21, 2008
257	China GrenTech	GRRF	NASDAQ	Tech. Hardware & Equip.	Mar 29, 2006
258	China Techfaith Wireless Communication	CNTF	NASDAQ	Tech. Hardware & Equip.	May 05, 2005
259	China Wireless Technologies	CHWTY	OTC	Tech. Hardware & Equip.	Sep 12, 2006
260	Foxconn International Holdings	FXCNY	OTC	Tech. Hardware & Equip.	Oct 20, 2008
261	Spreadtrum Communications	SPRD	NASDAQ	Tech. Hardware & Equip.	Jul 02, 2007
262	Vimicro International	VIMC	NASDAQ	Tech. Hardware & Equip.	Nov 18, 2005
263	7 Days Group	SVN	NYSE	Travel & Leisure	Nov 20, 2009
264	Air China	AIRYY	OTC	Travel & Leisure	Jun 30, 2006
265	Beijing Capital International Airport	BJCHY	OTC	Travel & Leisure	Nov 03, 2008
266	China Eastern Airlines	CEA	NYSE	Travel & Leisure	Jan 30, 1997
267	China Lodging	HTHT	NASDAQ	Travel & Leisure	Mar 31, 2010
268	China Southern Airlines	ZNH	NYSE	Travel & Leisure	Jul 24, 1997
269	CTrip.com International	CTRP	NASDAQ	Travel & Leisure	Dec 12, 2003
270	eLong	LONG	NASDAQ	Travel & Leisure	Nov 02, 2004
271	Guangshen Railway	GSH	NYSE	Travel & Leisure	May 16, 1996
272	Home Inns & Hotels Management	HMIN	NASDAQ	Travel & Leisure	Oct 31, 2006

Source: BNY Mellon

The list as presented here is organized according to industrial groupings. This highlights the range of Chinese economic sectors with representative companies offering stocks on U.S. markets. Industrial classifications have been kept per BNY Mellon's original categorizations. In certain cases, however, as sometimes happens with generalized labeling, classifications can be so generic that they ignore more functionally accurate industrial segmentations. Classifications can also split up what are in fact related companies among different groupings. For example, the cohort of China's closely followed private education companies as of 2011—Ambow (NYSE:AMBO), China Distance Education (NYSE:DL), ChinaEdu (NASDAQ:CEDU), Global Education (NASDAQ:GEDU), TAL Education (NYSE:XRS), New Oriental Education (NYSE:EDU), Noah Education (NYSE:NED), and Xueda Education (NYSE:XUE)—can be found in the *DR Directory* under "General Retailers," "Leisure Goods," and "Support Services."

Acknowledging such limitations, the directory listing still provides a useful window into the supply and demand for Chinese equities traded on U.S. markets.

- The top three categories of ADR issuers are "General Retailers" (with 20 companies), followed by "Real Estate Investment & Services" (18), and "Support Services" (17).
- In the middle bracket, seven categories contain between 10 and 15 Chinese ADR issuers: "Alternative Energy" (15), "Software & Computer Services" (14), "Food Producers" (13), "Construction & Materials" (11), "Industrial Transportation" (11), "Mining" (11), "Mobile Telecommunications" (11), Media (10), and "Travel & Leisure" (10).
- Fourteen categories contain less than ten but at least five ADR companies: "Pharmaceuticals & Biotechnology" (9), "Technical Hardware & Equipment" (9), "Automobiles & Parts" (8), "Financial Services" (8), "Leisure Goods" (7), "Banks" (6), "Chemicals" (6), "Food & Drug Retailers" (6), "Oil & Gas Producers" (6), "Oil Equipment, Services & Distribution" (6), "Electricity" (5), "General Industrials" (5), "Healthcare Equipment & Services" (5), and "Industrial Engineering" (5).

Companies from the top-three bracket all relate to tertiary, service-based sectors of China's economy. Their disproportional representation among ADR issuers is not surprising. These sectors play critical roles in driving the high rates of urbanization and new consumption patterns that characterize what some consider the "economic miracle" of modern China. Most of the ADSs for "General Retailers" and "Real Estate Investment & Services" trade over the counter. That makes the "Support Services" category (where all but three AD Shares trade on the NYSE or NASDAQ) a better reflection of the U.S. stock market presence of Chinese issuers from the top bracket. Companies from this grouping include human resource recruiter 51job (NASDAQ:JOBS) and Internet social networking platform Renren (NYSE:RENN).

Within the middle bracket of ADRs there are issuers from basic industries—"Construction & Materials," "Industrial Transportation," and "Mining"—along with those from entertainment, consumer goods, and hospitality-related industries—"Food Producers," "Media," and "Travel & Leisure"—and those that operate in fields of advanced technology—"Alternative Energy," "Software & Computer Services," and "Mobile Telecommunications." It is in the latter categories of high technology where ambitions run especially high. China Mobile (NYSE:CHL) is the earliest of the advanced technology-related firms from China to list in the United States. Its global IPO in 1997 represented a singular watershed event that opened the floodgates for the wave of Chinese issuances abroad that finally began gaining wide-scale momentum ten years later. This book extensively details the myriad influences on China, the United States, and the world that emerged in the wake of China Mobile's listing in Chapter 3.

Within the lower and broadest bracket of 14 categories containing between five and nine ADR issuers, there is a wide mixture of constituent firms. Here a number of categories are in fact related and, if combined, would indicate a stronger U.S. securities market presence for certain Chinese economic sectors.

For example, if "Banks" were included with "Financial Services," that combined category would actually contain 14 ADR issuers. Another 14 ADRs would also constitute a combined "Healthcare Equipment & Services" and "Pharmaceuticals & Biotechnology" grouping. If considering the general field of energy, then there are 17 issuances divided among "Oil & Gas Producers," "Oil Equipment, Services & Distribution," and "Electricity." Although not large in number of issuers, another category worth calling out in this bracket is "Technical Hardware & Equipment," which contains five ADRs listed on NASDAQ and four traded OTC. Of these, fabless (fabrication-less) semiconductor maker Spreadtrum Communications (NASDAQ:SPRD) particularly stands out. Spreadtrum serves as a strong example of the long-term ripple effects generated by the splash of China Mobile's pioneering debut. From its foundation as a tech start-up to addressing the challenges of being a listed company, Spreadtrum further illustrates the wide range of forces that converge and influence one another through the Sino-American public equity engagement.

Within the entire universe of ADR issuers, 122 list shares on exchange markets (70 on the NYSE and 52 on NASDAQ) while 150 trade on the off-board market. The number of new issuances surged in 2007 from a typical annual level of single and low double digits. That year's 27 ADS issuances nearly tripled the volume of 2006. The 65 ADS issuances in 2008 represented more than a doubling over 2007 (see Figure 1.1). This rapid growth in activity occurred during an especially bleak period for equity markets in the United States. For those Chinese ADR issuers that debuted through IPOs during the lean years of 2008–2009's Great Recession, they acted as a force of rejuvenation in the U.S. securities markets—though the results even then, before deeper-seated controversies came to light, often were mixed.

U.S. China Issuances Measuring Up

There are a number of ways to view the performance of Chinese share issuances in U.S. markets. The results of various individual companies are explored throughout this book. In terms of an aggregate picture, MSCI Indices (a leading U.S.-based compiler of global stock performance information) has among its more than 20 China indices the MSCI Overseas China Index. As of August 2011, that universe of Chinese stocks comprised six mid-caps (i.e., earning capitalizations

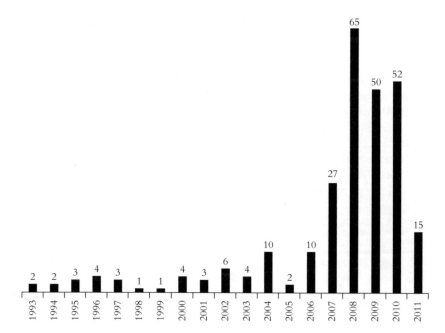

Figure 1.1 Annual Number of China ADRs, 1993–Q3 2011
SOURCE: BNY Mellon

of between $2 and $10 billion), one small-cap, and one large-cap company. These shares listed predominantly on NASDAQ. One of the
mid-caps, New Oriental Education, listed on the NYSE. Only the
small-cap is listed on a market outside the United States: COSCO,
which is traded on the Singapore Exchange.

The seven U.S.-listed companies of the MSCI Overseas China
Index contribute 98.6 percent of the index's weight, which effectively
makes it an index of select Chinese issuances in the United States. The
breakdown of the constituent issuers is listed on Table 1.2.

An admittedly highly select, small pool of companies (and over
50 percent dominated by the mass of a single company, Baidu—the
"Google of China"), the total returns of the MSCI Overseas China
Index do at least illustrate the kind of earnings that are possible with a
bet on China through the U.S. markets. Since May 2008, this particular
bundle of almost exclusively U.S.-listed Chinese shares has returned 66
percent (22.85 percent on a precisely annualized three-year basis). Against

Table 1.2   MSCI Overseas China Index Constituents (as of August 2011)

	Market Cap ($ b)	Index Weight (%)	Sector Weight (%)	GICS[1] Sector	ADR Issuer (Y/N)
Baidu (NASDAQ:BIDU)	39.4	59.97	75.7	Info Tech	Y
Sina (NASDAQ:SINA)	6.2	9.46	11.9	Info Tech	N
Ctrip.com (NASDAQ:CTRP)	6.0	9.11	47.1	Cons Discr	Y
NetEase.com (NASDAQ:NTES)	3.9	5.99	7.6	Info Tech	Y
New Oriental Education (NYSE:EDU)	3.6	5.41	27.9	Cons Discr	Y
Focus Media (NASDAQ:FMCN)	3.2	4.84	25.0	Cons Discr	Y
Sohu.com (NASDAQ:SOHU)	2.5	3.80	4.8	Info Tech	Y
COSCO (SIN:F83)	0.9	1.43	100.0	Industrials	N
Total	65.7	100.0			

SOURCE: MSCI

[1]GICS: Global Industry Classification Standard; Info Tech: Information Technology; Cons Discr: Consumer Discretionary

Figure 1.2   MSCI Overseas China Index Cumulative Performance, May 2008–August 2011
SOURCE: MSCI

a benchmark MSCI China Index and the broader MSCI ACWI (which measures equity market performance in developed and developing countries), this group of U.S.-listed Chinese stocks is a clear performance leader. The Overseas China Index provides a simple but telling example of how, if one chooses well, there can be real payouts from wagering on China through the Sino-American public equity dynamic.

Chapter 2

Realities, Theories, and Gung Ho

The Ying and Yang of Chinese Issuances

The U.S. saw an influx of Chinese growth IPOs, which dominated both the best- and worst-performing lists.

—Renaissance Capital[1]

Development arises from the contradictions inside a thing.

—Mao Zedong[2]

The China Wave

What has made Chinese stock listings such a hot topic in American finance comes from the impact of Chinese IPOs that surged in the United States toward the end of the first decade of the twenty-first century. This jolt of liquidity events from new Chinese issuances coincided with a time when U.S. stock markets were struggling for a fresh infusion of listing activity during and after a highly debilitating global financial crisis unleashed in 2008. Though within a few years Chinese listings would be forced to contend with a spate of negative market sentiment driven by foreign investor doubts over transparency, governance, and accounting practices, when the first wave of Chinese issuances hit American shores, it was met with enthusiasm.

The volume of IPO deal flow from the People's Republic (PRC) began making an impression on Wall Street in 2007, a period of relative market buoyancy before financial markets around the world crashed in 2008. Chinese stock issuances in the United States in 2007 increased more than three times over 2006.[3] China contributed half of the 25 best-performing IPOs of 2007, with two of the top three performers hailing from China's world-leading solar energy technology manufacturing sector: JA Solar (NASDAQ:JASO), which earned investors a year-end return of 365 percent), and Yingli Green Energy (NYSE:YGE), which returned 252 percent).[4] National drugstore chain China Nepstar (NYSE:NPD), online real estate broker E-House (NYSE:EJ), and financial information technology (IT) software developer Longtop Financial (NYSE:LFT) generated buzz as well.

In the next year, coinciding with the onset of the Great Recession brought on by the global financial crisis, these outstanding 2007 Chinese issuances retreated from the stellar initial impressions they had made and began a trend of market underperformance. The reasons vary but generally point to how both Chinese issuers and U.S. markets are, in many cases, still finding their way towards generating more consistent valuations.

Ironically, financial software and services provider Longtop had been the exception to this cohort of underperformers. That lasted until second quarter (Q2) 2011, when a number of skeptics and eventually the company's own auditors declared the company's financial numbers just too good to be true, finding evidence of large-scale fraud. This resulted in suspension of trading the company's stock and then its removal in August 2011 from the NYSE's main board altogether. Investor losses in LFT exceeded $1 billion. The fallout the debacle created for U.S.–China financial relations was unprecedented, a situation explored in detail in Chapter 6.

But during what history will record was at least the first surge of Chinese stock issuances in the United States running between 2007 and 2010, new Chinese listings were seen in heroic proportions. When the global financial crisis that had been rearing its head since 2007 fully burst out in 2008, IPO activity around the world plummeted, as did the performance of stock markets generally. New issuances on global exchanges fell by more than 50 percent based on deal numbers and plunged by nearly 70 percent based on funds raised.[5] In the U.S. markets, only four new Chinese issuers—computer-based testing services provider ATA Inc. (NASDAQ:ATAI); solar wafer manufacturer ReneSola (NYSE:SOL); online education company China Distance Education (NYSE:DL); and TV advertising agency China Mass Media (NYSE:CMM)—dared to list during the market bust.

Yet even such meager IPO numbers were significant during those dark days. Demonstrating both the poor market conditions in the United States at the time as well as the persistent appetite for new Chinese listings, Chinese issuances actually remained essentially unchanged as a percentage of total U.S. IPOs across the "break-out year" of 2007 and the "wipe-out year" of 2008. Chinese stock debuts in U.S. markets for 2008 accounted for almost 13 percent of all IPO deals, only a fraction off from 2007's proportion of 13.6 percent (see Figure 2.1).

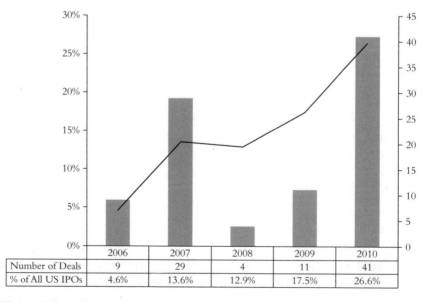

	2006	2007	2008	2009	2010
Number of Deals	9	29	4	11	41
% of All US IPOs	4.6%	13.6%	12.9%	17.5%	26.6%

Figure 2.1 China-based IPO Deal Flow in U.S. Markets, 2006–2010
Source: Renaissance Capital

By 2010, companies operationally based in China were contributing more than one-quarter of all IPO deals in the United States. Part of this came from disparities in basic economic conditions. Gross domestic product (GDP) in the world's major developed economies stagnated and shrank throughout 2008 and 2009. U.S. GDP flatlined at 0 percent growth in 2008 and then contracted by 2.6 percent in 2009. The usually stalwart German economy grew by a mere 0.7 percent in 2008 and then shriveled by 4.7 percent the next year. Japan fared even worse: a 1.2 percent contraction for 2008 followed by a withering 6.3 percent shrinkage in 2009.

While the world's other major economies stalled or declined, China Inc. raced ahead with 9.6 percent growth in 2008. It followed this by slightly lower (but still uniquely robust) 9.2 percent expansion in 2009.[6] Any U.S. firms that might consider going public with share offerings during this time period faced a severely negative domestic economic environment. By contrast, Chinese firms were operating within the best macroeconomic conditions on the planet. The biggest challenge facing such firms concerned choosing an exchange that offered the most attractive benefits. Despite a bleak economy, U.S. equity markets still appealed to Chinese companies eager to tap international investors. Investors, likewise, were eager to tap into China's high-flying growth.

Big-Stakes Games

A game changer (in many senses of the word) for Chinese IPOs in the United States came from ChangYou.com (NASDAQ:CYOU). One of China's biggest developers and operators of online games, the company on April 7, 2009, completed a surprisingly well received IPO on NASDAQ's Global Select Market, a segment of the NASDAQ exchange that boasts "the highest initial listing standards of any exchange in the world." Two years after its stock debut, CYOU was more than 100 percent above its listing-day price and was outperforming the NASDAQ index by a healthy double-digit margin. ChangYou had issued its American Depository Shares (ADSs) as an indirect but still 70 percent absolute majority-controlled subsidiary of the Beijing-headquartered, Delaware-registered, and already NASDAQ-listed

Sohu.com (NASDAQ:SOHU), a major Chinese online and mobile media group. At the time of ChangYou's listing, the U.S. IPO market had run dry. The company contributed the third U.S. IPO of 2009, on the heels of a Q1 2009 rate of stock issuances that amounted to barely 3 percent of the 68 IPOs in Q1 2007.[7]

ChangYou was an unlikely candidate for rejuvenating a moribund U.S. IPO market. Despite its pedigree as a semi-spinoff of an established—and strongly valued—U.S.-listed company, ChangYou operated only a single game, Tian Long Ba Bu, whose classical Chinese martial arts storyline was not exactly well known to typical U.S. stock market investors. Yet ChangYou held out an enticing investment story that transcended the risks of its singular and unfamiliar product offering. Tian Long Ba Bu represented China's second most popular locally developed MMORPG (massively multiplayer online role-playing game), an interactive online game played by up to hundreds of thousands of participants simultaneously. The company presented a homegrown, original outcropping from China's Internet market, which less than a year previously had surpassed the United States to emerge as the largest national online user base in the world. International Data Corporation (IDC) estimated the value of China's online game market that year at $2.4 billion, with predictions that it would climb to $3.4 billion by 2012. Further predicting that the paying online gamer penetration rate in China by 2012 would remain less than 60 percent, IDC's analysis (which was laid out in the CYOU share offering prospectus) showed plenty of room for converting more players into paying customers.[8]

Even if operating only the second most popular locally produced and third most popular MMORPG overall in China, ChangYou offered something much vaster in scope to investors: a slice of the seemingly irrepressible China growth juggernaut. CYOU shares debuted at the top of their estimated price range of $14 to $16 per ADS. They climbed as high as 50 percent to $23.93 before closing at $20.02—still a 25 percent pop—on their first day of trading. Listing 7.5 million ADSs, the little-known company that had only one game in its portfolio raised $120 million.[9] Though far from being blockbuster, these results nevertheless enlivened a languishing U.S. IPO market and pushed interest for U.S.-listed Chinese shares into the mainstream of global finance.

Following ChangYou, another ten Chinese companies would go public on the NYSE or NASDAQ in 2009. Those 11 Chinese listings provided the lion's share of all 14 foreign IPO stock issuances in the United States that year. As CYOU shares were soaring 135 percent above their IPO price (making CYOU the top performing U.S. stock debut for 2009), China's number-one game operator, Shanda Games Limited (NASDAQ:GAME), followed up with its own U.S. issuance and went public in late September. Shanda Games raised just north of $1.0 billion, becoming the first billion-dollar U.S.-listed IPO in 2009 and the largest U.S. offering by a Chinese Internet firm.

Shanda Games entered life as a public company with an impressive fund raise, plus having the best imaginable ticker symbol for its industry. (How can an online gaming company go wrong with a stock called "GAME"?) Like ChangYou, it enjoyed strong parent corporation backing as an offshoot of another high-performing U.S.-listed Chinese company, SNDA (NASDAQ-traded Shanda Interactive Entertainment). Despite these advantages, the price for GAME slid 14 percent immediately following the stock's debut at $12.50 per ADS. The issuance had been at the top of the price range when, at the last minute, the company chose to expand the volume of ADSs offered by about one-third, to more than 83.5 million.[10] The stock's priciness, combined with the swollen size of the share offering, probably worked against any springboarding off the IPO level. Over time, other factors contributed to dragging down the price, especially investor concerns about murky corporate governance.

By mid-2011, GAME shares were heading toward a price level of less than one-half their debut. By comparison, CYOU shares had tracked up to around $40, in excess of double their price at the time of their more modest IPO. In Q4 2011, management of GAME's parent company, Shanda Interactive (which was dominated by the chief executive and members of his family), had grown so disappointed with the group's U.S. market performance that they announced their intention to pull SNDA from its U.S. listing and take the company private via management buyout of the 32 percent the company shares that they did not already own.

Echoing the divergent fates of ChangYou and Shanda Games, 2009 saw three of the five best-performing IPOs and three of the five worst-performing IPOs in the United States turned in by Chinese issuances. Even with this unevenness (and, in hindsight, lack of sufficient vetting for some Chinese stocks to ensure that they were in line with U.S. market expectations), stock debuts from China-operating companies were helping to replenish deal flow in the stalled U.S. equity marketplace. America was suffering through what had become "the worst economic downturn since the Great Depression."[11] Chinese stock listings were providing a valuable market stimulus, not only by their numbers but the type of growth-oriented returns they offered. As the IPO research firm Renaissance Capital observed in its annual review for 2009:

> There were stark differences in the characteristics and indus-tries of IPOs originating from the dominant global players, the U.S. and China. U.S.-based IPOs were led by LBOs [lever-aged buyouts] and mortgage REITs [real estate investment trusts], reflecting private equity investors' need to delever-age on one hand and financial opportunism on the other. In contrast, Chinese IPOs, whether debuting in the U.S., China or Hong Kong, raised money to pour into China's domestic infrastructure, its nascent pharmaceutical industry, and other consumer-oriented enterprises. In a nutshell, the U.S. IPO market activity has largely been geared to healing the excesses of overleveraging in private equity and real estate, while the Chinese IPOs reflect a growth economy.[12]

China's investment story sold well to investors hungry for IPO activity and attractive upside. On its way to becoming the world's sec-ond largest economy (China overtook Japan for the number-two spot in 2010), equity stakes in Chinese companies seemed to offer the safety that came from a major economic power while providing the return profile of a rapidly developing emerging market. It was nothing less than a "China Miracle," as billionaire turnaround investor Wilbur Ross called it. Ross went so far as to argue that "Chinese companies deserve a premium, a multiple over Western companies."[13]

Chinese stocks weren't hot just in America; they were the hottest offerings anywhere. No longer poor cousins to equity markets in the United States, the stock markets of Greater China (Hong Kong, main-land China, and Taiwan) were best positioned to absorb this surge in new issuances and ended up grabbing most of the economic benefits (see Figure 2.2). For the first time in history, companies listing on bourses of Greater China created more—significantly more—wealth than what the U.S. exchanges were producing. U.S.-listed IPO value in 2009, at $25.2 billion, totaled less than half of $59.7 billion worth of shares that listed on the Hong Kong, Shenzhen, Shanghai, and Taiwan markets.[14]

Ying–Yang IPOs

The momentum driving China IPOs in 2009 continued well into 2010—and with a vengeance. The value of IPO activity in Greater China jumped upward by 141 percent. Raising a whopping $129.0 billion, IPOs that occurred in the China region dwarfed the $39.0 billion raised in the United States by more than three times. Take out the $15.8 billion raised by the relisting of common shares on the NYSE through the denationalization of General Motors (NYSE:GM), and the U.S. IPO market that year was a relatively paltry $23.2 billion.[15] On the basis of stock market listings, China's mixed public–private economy was running circles around the traditionally free market capitalist system of the United States.

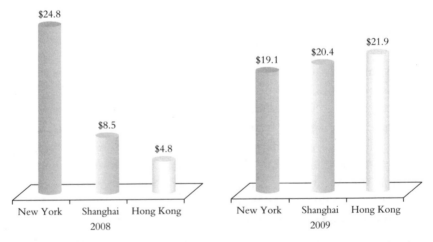

Figure 2.2 What a Difference a Year Can Make: IPO Funds Raised by Stock Exchange, 2008 vs. 2009
Source: PricewaterhouseCoopers

The nearly $130 billion in accumulated value for China IPOs in 2010 was almost twice that of the $65.2 billion raised in the United States during 2007, the last good year before markets crashed. Yet Chinese companies had not given up on America's more established and prestigious NYSE and NASDAQ markets. Chinese IPOs still helped drive U.S. exchange listings, providing 72 percent of all new foreign issuances in 2010. The feeling on Wall Street was that the resurgence of traditional "financial sponsor–backed" IPOs (offerings organized by cash-outs from private equity funders) and Chinese listings were moving the market forward.[16]

Following a record-setting 30 China IPOs in the United States for the year-to-date 2010, the Chinese government–controlled *Beijing News* ran a special report on the phenomenon in late November. Alluding to the then recently established Growth Enterprise Board, or "ChiNext"—supposedly akin to NASDAQ in its receptiveness to newly operating, high-growth firms—located in Shenzhen, the report's lead commentator, Wang Haitao, critically pondered China's dearth of capital market opportunities in an essay titled "Is NASDAQ Closer than Shenzhen?" He summarized the core issue at hand in terms of basic economics: "If a market restricts supply, or uses restrictive requirements to determine what is 'attractive or ugly,' then that market will inevitably experience supply problems."[17] Wang was making oblique but unmistakable reference to the overly discriminative requirements for listing within China, a state of affairs that can lead to pushing what the central government considers "inappropriate" but equity investors might well consider "deserving" Chinese firms to seek their equity capital from markets abroad. The newspaper report looked at more specific matters, too, such as the prohibitive costs and length of time required for a domestic listing and how foreign markets might better value a company's future earnings potential or be more receptive to companies active in innovative industrial spaces such as the Internet and private education.

By far the biggest criticisms typically heard in regard to China's domestic IPO process overall concern onerous listing requirements for companies—such as three-year track record of profitability to debut on any main board—and a system viewed as lacking in transparency and impartiality. "Mainland companies that want to list but do not meet the requirements," notes the *South China Morning Post*, "often bribe their way through the regulatory bureaucracy, or call on private equity companies or someone with political connections to influence approvals."[18] After listing, Chinese public companies further must contend with a market environment that not infrequently shows itself to be plagued by insider trading and price ramping.

Quality issues with China's stock markets had been known for years, but by the end of 2011, just how bad things could get were starkly revealed. In December, news broke of a government investigation of a record-setting RMB57 billion ($9.0 billion) pump-and-dump scheme. The scandal embroiled 30 securities analysts and 44 brokerage outlets suspected of colluding to fix the value of some 552 stocks. Given the extreme caution that Chinese market regulators take before pursuing cases of this nature, the alleged figures point to probable serious market distortions of great depth and breadth. Public revelation of such events is positive, in one sense, because it shows an increasing determination by Chinese regulators to expose these issues. Yet it also illustrates the susceptibility of China's stock markets to blatant manipulation.

Even with the more structurally stable trading environment found in American stock markets, as Chinese issuances on U.S. bourses gained momentum, issuers and investors have found good news often accompanied by bad. The 2009–2010 pipeline of Chinese stock debuts unleashed some great-performing IPOs that not infrequently bumped up against moderate- to poor-performing ones. Witness the way a Marketwatch.com story in 2010 remarked in the same sentence how "[s]hares of Internet service firm China Cache International Holdings skyrocketed in their U.S. market debut Friday, while a larger China deal, from a manufacturer of wind turbines, fell flat."[19]

Back to back, in both 2009 and 2010, the end-of-year return on IPOs disproportionately placed Chinese companies among the best and worst performers. According to Renaissance Capital data, three of the top ten IPOs for 2010 were by Chinese companies; a fourth, Colorado-based rare earth oxide producer Molycorp (NYSE:MCP), also distinguished itself with clear association to China. Yet in the case of Molycorp, this issuer highlighted how it specifically operates *outside* of the PRC. This reassured investors and helped catapult its share price to a top-ranked return of 256 percent on the back of market anxiety over Chinese government export controls on rare earth minerals. Conversely, four of the ten poorest year-end returns on IPOs in 2010 also came from China-related companies.[20]

The yin–yang from this mixed bag of U.S.-listed China-themed IPOs is not, by itself, necessarily problematic. Most of the new batch of "China concept stocks" (so named because the companies they represent usually are registered offshore but conduct most of their business in mainland China) that were going to market in the United States constituted high-growth, small-cap offerings. Stocks of that nature tend to be more speculative and encompass greater risk. Add to this China's commercial operating environment—which, regardless of the country's status as an economic superpower, remains very much in a developing-world phase of evolution. The propensity for the newly listed China small-cap issuances to delight as well as disappoint thus hardly should surprise. Although market-based reforms began in 1979 under the PRC's system of "socialism with Chinese characteristics," officially sanctioned stock markets did not even start operating until 1991. The Chinese people have demonstrated superb commercial acumen for thousands of years, yet a market-based equity culture of dispersed corporate ownership is extremely new to China. As highly developed U.S. capital markets increase their interactions with recently minted China operating companies, the learning curve for both sides will remain a steep one.

Market Détente

Whether one is a bull or bear on China, the nation's critical significance to the global economy cannot be dismissed. At the outset of the twenty-first century, the PRC has emerged as the world's second largest economic power, the leader in many key industries, and the principal engine for worldwide economic growth. China's rapid rate of economic expansion will eventually slow down, of course. Yet China's economic fundamentals point to the country, for the foreseeable future, unlikely ever to relinquish its role as a dominant commercial power on the world stage.

In a similar vein in regard to America, although the nation is often seen as a stumbling if not declining giant, the United States still demonstrates a remarkable—indeed, exceptional—capacity for rejuvenation and continued economic vibrancy. By most critical measures, the global economic and political leadership of the United States has yet to show any signs of serious deterioration. Both the United States and the PRC are positioned to occupy the two leading positions in the global economy for years to come. This makes constructive means for economic interaction between these two commercial superpowers all the more important.

Not that bragging rights to who exactly is the "number one" and who the "number two" in this relationship is that vital a distinction, some clarifications of rank are useful in underscoring the nature of how the countries are positioned vis-à-vis each other.

One of the most oft cited figures to portray Chinese ascendancy and American decline is GDP, the most common yardstick of a nation's economic fortitude. Depending on the data one uses, China will surpass the United States in GDP size by as early as 2016 or as late as 2030. If applying the more subjectively calculated purchasing power parity (PPP) figures estimated by the International Monetary Fund, China's PPP-based GDP will total $19 trillion in 2016. This will relegate the U.S. PPP-based GDP of $18.8 trillion to second place for the first time since America's rise as a superpower.[21] Leaving aside the assumptions and distortions that PPP estimates require, a more important point is that whenever such a GDP "takeover" by China occurs, unless the country makes a quantum leap in individual productivity, it will continue to lag the United States on a per person (or "per capita") basis.

How so? In order to make a truly equal comparison in the context of a global economy increasingly driven by individuals' production and consumption patterns, China's nearly $19 trillion in GDP should be divided by the nation's massive population of nearly 1.4 billion people. This means that the PRC's national wealth in 2016 will equate to just under $14,000 per capita. In contrast, 330 million Americans that same year will share their national economic output at the rate of about $57,000 per capita. On average, people residing in the United States will remain four times more economically enriched than those residing in China. Well into the foreseeable future, no reliable data dispute the United States maintaining a clear lead in per capita GDP. That means that averaged out pound for pound, the United States will continue leading the pack in the global economy.

Such comparisons should not detract from China's obvious dominance in terms of aggregate GDP, leadership in various market categories, and unrivaled growth across many measures. Both China and America are set to continue to occupy leading economic roles in the world, but the role of each will vary in nature and significance.

Patterns like this likewise emerge with figures regarding China's recent rise to the top of the world league tables for IPOs. An individual company's IPO is a one-time event for a stock market. Although public offerings are critical for market vitality, a stock market's fundamental strength comes from its total capitalization value. In this regard, the greatest share of worldwide stock market value remains in the United States. According to the World Federation of Exchanges, as of mid-2011, the $17.9 trillion in combined capitalization of NYSE and NASDAQ contributed nearly one-third of the global total for equity market capitalizations. The Greater China exchanges of mainland China, Hong Kong, and Taiwan, though repeatedly upping their capitalizations with eye-popping IPOs, still represent just around 13 percent of global stock market capitalized value.[22]

There are also distinguishing qualitative differences in areas like governance and liquidity. In a 2010 occasional report on the state of corporate governance in Asia, CLSA Asia-Pacific Markets presented the results of a detailed country-by-country analysis undertaken in collaboration with the Asian Corporate Governance Association. "Corporate-governance standards have improved over the past decade," the researchers found, "but even the best Asian markets remain far from international best practice." Surprising in light of the advanced state of development that many Asian economies—namely Japan, Korea, Singapore, Taiwan, and Hong Kong—have achieved, the report concluded that the region's stock markets "still lack effective rules on fundamentals such as independent directors and audit committees. Not enough has been invested to make best practices work."[23]

A host of complementary similarities and differences between the PRC and the United States produce the attractive forces that drive repeated pairings of Chinese stocks and American stock markets. Yet since the beginning of Chinese listings in the United States, critics have also charged that the combination is a mismatch. They argue that Chinese companies should list on Chinese markets where they will be better understood by regulators and investors. The often low, single-digit price-earnings (PE) ratios that Chinese shares have been attracting in U.S. markets compared the usually high PE multiples they command in mainland markets or Hong Kong lend credence to that view. So does the notoriety of China stock frauds perpetuated via U.S. stock market listings, which by mid-2011 had greatly tempered foreign investor appetite for overseas Chinese issuances.

These negative assessments, though not without merit, ignore larger macro considerations. In a truly global economy, capital and products (in this case, financial securities) should be able to move about freely and come together at venues that attract buyers and sellers. The dance of money and equity that occurs with Chinese shares on U.S. stock markets is but one of many such phenomena in an interconnected global market system. Nothing yet has indicated that the net benefits in economic wealth and information sharing generated by the exchange of Chinese equities in the United States do not outweigh the damage caused by Chinese stock scandals, as painful as those are to the investors concerned. Even the scandals themselves have provided important sources of learning and improvement for the Chinese and U.S. economies moving forward.

Nevertheless, tensions in the dynamic persist. Even with all the forces that drive the trade of global cash and Chinese equity in the United States, market participants and regulators often seem guarded if not deeply suspicious about the methods and motivations of various players. Differences in expectations for disclosure and accountability are particular flash points. The balancing of supply and demand factors has only been possible because of a carefully negotiated détente—a cordial and willing engagement between Chinese and Western interests but not one where each side fully accepts the other's economic worldview.

Despite the appearances of gleaming office towers, super highways, stylishly Western-attired urbanites, and factories turning out every conceivable type of manufactured good for the planet to consume, the structure of China's economy—its financial system in particular—differs markedly from that of Western developed nations. A common assumption seems to prevail among American policy makers and commentators that China is as willing to copy the U.S. economic system as it is so many Western-branded goods. U.S. officials and experts have shown themselves eager to impart wisdom for ways that China could improve itself by becoming just "more like us." Such proselytizing, while never really all that much appreciated, was at least tolerated in China for a while. Yet a large part of the Chinese leadership stopped bothering to listen around the time of the Great Recession. Apart from China's political establishment, popular sentiment also has been tuning out what to many in China has sounded like an American siren call to embrace free markets and Wall Street-style capitalism. Blockbuster bestselling books such as *Currency Wars* (2007) and *Unhappy China* (2009) elaborately portray the political economic structure of Western democracies as fundamentally, even *conspiratorially*, antagonistic to China's interests.

As Song Xiaojun, former People's Liberation Army Navy officer and the lead coauthor of *Unhappy China*, sees things, 2008 provided a turning point in China's view of itself and with the World Beyond China. Surveying matters ranging from tensions with the West over Beijing's hosting of the Summer Olympics to the global financial crisis, Song argues that "events have truly coincided, a kind of divine sign that China has an opportunity to push forward a grand vision."[24] Although the "grand vision" that Song and his collaborating authors advocate is not explicitly detailed, it is implicitly based on avoiding the perceived failures of liberal economic trade policies. This line of reasoning contends that the financial crisis has exposed the U.S. economic model to be not just flawed but failed. "I believe," writes Song's better-known coauthor, Wang Xiaodong, "that the global financial crisis demonstrates that American society is totally decrepit from top to bottom."[25]

The logic of *Unhappy China* typifies the gist of populist concepts that perceive a resurgent China deserving of bragging rights as a nation of power and influence. This follows years of indignity suffered through a cascading series of setbacks that began with China's defeats in the Opium Wars of the mid-nineteenth century. In the wake of latter-day worldwide financial turmoil, calls have resounded within the PRC to counter American economic hegemony to have China take greater control of its own destiny on the world stage. The most vocal rallying cry has been for transformation of China's RMB currency into a global standard of exchange. (Never mind that internationalization of the RMB would, in fact, expose the country more, not less, to the vicissitudes of the still liberally oriented workings of the world economy.)

Regardless of any lingering sense of dissatisfaction with Western economic policies in general and with that of America's financial system in particular, China's entrepreneurs more than its pundits help drive the direction of the nation's economy. And Chinese business leaders have been beating a path to Wall Street in spite of the underlying political tensions. What they and their global investors make of the opportunity to share in the risks and rewards of commingled equity ownership of Chinese enterprises via U.S. equity markets will determine much about how China and the world outside use the levers of global economic integration to mutual benefit.

Breaking Molds

Commingling of this sort does not in any way resemble other notions of financial integration like "Chimerica": a simplified concept of Chinese and American economic bonding that claims global asset prices have boomed because low labor costs in China have increased capital returns on Wall Street.[26] Nor is it about a G2 "club of two," which implies that the United States and China, mainly by virtue of their status as the world's two dominant economies, enjoy a special relationship—under the shadow of which, presumably, the rest of the world should be grateful to exist. The kind integration formed by equity exchange does not involve codependency or special powers between China and America. Instead, it is about dynamism, movement, trial and error, and decisions—risky decisions—concerning how information and equity capital traded on the most robust and liquid stock markets in the world is deployed to empower companies and industries in the fastest-growing major economy in the world. The main actors are China and the United States, but the effects traverse far beyond their borders.

The emerging relationship between the two powers is hardly inevitable, but it is strategically important for all concerned. That is why resolution of regulatory conflicts, discussed in Chapter 6, should be resolved as a priority. The newness of interconnections between U.S. equity markets and Chinese companies means that the relationship does not follow any particular model. The Sino-American equity dynamic defies narrow labels because it is a fluidly transpiring complex series of interactions; patterns of unfolding cause and effect that match developed world capital with developing world growth. It goes far beyond cost inputs and asset appreciation. It gets to the logic and actions behind the shares and capital that are reciprocated, not always smoothly and sometimes with great frustration, but that are actively exchanged nonetheless. Although there are ground rules that involve basic concepts for fair trading—transparency, disclosure, and veracity—there is no requirement that either side adopt the other's socioeconomic framework. In the transacting of cash and equities, the two largest national powers in the global economy are moving more closely in sync. This is not about static economic consolidation, it is about an evolving financial synergism.

Both Eastern and Western critics have seized on the financial meltdown of 2008 as an indictment against the Anglo-American model of "shareholder capitalism": the increasingly influential economic framework that deemphasizes intervention of the public sector in favor of shareholder-funded and controlled private enterprise to power a market-based economy. New America Foundation's Michael Lind assertively declared as late into the postcrisis period as March 2011—a time typified by more measured appraisals—that the "Thatcher-Reagan-Blair-Clinton model of capitalism is a failure."[27] Even if extreme, Lind's statement captures a sense of the profound frustrations felt over the status quo of capitalism in the developed world, exhibited by phenomena like the Occupy movement that began with protests on Wall Street in September 2011. Throughout the financial crisis and its aftermath, the U.S. U.K., and other shareholder-oriented economies undeniably revealed severe weaknesses in their varying flavors of equity-based capitalism. Nevertheless, the issues brought to light by these and other Western economies (including those employing alternative "stakeholder capitalism" models) point to failures in government policies, regulatory oversight, and corporate management—factors that on their own do not indict the powers of the marketplace and laissez-faire capitalism but rather how such powers are monitored and regulated.

What is so remarkable is that against a backdrop of eulogies and general exasperation with the Anglo-American model of shareholder capitalism, the last Communist-controlled major economy on the planet and the world's leading democratically governed economy have been conducting the purist of transnational shareholder capitalism engagements. They have been writing a new page in the history of equity-driven global capitalism rather than the last.

Adam Smith's China Bet

Adam Smith, the moralist philosopher whose thinking was later praised or vilified for underpinning the dominant economic rationale that permeates our world today, expressed an admiration bordering on awe for China in his magnum opus, *An Inquiry into the Nature and Causes of the Wealth of Nations*. Published in 1776, *Wealth of Nations* simultaneously praised China while questioning its prospects for continued development, not unlike the mixed sentiments about China's future outlook expressed by many contemporary observers.

In the first section—or "book," in the parlance of the time—of *Wealth of Nations*, Smith observes, "China has been long one of the richest, that is, one of the most fertile, best cultivated, most industrious, and most populous countries in the world." As if sighing while penning his text, he added, "It seems, however, to have been long stationary. Marco Polo, who visited it more than five hundred years ago, describes its cultivation, industry, and populousness, almost in the same terms in which they are described by travelers in the present times."[28] Smith assessed China to be "a much richer country than any part of Europe," which meant it would have been a natural candidate to serve as a model for emulation in his *Wealth of Nations*.[29]

Smith's view of China's economic stagnation prevented this. The world's first economist predicted that China's economic power would be eclipsed eventually, owing to how it was standing still while Europe was managing "gradual" economic progress and North America was leaping ahead as a "rapidly progressive" region.[30] Smith essentially saw China as constrained by its own success. For example, the country's world-leading advanced communications infrastructure, its "multitude of canals," so efficiently linked together China's internal domestic markets that external markets in foreign lands were ignored. The system was, in Smith's appraisal, the best in the world. He remarked, "By communicating with one another [they] afford an inland navigation much more extensive than that either of the Nile or the Ganges, or perhaps than both of them put together." All these civilizations of ancient grandeur, however, had been doomed by insularity. Smith noted that it was "remarkable that neither the ancient Egyptians, nor the Indians, nor the Chinese, encouraged foreign commerce, but seem all to have derived their great opulence from this inland navigation."[31] This reluctance to trade beyond national borders, an unwillingness to proactively engage other states in commercial relations and instead turn inward, to rely purely on domestic markets for development, was in Smith's analysis a road to ruin.[32]

It was not until two centuries after the appearance of the *Wealth of Nations*, as part of a Communist China's new policies toward reform and openness launched in 1979, that the nation began, gradually, to participate in reciprocal foreign trade. The crowning achievement of those policies is typically perceived as China's admission to the World Trade Organization, which the PRC accomplished in late 2001 through the Doha Round of WTO membership negotiations. This occurred after a decade and a half of protracted lobbying and discussions—conducted especially among China, the United States, and the European Union—to satisfy concerns about equal access to markets among these major economic powers. Undeniably a watershed event, China's admission to the WTO was actually predated by its less-celebrated entry into another major international trading mechanism, global equity capital markets.

Chinese state-owned enterprises (SOEs) had been listing in U.S. stock markets since the early 1990s. But the first IPO of a major SOE to garner worldwide attention and set the stage for the later widespread embrace of U.S.-listed Chinese stocks came from China Telecom (Hong Kong) Limited (NYSE:CHL), now known as China Mobile. China Mobile's high-profile simultaneous debut on the Hong Kong and New York stock exchanges during the tumultuous sweep of the Asian financial crisis in October 1997 made people pay attention to the "China story." By the time the PRC joined the WTO in 2001, China Mobile plus another four strategically vital, Communist Party of China (CPC) controlled, and central government–managed SOEs had already become members of the NYSE: PetroChina (NYSE:PTR), China Unicom (NYSE:CHU), Sinopec (NYSE:SHI), and China National Offshore Oil Corporation (NYSE:CEO). China Mobile plus these four listings marked the early formation of a grouping of industry leaders from China known in Chinese as first-tier companies of the nation (国家一流企业) or more commonly referred to in English as China's national champions.

The phenomenon of Chinese SOEs—which detractors are quick to point out are not just government owned but ultimately owned by the CPC—issuing only a token minority of their shares in a U.S. stock market has attracted controversy from the beginning of these stock listings. Regardless, by "going public" in the United States, even if only marginally issuing shares to foreign investors, the SOEs have exposed themselves to the expectations and demands of outside shareholders. The process has also effectively brought the CPC leadership into the heart of global capitalism, fostering important linkages from deep within China's economy to external markets and breaking through the insular homeostasis that Smith had originally argued was the key factor in suppressing the nation's economic growth.

Gains, Rules, and Risks

Endemic to why we even bother to interact economically is, according to the classically liberal philosophical viewpoint, the idea of *gains of trade*, which holds that transacting parties are always better off when they enter into a voluntary exchange. The principle of gains of trade supports equality and fairness in economic relations, standing in contrast with the concept of *mercantilism*, which advocates unbalanced trade based on export promotion and import restriction. The expectation of multiplicative, transcending gains enriching not only transacting parties but society as a whole infuses the rationale of Smith's *Wealth of Nations* as it does subsequent classically liberal and latter-day neoliberal economic theory. Upholding a laissez-faire ideal of limited government intervention in the market, gains of trade rationalizes the relatively porous borders that characterize today's global economy.

Of course, in practice, no one—people, institutions, or governments—adheres to the principle of open markets absolutely. This is especially the case for stock markets, the most emblematic of free-wheeling, shareholder capitalist institutions. Among all the world's equity exchanges, before a company earns the right to list its shares for sale to the general public, the firm first must demonstrate to market operators and government regulators that it meets minimum requirements. These mainly concern proving that the company is a legitimate enterprise and is prepared to adequately disclose its financial details.

In the United States, in addition to the listing standards imposed on issuers by the NYSE and NASDAQ, evolving acts by Congress have further extended the hand of government into public equity markets. America's national legislature enacted the Sarbanes-Oxley Act of 2002 (with its critical Title I provision that added a new level of government authority with the creation of a Public Company Accounting Oversight Board) after a string of major U.S. accounting scandals. The Dodd-Frank Wall Street Reform and Consumer Protection Act (which strengthens regulatory powers and instituted greater financial market transparency) entered the law books in 2010 as the United States recovered from the worst financial crisis since the Great Depression. Also in response to concerns about accounting malfeasance, in 2003, the NYSE and NASDAQ raised their corporate governance standards by bolstering the independence of corporate board members and audit committees. Moving with the times, U.S. stock markets and their regulatory regimes have been repeatedly upping the bar for the listing of public companies.

Even with the increasingly tough requirement put on U.S. stock listings, transactions of a public company's shares are done on the basis of *caveat emptor*—buyer beware. Because of exemptions for foreign company issuers, the full extent of U.S. government and market requirements has not obliged all U.S.-listed China concept stocks. Add to that the challenges of physical distance, language barriers, cultural differences, and a dissimilar business environment that applies to issuers that do all or most of their business in the PRC. Whenever anyone puts money down on a Chinese stock issued in the United States, these risk factors are all at play.

Chinese issuers themselves face their own set of risk considerations. Even with certain exemptions, foreign issuers are still exposed to the investor scrutiny and regulatory powers of the U.S. markets. Paying for U.S.-registered certified public accountant (CPA) firms that have China-based auditors, bicontinental American legal teams, and other expenses incurred for compliance with rules and regulations provides for listing costs that are higher than what would be the case if a company was operating in the United States. On top of this is the primary risk that U.S. stock markets might not adequately value a Chinese issuance. Then there is the very real but often underestimated need by Chinese management to become sufficiently versed in U.S. regulations and market expectations about disclosure. Providing detailed "color" in corporate transparency and future guidance, crucial for most companies that hope to gain sustainable shareholder interest, is largely an alien concept in a Chinese business culture that prizes commercial secrecy. All told, the uncertainties for Chinese companies that go public in the United States are by no means insignificant. The bet on gainful trade from Chinese listings runs both ways.

Information versus Noise

A broader benefit to China, the United States, and the world at large comes from the vast amounts of information that each Chinese listing on a U.S. equity exchange generates. This is especially the case for companies that IPO on the NYSE or NASDAQ. From the prospectus a private company files prior to its IPO, its "Registration Statement under the Securities Act of 1933," to its regularly issued quarterly and annual reports, occasional filings with the U.S. Securities and Exchange Commission, and other legally required or strategically issued announcements as a public company, pertinent details of the firm's operations and the industry in which it competes are openly disseminated. Depending on the interest the stock generates, bloggers, commentators, journalists, and analysts will produce additional material that examines and, to varying degrees, influences the share price. Of course, the most voluminous and actively tracked type of data is the share price itself, which provides a composite reflection of evolving investor sentiments toward the company's current performance and expected future profitability.

In the classical understanding of market pricing, there was an acknowledged imperfection in the mechanics at work. Market prices for commodities are not produced "by any accurate measure," Smith observed, "but by the higgling and bargaining of the market." This process, he contended, while "not exact, is sufficient for carrying on the business of common life."[33]

By the time the world had moved from the preindustrial era of Smith's time into a postindustrial one where circulating flows of information had dramatically increased in terms of speed and content, markets for information-intensive stocks and other financial securities had come to be seen to function as if they moved according to flawlessly executed machinations. A seminal paper written by Eugene Fama at the University of Chicago and published in 1970—coincidentally the year prior to the establishment of NASDAQ's instantaneously transacting electronic trading platform—defined an efficient market hypothesis, or EMH. The EMH simply, but significantly, posits that "security prices at any time 'fully reflect' all available information."[34] Although an extreme view (the notion that prices can at *any* time *fully* reflect *all* available information implies an impossibly all-knowing perfection of the marketplace), EMH has entered the shared mind-set of many market participants. It also serves as the basis for other influential financial frameworks, such as the capital asset pricing model (CAPM) and the Black-Scholes option pricing formula.

Others have extensively documented weaknesses in key assumptions that underpin the EMH. An entire field of behavioral economics arose not long after the theory's postulation to detail ways that risky decisions in finance—also known as betting preferences—can derive more from human irrationality than coldly logical deduction. No less a luminary from the economics establishment than Fischer Black, the co-creator of the Black-Scholes formula that seems to lend great credence to the EMH, pointed out that markets can easily operate inefficiently because investors often use irrelevant information, or "noise," and "trade on noise as if it were information."[35]

Collateral economic damage from centuries of repeated bubbles and panics that swing between overinflated or excessively depressed stock markets bolsters the argument that emotionality more than rationality moves share prices. Early on in the twentieth century, the successful stock market investor and paradigm-shifting economist

John Maynard Keynes famously commented in his groundbreaking work, *The General Theory of Employment, Interest and Money*, that most human decisions are "the result of animal spirits—a spontaneous urge to action rather than inaction, and not as the outcome of a weighted average of quantitative benefits multiplied by quantitative probabilities."[36]

Noise and irrationality typify many views on China from the world beyond its borders. The nation's exoticism has long inspired contradictory interpretations that range from fawning admiration to condemning vilification. Today, China bulls and bears spar in the market with alternative explanations of what the exact same data about Chinese companies and the Chinese economy truly implies.

The danger of using either bullish or bearish interpretations to understand China is that any fixed frame of reference, as with any attempt to model complex realities, can confuse rather than enlighten. The financial historian Charles Kindleberger reminds us that otherwise informed investors can be led to irrational decisions when they "choose the wrong model, fail to take account of a particular and crucial bit of information, or go so far as to suppress information that does not conform to the model implicitly adopted."[37]

Complete objectivity on any subject might be unattainable, but in the case of China, which is so easily misinterpreted by foreign observers, extra efforts should be taken to see matters in context. Otherwise investors and observers alike face the heightened risk of basing assessments of Chinese companies and industries more on noise than on genuine information. The following chapters of this book are part of an attempt to cut through some of that noise and, hopefully, provide a measure of true insight into what exactly underpins the dynamism of the United States–China public equity relationship.

Real "Gung Ho"

To conclude this chapter on pertinent theories and realities concerning Chinese stock listings in the United States, a brief detour into comparative pop culture and military history can demonstrate a centrally important point.

When Americans talk about someone being "gung ho," they mean, according to Merriam–Webster, someone "extremely or overly zealous or enthusiastic."[38] *The Oxford Essential Dictionary of the U.S. Military* defines the term in the context of a quintessentially American Hollywood film character. In its entry for "Rambo," the dictionary explains that as slang, Rambo means "a figure of extreme bravado, 'gung ho' personified."[39]

Despite the very peculiar American connotations associated with the word in English, gung ho in truth comes from a Chinese term for socialized industrial production, 工合. (In the original, it is pronounced like "goh-ng huh" in Mandarin and written as *gonghe* in standard romanized Chinese spelling today.) Credit goes to real-life American military hero and a progenitor of U.S. Special Forces guerilla warfare, Marine Lieutenant Colonel Evans Fordyce Carlson, for introducing the term to the modern American English vernacular during World War II.

Prior to the war, Carlson had picked up the phrase while serving as a military observer with the Chinese Eighth Route Army during China's struggle against Japanese invasion. Under the commander in chief of CPC forces, Zhu De, the Eighth Route Army carried out daring, small-scale attacks launched behind the lines of Japanese occupied territory. The effectiveness of the Chinese Communist military strategy, Zhu's egalitarian leadership style, and the rank and file's cooperative *esprit de corps* commitment to fight against great odds deeply impressed Carlson. The American officer associated this style of guerilla combat with what he had understood was the meaning of "gung ho." He later employed the phrase as the name for his own brand of battlefield philosophy. It thereby became the inaugural rallying cry for the Marine raiders Carlson organized in the Pacific Theater during the Second World War. Afterward, it was associated with the U.S. Marine Corps' special brand of battle readiness and a go-for-broke fearlessness more generally. Over time it has emerged as part of the distinctly American vocabulary without any immediately recognizable association to its Chinese roots.

What is particularly remarkable about the etymology of American gung ho is that the word's inspiration came from not just China but very clearly the era of *Communist China*. The term "Gung ho" (spelled with a capital "G") as Carlson encountered it was simply the Anglicized acronym of a production system known officially as the Chinese Industrial Cooperatives (CIC). "Gung ho" CIC enterprises supplied war materiel to Eighth Route Army troops. Carlson saw "Gung ho" written out in Chinese and English as part of a production trademark that was slapped on the vehicles and boxes containing supplies used by Chinese military forces. The phrase was in effect a signifier of early-stage Maoist industrial collectivization that was brought to the front lines of China's fight against foreign aggression. Those political overtones of course were thrown out when the Marines adopted the slogan, but the original sensibility for a cooperative, can-do spirit while confronting mortal threats endured.

The shared but distinctly differing use of "gung ho" serves as a reminder that the PRC and the United States can differ in their interpretations and use of exactly the same thing and still make matters work to their respective interests. China is unlikely to ever become "just like America" no matter how much it makes use of American institutions, such as U.S. stock markets. In light of China's deep roots as a *communitarian* society—which predate by thousands of years and facilitate its current political organization as a market-oriented *communist* state—the PRC is not likely to fully embrace the trappings of shareholder capitalism even if it continues to strengthen the role of private enterprise in its economy. Despite these and many other differences that will be explored in the following pages, the interaction of Chinese equities and U.S. stock markets can bring about enormous gains for all involved. If a sometimes uneasy détente can be augmented by a little "gung ho" (variously interpreted), then the Sino-American public equity dynamic will progress much more smoothly. A bicultural gung ho ethos shows how dissimilar worldviews held by China and the United States can not merely coexist but act symbiotically to support the success of each side.

Chapter 3

China Mobile

The Big Bet

Listing China Telecom will be the first course of a big banquet . . . bigger courses will be served later.

—Wu Jichuan, Minister of Posts and
Telecommunications (1997)[1]

Home to a cellular phone market approaching one billion subscriptions, the sheer numbers describing mobile phone usage in China tower above those of other national markets. In this sector of the world economy, China's "rise" to global prominence came about more like an upward sprint. In the year 2000, China's 85 million-strong mobile phone subscription base stood at about three-quarters the size of that of the United States (see Figure 3.1). Since then, cellular subscriptions in China have been bounding upward at a compound average growth rate (CAGR) of 26.0 percent, compared to a 9.8 percent CAGR for the United States. By 2010, China's market was ten times larger than it was in the last year of the twentieth century. In this sector of advanced telecommunications, China now dwarfs the previously world-dominant

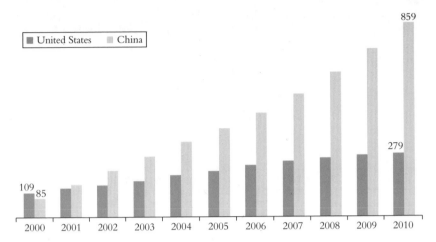

Figure 3.1   U.S. and China Mobile Phone Markets: Millions of Subscriptions, 2000–2010.
SOURCE: International Telecommunications Union

United States by a factor of three to one. Signs indicate that plenty of additional growth lies ahead.

China Mobile (NYSE:CHL), first listed on the NYSE as China Telecom (Hong Kong) Ltd., dominates this massive market as China's largest cellular network operator. The company services over 580 million customer accounts, close to 70 percent of the total. The company's subscription base is almost twice the size of the entire population of the United States. By the middle of 2011, China Mobile's stock market capitalization approached $190 billion on the back of 2010 operating revenue of RMB485.2 billion ($75.1 billion).[2] The world's next largest mobile phone carrier, Singapore Telecommunications (which counts 403 million cellular customers across various nations), earned revenues of about $18 billion—less than a third of China's top operator—over a similar period.

In a basic sense, China Mobile's outsize statistics reflect the vast scale and potential of the Chinese economy. More specifically, in relation to China's gargantuan mobile phone subscription base, China Mobile represents not just the leading operator in the market; the company effectively *created* the market. Through a uniquely structured, precedent-setting overseas stock listing, China Mobile gave birth to the nation's first interregional mobile phone system and the beginnings of the world's largest wireless communications marketplace.

First Dish in an IPO Banquet

As hard as it seems to imagine now, toward the end of the 1990s, China severely lacked anything close to a modern telecommunications infrastructure. At the time, businesses, investors, and governments in advanced nations had become enthralled by the prospects of something called the "New Economy," the notion of an economic system that thrived on interlacing networked flows of information to create gravity-defying levels of prosperity. Although a long way from getting caught up in anything like the dot-com mania that swept the West, China's government clearly recognized the advantages of building out a global-standard telecommunications capacity.

By 1994, the nation had attained a teledensity (number of main telephone lines per 100 residents) of 2.3. That tallied higher than the average for low-income countries (a grouping that includes the poorest of the poor) but scored five times less than middle-income countries (typified by the nations of Central and South America and Eastern Europe).[3] Addressing the telecom gap in its Ninth Five Year Plan (1996–2000), the Chinese government sought to aggressively expand the penetration rate of the nation's fixed-line and mobile communications systems.

China aimed to grow its teledensity at a 10 percent annual rate. With its enormous population, this translated to adding the equivalent of a U.S. regional Bell Operating Company every year. Looked at another way, the government had the task of building more capacity than the entire telephone network of France every two years.[4] Attaining these goals of size and speed would incur extremely heavy costs, as the authorities already knew too well. By 1997, the country was spending $12 billion annually on construction of new phone networks. Depreciation on equipment alone was running at $4 billion per year, expected to increase to $7 to $8 billion by 1998.[5]

Since the 1980s, privatization of government-owned monopolies had become a favored means to reorganize, modernize, expand, and recapitalize telecommunications systems around the world. In a nation where communist ideology and centuries of political tradition advocate government ownership and control of key economic assets, the Chinese leadership did not seriously entertain the possibility of full-scale privatization of its telcos. In preparing for global competition in the twenty-first century, China decided to do things differently, without any existing playbook to guide the transformation of its telecommunications infrastructure. To add to the challenge, in the case of its embryonic mobile phone system, networks in China were divided according to provincial jurisdictions. This increased the difficulty of coordinating the finance necessary to support development of a truly nationwide mobile phone network.

It would be the international stock markets—those hotbeds of unruly capitalism—that would provide an acceptable solution. Working closely with a large team of domestic and foreign (mainly American) financial advisors, China's Ministry of Posts and Telecommunications (MPT) devised a novel means to raise capital through the overseas listing of a minority of shares in an entity called China Telecom (Hong Kong) Limited (CTHK).

With a complex, multitiered structure that required great faith on the part of investors to accept, the global float of CTHK shares as the means to launch China's telecommunications restructuring represented a risky enough proposition in its own right. Yet much more than vast sums of capital and the prospects for China's first national mobile phone network rested on the outcome of the IPO. The authorities decided that if the share issuance worked as planned, it would set a framework for other strategically important state-owned enterprises (SOEs) to follow. The stock debut would serve as a litmus test for whether the government considered international equity market listings and the admittance of foreigners as co-shareholders to be an acceptable means for expanding the nation's economic reforms.

Apart from the raw ambition behind the basic parameters of the CTHK listing, its most remarkable (or, if one prefers, its most audacious) feature concerned how this company, one that functioned as a shell for funneling overseas investment, could possibly raise capital without actually owning any assets. CTHK's future earnings potential—the fundamental rationale for any equity investment in a company—hinged on this shell company taking shareholders' money to first acquire an initial platform of just two provincial mobile phone networks (see Figure 3.2). The driving idea behind that acquisition was to use the two provincial networks as an operating base from

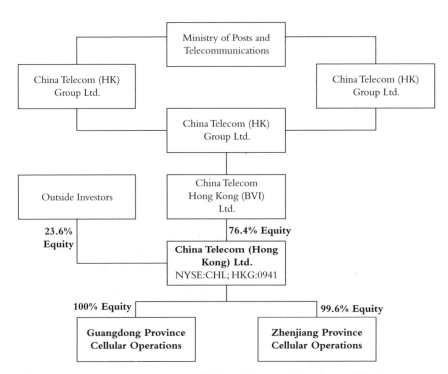

Figure 3.2   Post-IPO Structure of China Telecom (Hong Kong) Ltd.
SOURCE: China Telecom Prospectus

which CTHK could then add other regional carriers and slowly build out a truly nationwide network system. All that was fine in theory, but by going out to overseas stock markets without any assets in hand and all expected revenue growth contingent on a series of unguaranteed acquisitions, an unusual degree of execution risk distinguished the CTHK deal. Undeterred, the underwriters priced the stock far beyond prevailing market levels, at an amount close to 30 times the forecasted earnings per share. At the time, other Asian telecom growth stocks traded at 10 to 15 times forecasted earnings.[6]

China's MPT decided to offer approximately 25 percent of CTHK's enlarged share capital through a global float of 2.6 billion shares. The MPT and its bankers set a date in late October 1997 for a dual IPO on the NYSE and the Stock Exchange of Hong Kong. The NYSE debuted the equivalent of 277.8 million China Telecom shares in the form of American Depository Shares (at 20 ordinary shares per ADS), and the

Stock Exchange of Hong Kong (SEHK) debuted some 144 million shares. The stock market listings drove the momentum of the deal, while institutional and strategic investors—eager to get at least some stake in even only a semiprivatized Chinese mobile phone operator— snatched up the mother lode of nearly 2 billion shares on offer.

Once listed, CTHK intended to purchase and merge the mobile phone networks of Guangdong and Zhejiang. The nearly 3 million subscribers contained in these two prosperous southeastern provinces constituted 28 percent of China's entire mobile phone user base in 1997.[7] Following these cornerstone acquisitions, as a newly capital- ized transregional mobile phone operator, the company would pro- ceed to roll up other provincial networks until it arose as a nationwide operator. As already pointed out, this constituted an extremely bold proposition from the perspective of global capital markets. The trans- action required essentially no money down on the part of the Chinese government, which would remain the majority owner of CTHK. In return for seeding operations of a Chinese state-owned company, foreign investors would receive only a minority stake in an assetless enterprise. For outside equity funders, the deal made sense only if they sufficiently believed that the company would provide them satisfactory returns as it focused on creating a large-scale mobile telephone system for the people of China.

Aiming to raise $4 billion to finance the company's ambitions, nothing of this size or scope had previously been undertaken for a Chinese stock listing. If the IPO succeeded, it held the promise not only to launch a world-class telecommunications market to pave the way for China's participation in the Information Age, but also to serve as a blueprint for the semiprivatization of a "national team" of SOEs intended to sustain China's rapidly developing economy. The restruc- turing of major—not to mention, compared to the near shell that CTHK presented, more substantial—SOE banks, airlines, and energy, mining, and other telecommunications companies hinged on the out- come of this one stock market listing. China's grand plan intended to draw in copious amounts of foreign capital, to be sure. Ultimately, however, the government sought to improve the performance of state enterprises through the increased scrutiny and global exposure that operating as foreign-listed public companies would entail.

The potential for investment by foreign corporations in these listed SOEs' also held strong appeal to the Chinese authorities. Strategic foreign investors offered the possibility of introducing advanced technology and better management practices to the SOEs. To these corporate investors, the chance for a stake in some of the major Chinese corporations driving China's transformation into a global economic powerhouse was perhaps even more enticing.

In sync with market anticipation for the listing of CTHK and what might follow, Wu Jichuan, the head of the MPT, colorfully stoked the interest of the foreign investment community prior to the IPO by remarking that the "listing of China Telecom will be the first course of a big banquet . . . bigger courses will be served later."[8]

Birth in a Maelstrom

CTHK's stock market debut and its promise to touch off a wave of foreign listings for major Chinese SOEs constituted wagers and stakes of a completely new order. As if the inherent risks of the deal provided insufficient uncertainty, the bet on this issuance, already under an intense spotlight, further had to contend with unprecedented financial turbulence.

On Wednesday, October 22, in New York and on Thursday, October 23, 1997, in Hong Kong, CTHK listed back to back on the NYSE and the SEHK. The irony of this timing, coming almost to the day of the tenth anniversary of the October 19, 1987, global stock market wipeout known as Black Monday, seems to have been an unheeded omen. The IPO indeed ended up confronting adversities of historic proportions. The Asian financial crisis, spreading across the region since July, began to wreck havoc in Hong Kong on October 20, with the launch of downward bets on the Hong Kong dollar by international currency speculators. Hong Kong's financial sector, already wobbly from the spiraling regional contagion, started reeling.

On the day of CTHK's listing, the benchmark Hang Seng Index plunged 1,211 points (10.4 percent)—this after having already fallen 6.2 percent the previous day.[9] Just three days of negative currency speculation vaporized nearly one-quarter of the value of Hong Kong's stock market.[10] The situation bode even worse for this latest share listing from mainland China because such Chinese "red chip" stocks were suffering worse than the market overall. Rumors swirled that mainland Chinese interests were going to cash out from their positions in Hong Kong—a territory that China had, after all, reacquired from Britain only three months earlier. Local investors raced for the exits to keep ahead of the anticipated sell-off.[11]

Against these typhoon-force headwinds of financial collapse, CTHK came to market. The company and its bankers had set the international issue price of its shares at HK$11.80 ($1.52) or $30.50 per ADS. With the New York market opening ahead of Hong Kong, the ADSs listed first. The new issuance had fallen to $28.00 by the NYSE's closing bell. Subsequently on the SEHK, the stock finished its inaugural trading day at HK$10.55, 10.6 percent off the issue price. The mainstream Western financial press described China's largest-ever equity offering as "tarnished" and "flopped."[12] Critics directed considerable ire at the IPO underwriter syndicate, led by Goldman Sachs and China International Capital Corp. (CICC), alleging that they had not only mistimed but also overpriced the deal.

When originally marketing the stock ahead of the IPO, the underwriters (in total numbering over 20 banks and financial institutions) had set an indicative price range of HK$7.75 to HK$10. Once the issuance reached 30 times oversubscription, they ratcheted up the range.[13] The estimated level of oversubscription would in most markets reflect strong demand. Yet for Hong Kong, it in fact fell far below the expectations for oversubscriptions on the order of 500 to 600 times. These multiples, although phenomenally high, better reflected Hong Kong's frenzied hunger for a marquee red chip stock at the time. Some interpreted increased pricing after "a mere" 30 times subscribed to be opportunistically greedy, not to mention foolish.[14]

In spite of a higher offer price and financial market convulsions, Hong Kong's excitable retail investors ended up flocking to the CTHK issuance, still oversubscribing it by a factor of 35.2 times.[15] Hoping to raise as much as $4.6 billion, in the final tally the controversial and complex mega IPO attracted slightly more than $4 billion. The raise would have fared much worse had not Goldman and CICC enlisted a cohort of 12 Hong Kong tycoon investors to commit to purchase 45 percent of the issuance at the IPO price and lock in those shares for a minimum of one year. This helped the deal transcend prevailing market conditions to stoke the oversubscription from individuals and sustain interest from global institutional investors.[16]

Whatever one chooses to say about the fairness or true merits of the IPO, the fall in the listing-day share price (10.6 percent) hardly labels the debut a failure, especially if considering that the overall market index dropped by nearly an identical amount that same day. Unfazed by panic borne from the Asian financial crisis, the debut achieved Hong Kong's biggest share flotation in history and the first "blockbuster" offering of Chinese shares in America. Having formally incorporated as a company in a jerry-rigged fashion only one month before its stock issuance—and listing with core assets entirely contingent upon the success of its IPO—CTHK went into a stressed and uncertain marketplace to emerge as the world's fifth-largest cellular telephone operator based on market cap.[17]

The stock's subsequent performance and the company's role in modernizing China's mobile communications market have well rewarded the faith placed in the IPO by investors and the Chinese government. At the time of CTHK's listing, expectations for robust growth in mobile phone usage throughout Asia indicated that China, along with Japan, would lead a regionwide boom. Some predicted that the two nations would account for most of the 170 million subscriptions estimated for Asia by 2007.[18] China, on its own, exceeded the 170 million subscription mark five years ahead of that estimate. Cellular subscriptions in China would reach nearly 550 million by 2007, just 10 years after the IPO of CTHK (see Figure 3.3).[19]

An investor brave enough to take a chance on an ADS of CHL on its listing day would by mid-2011 have had an equity stake worth $200 in return for putting down $30 and some change. Since the time of its IPO, China Mobile's AD share price has risen nearly 550 percent. It has not only outperformed the Dow Jones Industrial Average (60 percent increase) but also the stock of a high-performing developed market mobile phone operator such as Europe's Vodafone (130 percent increase), not to mention an anemically performing representative U.S. operator, Verizon (8 percent decline).

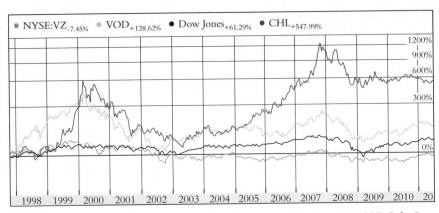

Figure 3.3   CHL Comparative Stock Performance, October 31, 1997–July 8, 2011.
SOURCE: Google Finance.

Ripple Effects

Despite the manifestly profitable long-term outcome for the CHL issuance, many reviews of CTHK's pathbreaking IPO ran from the mixed to the outright dismissive. One investment banker flatly summarized negative sentiment when declaring to the global capital markets newspaper *Euroweek*: "Far from heralding China's entry into the next century, the passage of this issue has come to highlight long–standing concerns about the intentions and depth of the Chinese reform program."[20]

In an article in the online magazine *Slate* headlined "Is There Anything U.S. Investors Won't Buy?" financial journalist James Surowiecki offered up a more insightful and balanced critique from the bearish chorus. Predating by some 13 years the *furor* that flared up over Chinese stock frauds in 2010 and 2011, Surowiecki doubted whether foreign ADR issuers would necessarily adhere to the standards of transparency and disclosure that investors were assuming applied to all equity instruments traded on a U.S. exchange. Acknowledging that American stockholders really only care about whether their shares go up in price, he posed and answered a key question:

If China Telecom's share price is going to double over the next year, why shouldn't you buy it?

If it is going to double, then you should buy. There, wasn't that easy? The problem, though, is that the ADR phenomenon has created a situation where U.S. investors are pouring billions of dollars into companies whose standards of financial disclosure and corporate governance are dramatically different from our own and which are, in some cases, nonexistent. That means, in turn, that it's hard to figure out whether a company will be profitable next year, let alone whether its stock price is going to double. And without full voting rights, there's nothing that investors—even institutional investors—can do if things go haywire.[21]

Looking back from a later vantage point, this assessment proved prescient in many regards. CTHK's stock was a winner, but Surowiecki was well justified to point out the need for mutually agreed to rules concerning transparency and governance.

Without sufficiently reliable and accurate information provided according to common terms of financial exchange, an investment takes on the characteristics of a crap shot—and one that might well be played using loaded dice. As longtime Wall Street observer Peter Bernstein has written: "Only the foolhardy take risks when the rules are unclear, whether it be [the game of] *balla*, buying IBM stock, building a factory, or submitting to an appendectomy."[22] Fortunately, the CTHK issuance benefited from a variety of positive fundamentals, principally a mind-boggling degree of pent-up demand for mobile phone service in China and sufficient commitment by the Chinese government to foster a globally competitive mobile communications sector. Not all China listings can be expected to enjoy the same supportive factors. For most Chinese firms, as with companies anywhere in the world, transparency, governance, and a well articulated strategy underpin a meaningful, if imperfect, valuation.

As part of the People's Republic of China (PRC) government's original intention to increase SOE competitiveness and management quality, China Mobile—the official name change from China Telecom (Hong Kong) Ltd. occurred in 2000—has improved its governance standards in gradual but meaningful increments. Results like this relate to some of the long-term, multifaceted upsides that betting

on China Mobile's listing brought out, something that most naysay-
ers either discounted or ignored. Steps in the direction of higher corporate governance standards for China Mobile have had to constantly
accommodate the administrative workings and political objectives of
the Chinese government, the company's largest shareholder, as the
government uses the company to spearhead its vision for development
of the nation's mobile phone infrastructure. Progressing shareholder
capitalism–based governance standards in such a context has made for a
difficult balancing act, but hardly an impossible one.

While minority shareholder considerations did not feature prominently in the company's 1997 global stock float, in 2001, China
Mobile started documenting its corporate governance policies in its
annual reports. In 2003, it began to pay shareholder dividends, starting at a 20 percent payout ratio. In 2004, it adopted the SEHK's Code
of Corporate Governance Practices. Though not yet going as far as
to conform to all the NYSE's listing rules for a U.S. issuer, in China
Mobile's annual reports and 20F filings with the SEC, the company
outlines areas where it deviates from NYSE standards. This demonstrates disclosure of sorts, yet obviously still below world-class norms.
In any event, the company cannot be faulted for taking advantage of
its ADS listing to give any false appearance of being a typical NYSE-
listed firm. The company plainly communicates where it does and
does not comply with U.S. practices; investors are obligated to assess
their own comfort level with that degree of compliance.

Beyond the more obvious signs of gradual improvements with
corporate governance at China Mobile itself, the company's interaction with the U.S. financial system directly paved the way for the
listing of a Chinese telco that became a model for how much more
robust corporate governance practices could fit within a Chinese SOE
framework.

Assimilating Global Standards

As intended, the China Mobile IPO opened the door for a slew of
major Chinese SOEs to partially list their shares in the United States,
with the NYSE chosen nearly by default for stock issuances by China's

national champion corporations. Fossil fuel companies PetroChina (NYSE:PTR), Sinopec (NYSE:SHI), and CNOOC (NYSE:CEO) conducted global floatations between 2000 and 2001. The second and third stages of the state telecom industry's privatization program generated IPOs for number-two mobile phone operator China Unicom (NYSE:CHU) in 2000 and the southern region fixed-line operations of China Telecom (NYSE:CHA) in 2001. Chalco (NYSE:ACH), the Aluminum Corporation of China, listed in 2001, followed by China Life Insurance (NYSE:LFC) in December 2003. When China Netcom (NYSE:CN) listed in November 2004, it brought to outside equity investors a chance to grab a piece of the last slice of China's national telecommunications infrastructure to be served up for a public offering. It also eventually ushered in a new ways of thinking about corporate governance at Chinese SOEs.

The origins of the Netcom name stretch back to the company's days as a private, Shanghai-based Internet service provider founded in the 1990s. In 2002, Netcom Ltd. combined with other fixed-line service providers, chiefly the monopoly telephone operations for the northern provinces spun off from China Telecom (which operated separately from the special vehicle CTHK that later became China Mobile). The merger came about as part of the industry reorganization that preceded China Telecom's overseas listings in New York and Hong Kong. Out of that final stage of industrial consolidation, China Netcom emerged as the junior half of a landline communications duopoly dominated by the better-positioned China Telecom, which retained China's most valuable fixed-line assets in the prospering southern region.

China Netcom also later debuted simultaneously on the NYSE and SEHK, with Goldman Sachs and CICC again acting as joint book runners and global coordinators as they had for CTHK/China Mobile; Citigroup (which had managed Netcom's earlier foreign acquisition of the bankrupt Asia Global Crossing) also joined as a book runner, the most important of role for an investment bank in an IPO. Netcom's November 2004 IPO raised $1.1 billion for 16.2 percent of the company's enlarged share capital. At the beginning of the year, reports indicated that the company planned to raise $2 billion or more for a 25 percent share floatation. This proved difficult as the markets saw the listing as a watered-down version of the 2002 share offering by

China Telecom (NYSE:CHA, again not to be confused by CTHK's 1997 offering of shares on the NYSE that trade under the ticker symbol CHL).

In the end, China Netcom adjusted its valuation downward to attract buyers, issuing the stock at a current price-earnings ratio of 6.5 (versus the 8.9 times current earnings that China Telecom's stock price was garnering at the time). It further sweetened the deal by offering to pay shareholders 35 to 40 percent of net profit as dividends (comparable stock then paid out at about only half those levels). The market very much perceived Netcom as a "me too" play, akin to being the runt of the litter in overseas-listed Chinese telecommunications issuances. These comparative weaknesses provided a silver lining to foreign investors as they compelled the firm's senior manager, Chairman Zhang Chunjiang, to find additional means to build investor confidence from the outset.

Not long after going public, at a fateful board meeting in August 2005, the chairman was about to approve an acquisition of assets from Netcom's government-controlled majority shareholder. Although a routine approval matter for a state-listed company, an independent director and head of Netcom's Corporate Governance Committee, John Thornton, did what in the context of a Chinese SOE was virtually unthinkable: *he objected*.

Thornton, a former group president of Goldman Sachs who had served as chairman of the bank's Asia operations during the fateful IPO of CTHK, did not oppose the acquisition of the assets as a bad business decision. He disagreed with how the company had proposed the transaction without independent review. Company lawyers argued that the acquisition did not legally require as high a degree of vetting as Thornton was requesting. The ex-banker contended that irrespective of the law, best-practice corporate governance dictated that such procedures be followed.

Later reflecting on the incident, Zhang admitted in an interview: "This was the first time I'd ever encountered opposition. It was a seemingly small incident that touched off something much bigger. It made me think about how we could set up a corporate governance structure that would put the capital markets at ease."[23]

What followed literally became a first-of-its-kind textbook case on how China could integrate American style corporate governance practices within a semiprivatized Chinese SOE. Zhang realized from Thornton's objections that Netcom would need to adopt new management processes but do so in a way that would not interfere with the objectives of the Chinese Communist Party serving as the ultimate majority shareholder. The company hired a team of advisors from the U.S. consultancy group McKinsey & Co. and one of China's top institutions of higher learning, Tsinghua University. With 7 out of 13 directors on the Netcom board serving independently, the company could also draw from a relatively broad base of unencumbered individuals at that level for help in achieving the delicate balances needed to implement substantial changes.

The combined efforts brought about noticeable results. The final version of a new corporate governance plan, though not without compromises to accommodate state interests, introduced greater transparency to China Netcom than any SOE had ever adopted before. Major improvements included a traceable validation process for approval of related party transactions. This kind of decision-making mechanism crucially facilitates governance in a company that frequently conducts business with a parent organization. The capital market–inspired reforms at China Netcom, entered into the annals of management scholarship as a 2008 Harvard Business School case study, established a new benchmark for corporate governance in Chinese industry.[24]

Since its merger with the nation's number-two mobile carrier, China Unicom, in October 2008, China Netcom no longer operates as an independent business enterprise. While it was in operation, the final and smallest IPO to spin off from the restructuring of China's telecom ministry delivered in unexpected ways. In addition to the company's unusually generous dividend policies, China Netcom shareholders were in a stock whose price tripled between its November 2004 debut and the June 2008 announcement of the company's acquisition. A more lasting payout—but, as explored in the next section, one hardly lacking in dramatic irony—came from the corporate governance structures that China Netcom demonstrated were possible for a Chinese government-owned enterprise (see Figure 3.4).

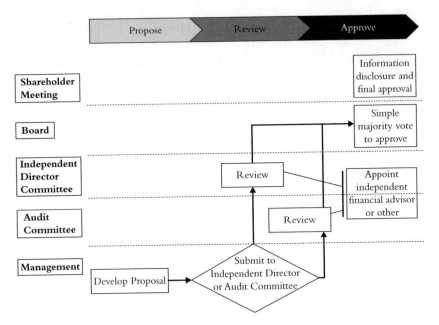

Figure 3.4   China Netcom: Connected Transaction Review Process
SOURCE: China Netcom, HBS Case Study

Of Men and Governance

In a bizarrely ironic sidebar to the institutional reforms spearheaded by Netcom's chairman Zhang Chunjiang, later events suggest that the man himself failed to adhere to the principles embodied by the governance policies that he implemented. In December 2009, the "public face of corporate governance in Chinese state industry" (as London's *Financial Times* had dubbed him) fell from grace under accusations of perpetuating "the largest corruption scandal in the telecommunications industry since the founding of the republic."[25]

According to the investigative Chinese business magazine *Caijing*, Zhang led a double life. Visible displays of principled corporate stewardship reportedly occurred alongside personal behavior of "coarse human relations and alcoholic indulgence." He allegedly maintained a number of mistresses, at least one of whom he installed at a senior position in Netcom. She presumably worked with other confederates as part of an insider cabal that allowed the chairman to cover up as much as RMB20 billion ($2.9 billion) in losses in the months prior to the $24 billion valued share-swap acquisition by China Unicom.[26]

The scheme purportedly hatched by Zhang and his accomplices involved inflating earnings so that on the basis of Netcom's impressive results, Zhang would move to the top position at China Unicom following the merger. He supposedly had intended then to cover up the losses along with his individual acts of graft from his new position of higher authority. The plan fell apart when, instead of going on to head Unicom, Zhang was transferred by the ministry to serve in roles of even greater importance (but utterly lacking in authority over Unicom's bookkeeping) as deputy general manager and party secretary at none other than the nation's top telecommunications company, China Mobile.

Zhang's overscheming seems to have led to his undoing. Earnings performance of Netcom was so exaggerated that he achieved reassignment at a level higher than the one for which he was aiming. Subsequently lacking the means to hide his transgressions, the very transparency and corporate discipline that Zhang had ushered in at Netcom caught up with him. Barely a year after the Unicom–Netcom merger closed, internal investigations uncovered Zhang's corruption, leading to his dismissal from all his posts and a later trial. In July 2011, a tribunal sentenced him to death—Chinese courts tend to make an example of high-profile corruption cases—but with a two-year reprieve. With good behavior, Zhang will likely see his sentence transmuted to a life term. Even with the reduced punishment, the former chairman of Netcom has the dubious distinction of twice serving as the face of corporate governance. In the second instance his guise has metaphorically assumed the form of an impaled head, which for his sake hopefully will remain purely a figurative image.

For all the sordidness of the affair and the blatant contradictions it brought to light about the former champion of corporate governance in China, Zhang Chunjiang's tenure at Netcom and perversely even the corruption scandal itself have contributed to the cause of institutional reform in China. However flawed as a captain of industry, Zhang did succeed in introducing valuable improvements to governance at a major U.S.-listed Chinese SOE. Moreover, Zhang's corruption case has elicited serious discussion as well as signs of action on ways to further carry out improvements to governance systems. This time it is not only representatives of overseas investors who are speaking out but also members of influential organizations within China's central government.

Lin Yueqin, an economist at the prestigious Chinese Academy of Social Sciences, commented in the *China Daily* (a leading English-language newspaper used by the government for communicating official viewpoints) that cases like Zhang's "stem from the current appointment system."[27] That is a relatively bold statement, one that echoes what foreign commentators regard as one of the biggest issues at listed SOEs: lack of independently selected senior management appointments that are not simply chosen by the Communist Party and then rubber-stamped by a company board. Lin has highlighted the significance of Zhang Chunjiang's case specifically to call for greater board independence. The same *China Daily* article described a trial program undertaken by China's chief SOE regulator, the State-owned Assets Supervision and Administration Commission (SASAC), to strengthen board independence and oversight of government-appointed managers at a number of state-owned corporations.

Zhang might have cynically hid behind false pretenses of commitment to corporate governance, but influential elements within the Chinese government appear to be seriously considering the advantages of increased transparency and accountability as a result of his multifaceted examples of good and bad governance practices.

Red Chip Scare

In addition to the adjustments that the Chinese government has undertaken to integrate U.S.-listed SOEs into China's economic system, elements of the U.S. government have also had to confront the implications of Chinese stock issuances for America's capital markets.

Chapters 5 and 6 look at how U.S. federal government regulators have been dealing with some of the major controversies that have surfaced over time. Early on, before tangible issues had time to emerge, there was some speculation within the U.S. Congress about what the potential downside to Chinese issuances might be. One of the more colorful opponents to Chinese listings came from the powerful House Rules Committee chairman, Representative Gerald "Jerry" Solomon of New York. Chairman Solomon, along with Senator Duncan Faircloth of North Carolina, earned a special place in the annals of the Sino-American equity dynamic for introducing to both houses of Congress the U.S. Market Security Act of 1997 immediately following China Mobile's NYSE IPO.

Solomon, a gung ho Marine veteran of the Korean War and a feisty Reaganite conservative, described his proposed legislation as "responsive both to current trends and forward looking to the age where economic warfare may supersede more traditional forms of warfare." His bill aimed to establish for Americans "a special watchdog agency specifically committed to making sure that no entity can engineer fluctuations that could bring our markets down."

Not one for mincing words—and since his decorated service in the war, perpetually antagonistic toward Communist China—the senior lawmaker charged the PRC, and *only* the PRC, as a probable culprit to wage "economic warfare against us through bogus offerings in our markets." Hardly warmed by MPT Minister Wu Jichuan's invitation to foreign investors to join in the extended feast of Chinese SOE IPOs, Solomon warned that the "communist government in China is in the midst of offering a whole string of their controlled businesses on the Hong Kong markets with the intent of listing them on the New York Stock Exchange. China Telecom is just the most recent to go up on the trading board in both places."[28]

To be fair, in a general sense, elements of Solomon's call to arms did not lack merit. His expressed chief concern to protect the access of investors "to the most accurate, fair, and sound information pertaining to stock listings so they can make educated, informed choices" was not only reasonable but insightful. If legislation of this nature had been applied not just to listings from China but to all stock issuances, U.S. investors could have been spared a number of high-profile domestic stock frauds that by that time were already brewing. Unfortunately, the U.S. Market Security Act viewed China as the only enemy and utterly overlooked more immediate threats then fermenting within America's own borders. The New York congressman—whose other China-related bill proposals for 1997 included H.R. 320, the Chinese

Slave Labor Act, and H.R. 87, which aimed to prevent international financial institution from providing any kind of assistance to China—was so convinced of the Chinese government's ill intents that he seemed incapable of perceiving any advantages whatsoever in interaction between Chinese SOEs and U.S. capital markets.

Just as exaggerated criticisms of America and the U.S. financial system by China's far right misconstrue the mutual gains available from closer cooperation, Solomon's paranoia of economic aggression by China ignored the tremendous potential benefits from strengthening Sino-American financial relations. The logic of probable "economic warfare" being launched by a foreign power from the platform of U.S. financial markets seems more reminiscent of stereotyped Hollywood portrayals of enemies to the American way of life than to any legitimate signs of threat. In fact, by the time of China Mobile's IPO, the James Bond film *GoldenEye* featured an impossibly powerful satellite communications technology that the forces of evil (backed by unreformed former Soviet Communists) intended to use to cause a "worldwide financial meltdown."[29] That plotline bears far greater resemblance to the reasoning of the U.S. Market Security Act than any sound economic analysis.

Of course, to question the rationale behind a stock issuance and the motives of an issuer, whether the listing source is the PRC government or IBM Corporation, demonstrates prudence. To assume, without probable cause, that an issuer intends capital market annihilation demonstrates something else. For reasons not fully fathomable, China often inspires these sorts of outlandish interpretations. The extremes that extend from overexuberance—that fantastically envisioned opportunity to supply "oil for the lamps of China"—to fearmongering—captured in that particularly odious phrase, "yellow peril"—chaotically tug upon Western perceptions of this seemingly inscrutable foreign power. Seeing China rationally, without favoritism or prejudice, to filter out the noise of any assessment, remains an ongoing challenge to America and the world at large.

Fortunately for the sake of progressive U.S.-Sino financial relations, Solomon's proposed act never materialized into law. Unfortunately for American investors, nothing targeting more tangible threats to the U.S. capital markets at the time did either. In the year of China Mobile's NYSE listing, fraudulent management practices at telecom companies such as WorldCom and Global Crossing, along with massive accounting malpractice at the energy-trading firm Enron, were concocting bigger toxic hazards to U.S. financial markets than anything a Chinese SOE partial stock float could ever stir up. After the considerable damage those U.S.-operating enterprises visited on the markets, financial legislation of another type emerged. This arrived in the form of the Public Company Accounting Reform and Investor Protection Act proposed by Senator Paul Sarbanes, later combined with similar legislation started by Representative Michael Oxley, and entered into the law books in 2002 as the eponymous Sarbanes-Oxley Act.

Headline-grabbing conflicts between Chinese stock issuances and this latest incarnation of U.S. governance standards, known as Sarbox or SOX, erupted in later years. They arose not out of a nefarious conspiracy hatched by scheming Communist authorities bent on undermining the global capitalist system, but out of fraudulent or insufficiently transparent behavior at certain Chinese companies, combined with structural differences between the regulatory regimes and business practices in China and the United States. Later chapters look more intently at these problematic aspects of the U.S.-China equity exchange dynamic.

The U.S. Market Security Act of 1997 provides another reminder of how anti-liberal, protectionist sentiments—more typically associated with Chinese conservatism—have also emerged within the U.S. polity as the Sino-American financial relationship has developed. So far, more balanced assessments have prevailed, allowing transformative events like the listing of CTHK/China Mobile and the IPOs of so many Chinese state- and privately operated enterprises that followed in its wake to continue to raise capital on U.S. equity markets.

Spillover Effects

In 2000, three years after CTHK's historic IPO and the very year that China geared up to overtake the United State in the number of mobile phone subscriptions, foreign brands held 93 percent of the China's

high-flying cellular handset market.[30] Over time, as China's telecommunications market matured and its manufacturing capabilities increased,
local Chinese handset makers entered the fray. Unlike the tendency in
some developing markets to pursue protectionist industrial policies—
and though encouraging indigenous high-tech product development and often favoring homegrown technology supply—in the telecommunications field, China has remained fundamentally open to
foreign suppliers. Figures indicate that throughout the first decade of
the twenty-first century, multinational handset brands such as Nokia,
Samsung, LG, Sony-Ericsson, Motorola, and Apple continuously occupied a majority share of the prized China handset market. Between
2009 and 2010, out of 16 major telecom infrastructure projects in the
PRC, European and American equipment manufacturers successfully
bid on 11 projects outright and shared 1 with local companies. The
announced contract value of six projects alone exceeded $5.5 billion.[31]

The mobile telecom–focused telecommunications infrastructure
in China that emerged after China Mobile's IPO is one illustration
of how the wagers made on the company's global stock issuance have
earned benefits far exceeding the basic gains of trade accorded to the
company and its investors. Putting aside a review of the fundamental and pervasively shared benefits created by a country with advanced
telecommunications capacity, Chinese mobile phone users—the most
immediate nonfinancial beneficiaries—along with the employees and
other stakeholders of foreign and Chinese handset manufacturers, have
been the most directly enriched group from the modernization and
growth of China's telecommunications sector.

In step with the transformation of China's mobile communications
market, the country has given birth to an array of increasingly globally
recognized handset manufacturers. Chinese brands such as ZTE,
TCL, and Huawei have developed products that now compete in
local Chinese and overseas markets head-to-head with more established foreign-branded products. In 2010, ZTE became the first
mainland Chinese cell phone manufacturer to place in International
Data Corporation's coveted "top five" worldwide ranking of mobile
phone shipments. ZTE's 51.8 million phone shipments earned it a
3.7 percent global market share and fourth-place position, surpass-
ing better-known Research in Motion, whose BlackBerry models

racked up sales performance slightly behind that of ZTE handsets with 48.8 million shipments and a 3.5 percent global market
share.[32] One very distinct end result of enlightened industrial policy
in China is that the basic openness and competitive environment
of the PRC's mobile phone market has stimulated technological development and product choice for the benefit of consumers
worldwide.

The momentum behind the impressive growth and economic
value generated by China's mobile phone market boom shows no signs
of stopping anytime soon. Through the repeated leaps that China has
been making with its mobile phone market development, as of 2010,
China's cellular penetration rate was about 65 percent, nearly 10 times
greater than the penetration achieved back in 2000 (see Figure 3.5).
Remarkable as that is, as the country's economy rolls forward faster
than that of any major nation on earth, demand for even more volume
and sophistication in China's mobile telecom products and services
sectors will likely grow apace.

Analysts estimate that mobile phone penetration in China could
more than double by 2015. China's penetration rate, measured by
number of mobile phone subscriptions per 100 inhabitants, still
measures only about 70 percent of the rate achieved in the United
States, indicating plenty of room for growth based on this mature

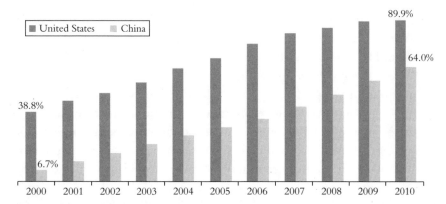

Figure 3.5 U.S. and China Mobile Phone Markets Penetration Rates,
2000–2010
SOURCE: International Telecommunications Union

market benchmark. Moreover, rather than merely playing catch-up with the developed world, China's mobile phone base is, in fact, leap-frogging it.

Mobile phone penetration in the United States (as with techno-logically advanced nations like Japan) has plateaued in recent years at around 90 percent. This occurs because long before cellular com-munications technology became available, developed economies such as the United States, Japan, and Western Europe already had robust telecom infrastructures in place. Developing nations such as China, by contrast, have created national cellular phone systems in lieu of sub-stantial preexisting fixed-line systems. Consumers in China also prefer to have multiple cellular phone numbers to better cover separate uses in business, travel, and personal life. Thus, achieving a penetration rate well in excess of 100 percent (based on more than one subscription per person) in China is very probable.

As it so happens, demand for fixed-line telephone services in the PRC is actually softening. This both signifies and additionally encour-ages higher demand for cellular services. If mobile phone network expansion into the country's rural areas—a vast internal market that remains relatively untapped—combines with a brisk uptake in data-intensive smartphones by urban users, these trends could take China's mobile phone subscriptions to new dimensions of usage intensity and technological sophistication. Business Monitor International, which issues projections at the high end of the estimates spectrum, predicts that mobile phone penetration in the PRC will reach 100 percent by 2013 and extend to almost 140 percent by 2015.

Should China achieve that level of mobile teledensity, the nation will have a mind-bogglingly vast market of 1.9 billion subscribers.[33] To put that in perspective, if one thought to phone in to say "*ninhao*" ("hello" in standard Mandarin Chinese) to each subscriber active as of 2015, it would take some 60 years to finish making rounds (and that would be only allowing for one second to utter each greeting continuously without interruption). Put in a comparative market per-spective, such a subscription base by 2015 for China *alone* will surpass the combined subscription total as of 2010 for *all* of the world's major developing nations that constitute the BRICI group: Brazil, Russia, India, China, and Indonesia.[34]

Quantity, Banditry, and Quality

China's ascension as a mobile phone powerhouse goes beyond sheer numbers. Quality and innovation, not frequently recognized as strong suits for Chinese industries, play growing roles as well. Simultaneously both the world's largest consuming market and production base for mobile phones, China's swelling supply and demand power has driven down global prices while pushing features and functionality, providing diverse benefits for consumers worldwide.

The more distinctive, and controversial, of China's contributions to the global cell phone industry are handset clones, popularly known as *shanzhai* (pronounced "shan-jai" and literally meaning "mountain hideout"). The *shanzhai*—a term that, as used in modern Chinese, reflects a whimsical purloining or humorous imitation of an original item—units burst onto China's local cell phone scene around 2005. Their appearance resulted from advances in software, industrial design techniques, and (something observers and analysts have especially emphasized) a radically low-priced all-in-one baseboard chipset—the electronic guts of a phone—made by a leading Taiwan microchip house, MediaTek. Taking these technical ingredients and mixing them with the plucky entrepreneurialism exhibited by innumerable micro-scale manufacturers clustered around the counterfeit product bazaars of Shenzhen (Communist China's first testing ground for market-based economics located next to Hong Kong), and very quickly, realistic looking imitation phones began popping up.

Displaying slightly off mimicry of leading foreign brands by labeling handsets with names like Nckia, Sumsung, Blockberry, and the Hi-Phone, *shanzhai* handsets stoked hot interest for their amazingly low, sub-$100 prices and fun features lacking in the genuine articles. Best sellers include phones with multiple speakers for a boom box effect, television reception capability, a built-in LED flashlight, or a camera lens that can add telescopic attachments. *Shanzhai* handsets also boast more practical functions, such as extended battery life, and can accommodate at least two SIM cards (which in China and most parts of the world do not require activation) so users can employ multiple subscriptions on a single device. Owing to low cost of entry provided by the MediaTek chipset and freedom to ignore the lengthy research and development (R&D) work, design approval, and production ramp-up required by a global handset brand, *shanzhai* phone makers can churn out new models in as little as 1 to 2 months. This compares with 6 to 12 months for internationally branded phones.[35]

The affordability of *shanzhai* clones and locally branded handsets carved out a new low-end segment in China and, via exports, in developing markets around the world. Between 2007 and 2009, while China's handset market crescendoed at a rate of 22 percent growth in handset shipments, category leader Nokia saw its sales level off at between 71 and 72 million units per year. JP Morgan analyst Alvin Knock estimates that the affordable Chinese-made phones powered by MediaTek chipsets captured the China-based sales increases that passed Nokia by.[36] As *shanzhai* phone production scaled up, China's cellular knockoffs started appearing on store shelves and hawker stands in India, Russia, and throughout Southeast Asia, igniting buyer fever for their affordable, feature-rich offerings. The telecommunications consultancy the Linley Group, in 2008 estimated that official statistics for worldwide mobile phone shipments undercounted by as much as 150 million units because the data overlooked the unrecorded output of *shanzhai* phones. Since then, the reach of seductively affordable Chinese clones has spread farther to Latin America, Africa, and the Middle East, launching booms in mobile telecommunications wherever they touch down.

Despite the products' roguish associations as pirated counterfeits, the rapid flexibility by which *shanzhai* phones gauge, respond to, and influence consumer tastes around the world makes them celebrated by a number of academics and industry observers who treat them as symbols of leading-edge creativity. According to this group of *shanzhai* advocates, the phones are seen as a sign of things to come from Chinese manufacturing at large and should serve as inspiration for foreign brands. Yongjiang Shi of Cambridge University believes that "developed nations and established companies" should look to China's experience with *shanzhai* phones "to reconsider the relationship between manufacturing and brand" and "capture emerging opportunities and create alternative brands in new markets."[37] The Silicon Valley–based global design consultancy IDEO sees China's quirky homegrown phone stylings and other knockoff products as major market opportunities, a chance "for international companies to introduce Chinese consumers to their brands, and then observe how local Chinese culture adapts their offerings."[38] Echoing some of the admiration once reserved for the lightning-fast production changeover capacity of Japan's "just in time" manufacturers, Vassar College's Yu Zhou remarks that China's *shanzhai* phone producers excel not so much by their technology but by "how they form supply chains and how rapidly they react to new trends."[39]

Considering that most Chinese phone cloners thrive mainly by means of imitation with some clever gadgetry thrown in, the ebullient praise of their innovativeness might seem a bit excessive. Yet not all Chinese *shanzhai* makers are content with relying on the product designs and brand imagery of others to serve as the canvas for their creations. Perhaps the best example of this can be seen with Beijing-based Tianyu Communication Equipment, which had its origins as a *shanzhai* cellular handset manufacturer but later emerged as a recognized brand-name manufacturer with its own fully operating R&D capacity. Tianyu's markets its K-Touch series phones in direct competition with more established brands at the low end of the market.

At the next level up in China's phone manufacturing base, major Chinese handset brands have moved beyond their traditional lower-end market orientation. They are positioning their product offerings higher to vie for the fatter margins available in higher-end segments and in developed-country markets. As the first Chinese manufacturer to rank as a Big Five global handset brand, ZTE has already set the stage for wider acceptance of self-developed Chinese mobile phone technology in mature markets. In 2011, the company released an Android operating system–based touchscreen phone for the United Kingdom's mid-market—another indication of ZTE's global ambitions and what might be possible for other leading Chinese mobile phone manufacturers.

Back at ZTE's home base in the PRC, China's three semiprivate, U.S.-listed cellular operators—China Mobile, China Unicom, and China Telecom—have been investing heavily in advanced infrastructure to upgrade the nation's capacity to carry later-generation communications traffic. In 2009 alone, they spent over RMB161 billion (equivalent then to just under $24 billion) to roll out the nation's third-generation (3G) networks, constructing 325,000 3G base stations in the process. According to China's Ministry of Industry and Information Technology (MIIT), that represents the fastest and most extensive build-out of its kind for any national market ever. By the ministry's reckoning, in addition to the RMB161 billion directly invested into the networks, the spending on the 3G rollout stimulated another RMB589 billion ($86 billion) in related but indirect investments. This likewise translated into directly boosting China's gross domestic product (GDP) by about another RMB34 billion ($5 billion) and indirectly by RMB141 billion ($21 billion).[40] An earlier McKinsey study on 2G cellular usage in China corroborates that the dividends for investments in the country's mobile phone infrastructure can be extraordinary. The researchers found that frequently mobile workers (a group ranging from taxi drivers to salespeople) in China boosted labor productivity by nearly 6 percent when using cellular communications. This equated to tens of billions of dollars in yearly economic returns for the nation.[41]

New Generations, New Markets

When China Mobile listed in 1997, the stock's investment thesis pivoted on infrastructure driving demand. This story sold well because of the dearth of telecommunications services in China prior to the introduction of basic cellular networks. For Chinese subscribers to migrate to more advanced, data-intensive 3G and 4G communications, however, the situation differs. Already basically satisfied with the simple voice and limited data services that prevailing 2G networks offer, most Chinese consumers expect more compelling reasons than merely the availability of next-generation network services before purchasing the more sophisticated and more costly to use mobile devices that those networks support.

This phenomenon is reflected in the take-up rate for 3G subscriptions in China, which has been rising but not as explosively as the frenetically paced infrastructure build-out had originally intended. MITT first predicted that, by 2011, 3G subscriptions would climb almost 15 times, to 150 million from a base of slightly more than 10 million in 2009.[42] Among the various estimates for actual 3G usage in China, even using figures from a higher range, 3G subscriptions in China had reached only around 50 million by 2010. According to official government statistics, 3G subscriptions in the first half of 2011 had just passed the 80 million mark. All these numbers suggest a level of growth that by the end of 2011 has fallen substantially short of the original target.[43]

To cross the technology gap, in the same way that China's *shanzhai* 2G phones ignited consumer interest worldwide, low-cost 3G and 4G solutions from Chinese manufacturers are likely to provide the trigger needed for Chinese and other developing-world consumers to move up to next-generation of smartphone handsets. Leping Huang at Nomura International, the research arm of the Japanese securities brokerage, reasons that affordable "smartphones for the masses" are the key component that has been lacking in China so far.[44] At the beginning of 2012, the most coveted smartphone among Chinese consumers, the iPhone 4S, was selling at a starting price of about RMB5,000 (nearly $800). On the basis of per capita GDP, the typical Chinese person at the time was averaging approximately $400 of economic output per month, which shows just how steep a cost proposition a top-of-the-line smartphone can represent to most Chinese.[45] Consistent with what Nomura's Huang has predicted, once there are enough smartphones selling at close to RMB1,000 (about $150), a dramatic reshaping of the world's largest cellular telecom market seems possible.

As China advances up the technology curve in mobile phone usage and production, this progress can be expected to be accompanied by other deep-seated transformations. One of the most interesting will be increased respect for brand integrity and protection of intellectual property rights—the very issues that have doggedly plagued China's trade ties with the developed world. The upgrading of China's mobile phone marketplace looks especially promising at this juncture for a number of U.S. companies and U.S.-listed Chinese stocks. San Diego, California–based Qualcomm (NASDAQ:QCOM) along with China-based, Sino-American–operated and U.S.-listed chipmaker Spreadtrum (NASDAQ:SPRD) enjoy particularly advantageous positions to capitalize on the generational shift. (The next chapter looks at Spreadtrum's controversial example of a latter-day China bet.) The U.S. technology colossus Google (NASDAQ:GOOG), whose clashing with

Chinese authorities over censorship regulations resulted in a period where its Internet search engine services in China were halted, has already become the leading smartphone operating system provider in the PRC via Google's popular Android platform. Where it has failed in one Chinese market, Google has resoundingly succeeded in another. Google technology has become for advanced mobile devices in China what Intel had already much earlier become for computers.

Silicon Valley's most iconic brand, Apple (NASDAQ:AAPL), is finding new opportunities in China's emergent 3G/4G space as well. Though priced out of range for the majority of Chinese consumers, the iPhone series has enjoyed market leadership in being a prestige status symbol for users who make the switch to smartphones. Similar to the situation with Google, it is Apple's phone sales, rather than the company's mainline computer offering, that have propelled its growth in China.[46] In 2011, Apple's branded retail stores in the PRC were attracting on average 40,000 visits per day—four times greater than that for a U.S. store—and generating the highest average revenues of any Apple stores in the world. Some observers go so far as to predict that China eventually will replace the value of Apple's home market in the United States and become the single largest market for Apple products in the world.[47]

In addition to all the new opportunities that next-generation mobile telephony in China has been creating for foreign and domestic brands, the structure of China's cellular marketplace has been becoming more competitive as well. 3G subscription numbers have divided according to a roughly 40 percent market share for China Mobile, with 30 percent shares going to China Telecom and China Unicom. China Mobile's heavily dominant 70 percent market share in total mobile subscriptions made it the logical carrier for the government to enlist to deploy the nation's homegrown 3G standard, Time Division Synchronous Code Division Multiple Access (typically referred as TD-SCDMA or simply TD 3G). China Mobile's government-mandated adoption of TD 3G left rival carriers China Unicom and China Telecom free to deploy networks built on international protocols known for faster data transfer speeds and that support a broader array of next-generation handsets. This has meant that moving into the smartphone era, China Mobile was supporting about 25 types of

3G devices, compared to 70 supported by China Telecom and more than 100 supported by China Unicom.[48] This bodes well for the prospects of competitive rivalry among carriers to boost market efficiencies and provide greater consumer choice going forward.

Nothing and Everything

Carl Walter and Fraser Howie, two experienced, longtime practitioners in and observers of China's financial system, have remarked that the listing of CTHK as an assetless, Chinese government–controlled regional telecommunications play was such a contrived deal that its success amounted to "truly pulling capital out of the air!"[49] A University of Hong Kong case study goes further, questioning whether the transaction merely amounted to "money for nothing" for outside investors. Rather than "making an opening of China's telecommunications operations to foreign involvement," the discussion paper asserts, "the offering appeared to be quite the opposite: a centralization and reiteration of Beijing's control over its telecoms network."[50]

To this day, Chinese government control over the nation's telecommunications infrastructure certainly shows no signs of abating. There should also be no illusions that corporate governance practices at China Mobile and other SOEs, though having improved significantly over time, have matched Western standards; they are still some ways off. "Off," however, is not an absolute indicator that the Chinese way is necessarily inferior. The China-born, Texas Tech–educated PhD and former chief executive of China Netcom, Suning "Edward" Tian, once loudly protested the seemingly arbitrary way in which senior appointments were made at the state-owned telco he formerly ran. Tian came to see things differently after his tenure with the company. As related by *Financial Times* correspondent Richard McGregor:

> Tian left the system with a more favourable view than he had had when he joined. "I feel I could justify this system now and understand how it has worked for 1,000 years," he said. "Ten years ago, I would not have a similar feeling." Tian compared his time at Netcom to his experience on boards in Western companies, where he said CEOs were chosen by busy directors

in consultation with headhunters. However political the process in China might have been, he maintained the vetting of
CEOs was generally more thorough in his homeland.[51]

China's "system," in its various guises, frequently does not match
Western norms. But that does not necessarily mean that more traditional Chinese management practices are incapable of helping to build
shareholder value.

The growth of China Mobile and the consumer and manufacturing sectors that have emerged around it saw the United States as the
world's leading cellular phone market overtaken by the PRC. Yet rather
than representing a loss to America and victory to China, the process has been rewarding to both sides. In the United States, Wall Street
has been far from the only winner, as leading American technology
firms like Apple, Qualcomm, Google, and Motorola (NYSE:MMI;
NYSE:MSI), among many others, have all seen their China-related
business rise in importance—for some to the point where China sales
have become their most strategically important and viable long-term
growth opportunity. Other foreign technology providers and consumers have reaped the rewards of new market access and increased
product choices. Meanwhile, China has experienced a complete transformation of its telecom product and infrastructure markets, going
from being far behind global standards to now ranking at the top.

Add to this how the controversial, market-battered IPO of
CTHK/China Mobile managed to debut during one of the darkest
hours of the Asian financial crisis and opened the door for the subsequent wave of Chinese share issuances on U.S. stock exchanges. The
listing of CHL shares was both a watershed historical event and a game
changer in the U.S.–China financial relationship.

In the context of Adam Smith's original assessment of China, the
world-leading yet inward-looking communications and navigations
system of past imperial eras has been succeeded by a multilayered,
intricately transnational communications edifice that has generated
an abundance of global wealth-creating activities. If he were alive and
writing today, Mr. Smith would no doubt have much on which to
compliment China's Communist rulers concerning the means they

used to build up the nation's telecommunications markets even if he would fundamentally disagree with their economic philosophy.

The next generation of mobile telecommunications that China is entering involves convergence of formerly separated spheres of information technology and processing. Computing power is branching out into new dimensions of affordability, portability, and connectivity found in mobile devices like smartphones and tablets; novel ways for accumulating, interpreting, modifying, and sharing data are expanding in availability. Although a latecomer to embracing the Information Age, since the Chinese government's bold experiment with the global IPO of China Mobile, the PRC has emerged among the leading nations in this evolution in content-based and content-generating interconnectedness. Even with a communications regulatory regime that differs markedly from the West, like all nations that are developing next-generation capabilities, adoption of this new framework for connecting people in China can be expected to set the stage for further transformations in the market and society as a whole.

In any final assessment, however risky and unorthodox the IPO of China Mobile was, the vast payoffs and broad range of value added in terms of financial returns, social advancement, global industrial development, stimulation of worldwide consumer markets, and increased competition and market access within China's world-leading mobile telecommunications sector should be factored in as well. The listing hardly proved to be a sucker's bet. The global stock float represents a gamble that clearly has paid out disproportionately to those who have been willing to play.

Chapter 4

Spreadtrum Communications

When the Chips Are Down

Not long after we moved into the big old hotel in the Rockies to spend the winter as caretakers, Danny started muttering something to himself over and over again, something that sounded like "Spreadtrum, Spreadtrum."

Then one evening as an icy mist enshrouded the hotel grounds, Danny wrote the word in red marker on his hand and held it up to the mirror, and we realized, to our horror, that "Spreadtrum" was the mirror image of "MURDER."

—Mark Gongloff, *Wall Street Journal*[1]

Mark Gongloff's satirical likening of the panic selling that hammered the stock of Spreadtrum Communications (NASDAQ:SPRD) in late June 2011 borrows imagery from the 1980 horror film classic, *The Shining*. The movie revolves around a boy, Danny, who comes under the spell of a visionary power, "the shining." Danny's mysterious acumen to perceive terrifyingly evil acts that escape the eyes of others ultimately saves him and his mother from an otherwise certain death at the hands of his murderously crazed father whose part (to give sufficient context to this opening epigraph) was memorably played with gusto by a master of the genre, Jack Nicholson.

After a streak of entirely unexpected but increasingly devastating short calls beginning in the summer of 2010, a 34-year-old American named Carson Block had gained in reputation as a "Danny" in regard to U.S.-listed Chinese stocks: a *wunderkind* capable of revealing the horrors of unscrupulous company management bent on defrauding investors. By the time Block had turned his gaze to wireless communications semiconductor maker Spreadtrum in mid-2011, shareholders were hanging on his every assessment of a Chinese stock's worth with a sense of trepidation and fear.

Block and a number of other short sellers enjoyed a string of highly publicized successes with their downward bets on U.S.-listed Chinese stocks, feeding a spate of short attacks that crested during roughly a one-year period from mid-2010 to mid-2011.

Short sellers ("shorts") essentially operate by borrowing shares from a stockbroker rather than purchasing the shares as long-term shareholders do. Shorts sell their borrowed shares on the market, receiving payment according to a stock's prevailing market value. Shorts are forever betting that the share price of a stock in which they hold positions will drop. This allows them to return their borrowed shares in the future by purchasing the loaned quantity for less money than they earned when they sold the borrowed shares. The profit mechanism in a short sale is thus highly speculative, which incentivizes short sellers to stimulate the market to drive a targeted share price down as far as possible. The bearish bets by short sellers are perpetually at odds with the bullish wagers of long-term investors, which are premised on belief in a company's future prospects and the assumption of increasing value for its shares.

Amid an atmosphere of highly charged arguments for bullish and bearish assessments of what China's economy actually represents, the role of China shorts has stoked long-standing controversies. The 2010–2011 swelling of high-profile short attacks and accompanying negative sentiment toward Chinese listings followed unexpectedly the 2009–2010s wave of China IPOs and the market's strong enthusiasm for China concept stocks.

Stirring the Waters

Block entered the investment world spotlight with an online report issued on June 28, 2010. Released under the name of Muddy Waters Research, this first in a series of short calls by this former Shanghai-based lawyer charged that NYSE Amex Equities–traded Orient Paper Inc. (AMEX:ONP) was "a fraud" whose "purpose is to raise and mis-appropriate tens of millions of dollars."[2] The stock subsequently shed nearly 50 percent of its value, careening downward from a level of $8.43 to $4.45 within a month. Over the course of a year, another four U.S.-listed Chinese stocks suffered the wrath of Muddy Waters' accusatory finger, which Block and his collaborating outside research-ers pointed at target companies through reports posted on the Muddy Waters website.

Despite having cultivated a reputation for savantlike perceptive-ness, Block's revelatory powers had dulled by the time Spreadtrum, the Chinese wireless baseband semiconductor company mentioned in the previous chapter, appeared in Muddy Waters' sights. Posting an open letter addressed to the chairman of Spreadtrum on June 28, 2011—a year to the day after Muddy Waters issued its inaugural report on Orient Paper—instead of charging blatant fraud and backing this claim by incredulity-arousing evidence, the Muddy Waters' short sale thesis had become far more timid. The summary assessment of con-demnation merely stated: "We believe that there is a high risk of material misstatements in the reported financials."

Muddy Waters' "shining" letter on Spreadtrum then laid out a number of interesting but only partially researched observations and a list of 15 questions. Far from inquisitorial statements that on their own would portray an image of an investment scam, the queries posed were pedantic, the sort any interested investor might use in order to better understand a company. *Why was a previous CEO fired? Did a previous CFO leave voluntarily? What are the growth rates for various product markets?*

How do auditors confirm cash accounts? Why and how is the company making certain acquisitions?[3]

So after one year in the game, the world's most influential China stock short had gone from issuing withering allegations such as those aimed at Orient Paper—

- Approximately $30 million at ONP has been misappropriated by management.
- ONP overstated revenue by 40 times.
- ONP overvalues its assets by at least 10 times.
- ONP inventory is overstated by millions of dollars.
- ONP overstates its gross profit margin by hundreds of basis points.[4]

—to asking the chairman of a target company for help in getting his facts straight:

- Is it fair to assume that SPRD's CFO voluntarily left his position?
- By how much did SPRD's markets grow in the previous year?
- Why are SPRD's operating cash flow accounts much larger than in the past?
- How did auditors confirm the sizes of each of the cash flow accounts?
- What was the reason for staggering an acquisition in two stages?[5]

The hellfire that had previously infused typical short attack pieces was absent. The questions posed by Muddy Waters were entirely reasonable but decidedly ordinary. What is so remarkable is that a body of basic observations about potential risk factors at a company capped off by a set simple questions could at the time induce so much fear in the market. As spoofed in the *Wall Street Journal*, the horror with which investors perceived the Muddy Waters letter illustrates the depths to which sentiments about U.S.-listed Chinese stocks had plunged by the first half of 2011.

Lynn Cowan, "IPO Outlook" columnist at the *Wall Street Journal*, wrote in May that year how Chinese IPOs had lost their sizzle and that investors had become "spooked by a rash of stock halts for U.S.-listed Chinese companies in recent weeks."[6] A special report that same month by Reuters titled "Chinese Stock Scams Are the Latest

U.S. Import" counted 21 Chinese companies listed on the NYSE or NASDAQ whose shares had been halted or delisted.[7] Floyd Norris, chief financial correspondent of the *New York Times*, wrote a probing article that condemned what he titled "The Audacity of Chinese Frauds."[8] The Motley Fool's editor/analyst Tim Hanson posted a piece where the headline asked "Is China a Complete Joke?" Hanson concluded *no*, stating "We continue to believe the country is making progress that will ultimately benefit patient, long-term investors."[9] Yet simply by posing the question, this well-known China stock commentator showed how far market momentum had gyrated from China IPO euphoria to stock scandal panic.

In the case of the mildly worded Muddy Waters open letter to Spreadtrum, the reaction of a jittery investor base was swift. By noon on the trading day that the letter appeared, Spreadtrum's stock plummeted 35 percent. A total of 36 million SPRD shares changed hands, 13 times the average daily volume. If Spreadtrum had been like any of the other China stocks excoriated in detailed short seller hit pieces of the time, the share price would have continued tumbling. Instead, the share price closed down a slight 3.5 percent on the day the letter was broadcast online.

Spreadtrum, it turned out, *was* a sign of something—not a sign of fraud, but a sign that probably the worst of the seriously problematic or blatantly fraudulent Chinese stock issuances had already been exposed. Having feasted during a one-year feeding frenzy and basking in the sort of exaggerated reputations that typically presage a correction toward more rational perceptions, the shorts were now beginning to overextend themselves in more desperate attempts to profit by stirring panic over flawed Chinese issuances.

A number of sell side analysts—who tend to take a more rigorous approach to financial analysis and try to find answers to basic questions about a company before publishing any research—responded to the market sell-off by pointing out that plausible explanations for the concerns raised by Muddy Waters already existed and that remaining unknowns could be fairly easily verified. Stefan Chang at Samsung Securities conceded that "the company needs to improve its transparency," which is a common theme that applies to many listed Chinese companies. Nevertheless, the company had already been sufficiently forthcoming with enough information as to enable the analyst to offer his own responses to the questions raised even before SPRD management had time to organize a conference call to issue official rebuttals.[10]

Morgan Stanley's Bill Lu, issuing a note following the conference call, likewise acknowledged some general concerns—"the company's elevated inventory levels," for example—but concluded that among the negative speculations that had sent the stock plummeting, "no new or valid concerns have been raised."[11] Within two days of the highly visible questioning of SPDR's financials, the stock was trading up 6.3 percent. Spreadtrum was the first company to bounce back during Muddy Waters' theretofore one-year perfect batting average for inciting the market to heavily lower its valuations for targeted Chinese stocks.

By the time the open letter on Spreadtrum circulated online, the market had developed near-Pavlovian conditioning to convulse at even a whiff of negative commentary from a recognized short seller. Momentum also played heavily in Muddy Waters' favor. Just weeks prior to the Spreadtrum letter, Block had publicly released an extensively detailed and condemning assessment of Toronto Stock Exchange–listed Sino-Forest Corporation (TSX:TRE). It declared the company's financing structure "a multibillion Ponzi scheme, and accompanied by substantial theft."[12] Sino-Forest's stock value plummeted more than 80 percent within a matter of days, followed by delisting, resignation of its senior management, and a spate of class action lawsuits against the firm.

The plunge in Sino-Forest stock took some of Wall Street's smartest names down with it, heightening Block's reputation as a diviner of Chinese stock fraud. John Paulson, who had earned billions along with financial deification for his phenomenally prescient shorting of subprime mortgage–backed assets in 2007, had been Sino-Forest's largest shareholder. Paulson & Co.'s flagship Advantage hedge fund, the world's third largest, had held up to a 14.1 percent equity stake in Sino-Forest estimated to be worth approximately $840 million prior to the stock's crash. The value of that holding declined over $700 million before the fund entirely disposed its ownership in Sino-Forest, just 15 days following the Muddy Waters report.[13] Although Paulson & Co. had unwound its position to a 12.5 percent stake by the time of the asset disposal, in a letter to fund shareholders, Paulson admitted to having lost $487 million since May 31 on the investment.[14]

Christopher Davis, a value investor known for intensely scrutinizing stocks and holding them for unusually long periods, stoically faced the stock's wipeout as TRE's second largest shareholder with a 13 percent stake held by Davis Selected Advisers. Bloomberg estimated that the value of that position dropped by about $680 million during the aftershocks of the short attack.[15] This rapid loss stands in stark contrast to the long-term returns posted by Davis's flagship New York Venture Fund, billed as "the only fund to have outperformed the S&P 500 Index over every 10 year period since its inception in 1969."[16]

In addition to massive losses incurred by Paulson and Davis on TRE, a number of earlier Muddy Walters' reports issued throughout February 2011 on China MediaExpress (NASDAQ:CCME) led to shareholder flight and an eventual delisting that gutted the value of a $13.5 million investment by former AIG chairman and Wall Street's best-known China hand, Maurice "Hank" Greenberg.[17] Problematic or fraudulent Chinese issuances, and upstart shorts like Muddy Waters that dug deep enough to expose them, were upending established reputations and overturning conventional wisdom about the reliability of supposedly well vetted information on China concept stocks.

Traumatic as it was, the market turbulence was also proving how phenomenally well U.S. exchanges ultimately function as venues for bringing out the truth about the companies that list there, incentivizing examination of how financial information is gathered and reported and the extent to which it can be relied. As subsequent chapters will show, how best to secure accurate data on U.S.-listed Chinese companies has long been a contentious subject. Regardless, the ongoing drive for accurate and insightful data is one of the greatest and most enduring benefits of the forces underpinning each and every China bet that is made in U.S. markets.

By so quickly and dramatically cutting down once high-flying stocks and outwitting some of the Wall Street establishment's best minds, Block along with other China short sellers had acquired new status and market leverage. Assessing Muddy Waters' so far perfect track record capped off by its short attack on Sino-Forest, Reuters observed:

Of the five companies Muddy Waters is known to have advised investors to sell, with all asserting some level of accounting irregularities, two have been delisted from the Nasdaq and one has not traded since April.

Of the two that continue to trade, neither has come anywhere close to approaching the levels they changed hands at before the reports.[18]

The remaining chapters of this book explore issues about properly understanding questionable Chinese issuances, how "getting" the China story these stocks represent requires avoiding the knee-jerk responsiveness of a skittish herd to instead carefully consider information that circulates around China concept shares. The need for and challenges of ensuring that accurate information is delivered to the market about these stocks is also examined. Before leaving a discussion of Spreadtrum, the rest of this chapter looks in depth at how the company's individual story relates to bearish interpretations of China concept stocks generally. Although the Spreadtrum story is obviously anecdotal, as was the case of China Mobile—a company whose rise and development in fact seeded the ground that made the birth and evolution of genuinely innovative high-tech Chinese firms like Spreadtrum possible—the Spreadtrum story also reveals many of the wider forces at play in the U.S.-China equity exchange dynamic.

The Basic Spreadtrum Story

Spreadtrum is among a plethora of multinational, hybrid Sino-foreign enterprises that have sprouted up in the fertile soil for mobile communications businesses of China's expanding and technologically advancing telecommunications market. It functions as a China-operating company that integrates Chinese and foreign (mainly American) capital and technology.

Three months before Spreadtrum had even established its headquarters around Shanghai in 2001, it had founded its research and development (R&D) facilities in Sunnyvale, California, in the heart of Silicon Valley. Datong Chen, the company's cofounder and chief technology officer, received his PhD from Beijing's Tsinghua University (China's near equivalent of MIT) and did postdoctoral research at the University of Illinois and Stanford. He helped establish Spreadtrum after cofounding in Silicon Valley the semiconductor image sensor device company Omnivision Technology (NASDAQ:OVTI), which successfully listed on NASDAQ in 2000.

The company's private equity financing was also transnational in nature. Between 2002 and 2006, Spreadtrum raised its Series B through D rounds of funding from key managers and a number of Chinese and U.S. venture capital firms, principally two Taipei-based VCs—Fortune Venture Investment Group and Pacific Venture Partners—and one of Silicon Valley's premier VC houses, New Enterprise Associates (NEA). NEA owned nearly 25 percent of Spreadtrum's stock when the company listed on NASDAQ in 2007. The IPO raised nearly $125 million, pricing at $14 per American Depositary Share (ADS), above the expected range of $11 to $13 per share.[19] Two of Wall Street's most respected bulge bracket investment banks at the time, Morgan Stanley and Lehman Brothers, led the underwriting.

During the economic and market turmoil of late 2008 to early 2009, SPRD stock traded briefly below $1 per ADS. The period also marked a time of management transition, with a new chairman/CEO/president, Leo Li, joining in 2008. Then there was, as Muddy Waters' letter pointed out, "a near simultaneous turnover in 2009 among SPRD's CFO, audit committee, and auditor." This was an event that the short seller later declared to be "troubling."[20] Yet such a verdict has to ignore the possibility that the departure of a CFO might have been part of ongoing senior management transitions—hardly unusual for the time, or for the technology, media, and telecommunications industry, or for the company's particular situation. The presumably worrying turnover in the audit committee moreover involved a single committee member, and this person was not even the committee chair—a point that would normally mitigate against any reason for immediate concern. As for a change of auditors, the company's "troubling" action there was to replace its reputable Big Four CPA, Deloitte, with another reputable Big Four CPA, PricewaterhouseCoopers (PwC). Keeping a major CPA on board as auditor usually would indicate that any immediate concern in that regard also was unwarranted.

Unless short sellers—or any investors, for that matter—bother to take a close look at a target company's evolving operating conditions and policies in context, its prospects can be misunderstood. The same applies for interpreting how well a company's investment strategies serve to strengthen its market position and enhance shareholder value.

Based on the information available, throughout 2008 and 2009, Spreadtrum appears to have made meaningful progress with building out its operations and market position. In January 2008, it completed acquisition of San Diego, California–based Quorum Systems, a company specializing in design of radio frequency (RF) transceivers that run on a power-saving CMOS (complementary metal oxide semiconductor) chip architecture. According to the company's Form 20-F annual report filed with the Securities and Exchange Commission, the Quorum merger brought to Spreadtrum a higher order of RF technology based on an advanced single-chip, multimode CMOS platform. The platform can be integrated in multiple markets that use differing mobile phone standards. Spreadtrum thereby became able produce chips covering not only the TD–SCDMA standard promoted by the Chinese government and China Mobile but also major foreign-developed transmission standards. The Quorum acquisition further provided Spreadtrum with a new base for R&D operations in the United States, giving it access to San Diego's advanced communications technology cluster.

None of this upgrading and expansion was cheap. The Quorum purchase required $55 million in cash and $15 million in stock, with up to an additional $6 million in cash for performance–based earn outs expected within two years following deal close. That price tag amounted to more than half the proceeds raised by the company's June 2007 IPO. Spreadtrum additionally reported spending "considerable R&D resources in 2008" to address quality issues. By 2009, it reported to be seeing improvements with its newer basebands compared with the older baseband products.[21] After successfully integrating Quorum's technology, in 2009 Spreadtrum launched the world's first single-chip RF transceiver that supported TD-SCDMA plus another three major mobile phone standards.

Following these developments, in March 2009, the company broke out of the sub-dollar price levels where its stock had been languishing.

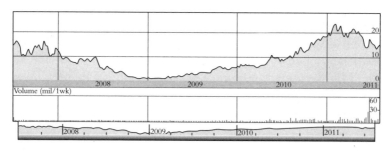

Figure 4.1 SPRD Stock Performance, July 7, 2007–August 12, 2011.
Source: Google Finance.

One could make the bearish assumption, as Muddy Waters did, that the stock's recovery resulted from accounting chicanery. Or one could consider how management changes and strategic deployment of capital could have built a stronger platform upon which the company managed to grow its revenue and resources. The bets can go either way, but without compelling evidence to support bear or bull assessments, one is making assumptions that could adversely impact investment risk in unexpected ways. The tepidness of the Muddy Waters' allegations were a signal that its accusations were more speculative than usual, though those who piled into the short-lived stock sell-off of SPRD probably failed to take that into account.

Spreadtrum's investment activities also warrant consideration in a wider context. Looked at from a macro level of the Sino-American equity exchange dynamic, Spreadtrum has returned multiple benefits, and in some cases actual cash investment, to the U.S. and global economies. In a fundamental sense, the company has used its IPO proceeds and ongoing market financing to build up its components' quality competitiveness, technical features, and cost efficiencies, which in turn enhances the value of communications products that are used all over the world. As part of specific strategic efforts to upgrade its technological capabilities, Spreadtrum has reinvested directly back into the United States through expansion of its internal R&D resources as well through acquisitions like Quorum. These expansive, iterative flows of capital and goods from SPRD represent the types of basic, reciprocating benefits that are possible with Chinese listings in America.

Another noteworthy feature in the way that a Chinese company like Spreadtrum is more inclusive than might be commonly assumed is the fact that the company's most vital resource, human capital, is distinguished by deep cross-cultural linkages. As of 2011, the core management team to a person had all previously worked at U.S. companies and had acquired at least part of their education in the United States. Although America's most famed China short seemed overly eager to bet against Spreadtrum, the company itself has a solid record of being long on the United States for its financing, technology, and talent.

Leading a New Chinese Industry

Beyond its own investment story, Spreadtrum also offers a narrative on how China has expanded its industrial capabilities into the very core of cutting-edge wireless technology.

Spreadtrum operates as a fabless semiconductor company. Its core business activities are to design, develop, and market baseband processor and RF transceiver components that run wireless communication devices such as mobile phones and wireless Internet routers. In terms of the types of components the company offers, baseband signals travel at low frequency while radio signals travel at high frequency; offering the two together means that Spreadtrum covers both sides of the wireless transmissions space.

The reason that baseband semiconductors are so important is that they encode and decode communications protocols, thereby enabling wireless devices to work. They also often serve as the hardware platform for a mobile unit's operating system and multimedia applications, the features that add the most value to wireless handsets. Spreadtrum's rather awkward-sounding English name derives from a modulation process known as spread spectrum. Spread spectrum technology varies the signals of frequency communications. That widens bandwidth, the "space" across which information flows, while minimizing signal interference. The effect produces better-quality communications.

Spreadtrum's "fabless" status refers to its role as a chipmaker that does not physically manufacture semiconductors, instead outsourcing actual production to a semiconductor foundry that maintains the highly capital-intensive wafer fabrication facilities required for manufacturing. A "fabless semi" operation focuses on design of the integrated circuitry of its chips. These firms are often referred to as "IC design companies" or "semiconductor design houses." Because Spreadtrum also markets and ships its branded components, its scope of activities in fact exceeds design work so the company does more than the typical semiconductor design house.

The world of semiconductor chipmakers is mainly composed of vertically integrated design-to-fabrication companies like Intel, Samsung, and Texas Instruments and design-based fabless companies like Broadcom, AMD, MediaTek, and Spreadtrum. Qualcomm, a well-known exception to the dichotomy, operates both fab and fabless facilities.[22]

Going fabless means that entrepreneurs can enter the industry without having to shoulder the burden of the enormously heavy capital investment required to establish a chip foundry. Popularization of mobile communications has created large-scale global component supply markets that in turn have spurred the growth of fabless companies that create mobile technology chips and "chipsets" (mounted arrays of IC components). Established fabless industry leaders—Southern California's Qualcomm and Broadcom and Taiwan's MediaTek—all focus on supply of wireless communications components. At the start of the twenty-first century, wireless chips had emerged as a prevailing hot sector within the semiconductor industry, not unlike what calculator memory chips and CPUs were to previous generations of computer development.

As detailed in the previous chapter, China has been rapidly transforming itself from a passive consuming and producing of mobile phone products to proactively shaping worldwide mobile communications. According to the research firm IHS iSuppli, shipments in 2010 of mobile handsets designed in China jumped by 60 percent. This growth in finished products has been propelling fabless semiconductor development as well. Fabless semis in the People's Republic (PRC) are expected to more than double their revenues by the middle of the decade, going from $5.2 billion in sales in 2010 to $10.7 billion in sales by 2015. As of 2010, Spreadtrum had already jumped to the front of the pack by becoming mainland China's first fabless supplier to exceed $300 million in annual sales, racking up nearly $350 million in revenue for that year.[23] To hit that milestone, Spreadtrum achieved an annual revenue growth rate of 230 percent—far ahead of China's overall baseband component shipment growth rate of 36 percent.[24]

When listing in June 2007, Spreadtrum was in the midst of an upward surge in sales, which reached new highs each quarter that year. Having phased out sales of a previous product line, handset boards, in late 2005, the company gained revenue, profits, and market share starting in 2006 through growing a customer base that purchased Spreadtrum's higher-margin stand-alone baseband semiconductors and chipsets. Revenues hit $26.2 million in the first quarter of 2007, then $32.2 million in the second, then $38.6 million in the third, and $48.5 million in the fourth. The company was charging ahead with 85 percent top-line growth for the year.

But not unlike a number of Chinese small-cap stocks that open strong at their IPO only to deflate and then languish, SPDR's share price bottomed for a period of time. It hit such lows that the company's ability to survive was questioned. In 2008, Spreadtrum faltered with overextended product lines, shipment delays, quality issues, and poor customer support. It lost key accounts and its market share dropped. Adding to its challenges, worldwide mobile handset sales fell with the onset of the global recession. Spreadtrum endured revenue slippage of about 50 percent each quarter during the second half of 2008. In the last quarter of the year, the company managed to eke out sales of just over $10 million. A gross margin that had been holding steady at more than 40 percent nosedived to an abysmal −26.8 percent. The company's bottom line incurred a net loss of $78.7 million, nearly a $100 million plummet from the net income of $21.1 million it earned in 2007. The share price careened downward to a low of 63 cents.

Pulling Back from the Brink

Faced with such dismal performance, the board of directors at a typical U.S.-listed firm would more likely than not abruptly replace the CEO and bring in new blood. In a typical Chinese enterprise, the authority of a chief executive (especially one whose power is concentrated as a company founder-cum-chairman/CEO/president as in the case of Spreadtrum) usually stays in place out of a traditional sense of hierarchical deference.

At Spreadtrum, the company responded through a senior manager change-out, but did so in phases and with the participation of the serving chief executive. The new chief, Liyou "Leo" Li, joined the company as president in October 2008, became CEO in February 2009, and ascended to chairman of the board in August 2010. The company's main founder, Ping Wu, stayed involved during the transition and relinquished those positions according to the same time scale. Through this phased approach, the company achieved American-style responsiveness but balanced it with Chinese-style leadership continuity.

Leo Li came into his roles of advancing responsibility at Spreadtrum with copious amounts of American education and industry experience. "Dr. Li" obtained his PhD in electrical engineering from the University of Maryland and added an MBA from National University in La Jolla, California. He developed a career in baseband semiconductors at a string of Southern California "Tech Coast" companies: Rockwell Semiconductors (since spun off as Conextant), Mobilink, Broadcom, and Magicomm. In joining Spreadtrum, he brought with him direct and deep understanding of the company's global industry and international customer expectations for global standard quality. The company greatly needed this type of expertise as Spreadtrum's miscalculations on industry demand for products and quality issues had been propelling its nosediving stock performance.

Li spearheaded a turnaround that addressed these matters straight on. Within less than a year of his arrival, Spreadtrum racked up sales of almost $40 million, returned to operating profitability, and restored its gross margins to around 40 percent. Within two years, the company's annual revenue approached $350 million, more than twice the amount for 2007. Its net profit of $67.2 million had more than tripled since 2007's level of $21.1 million. A high-flying Chinese tech play that had almost tanked a year and a half after its IPO was now roaring to new heights.

China Mobile and subsequently listed Chinese telecom carriers had proven China's viability and unparalleled strengths as a mobile phone marketplace. Myriad *shanzhai* makers along with a proliferating number of homegrown wireless handset brands had demonstrated the nation's competitiveness for developing and manufacturing the centerpiece goods of the worldwide mobile communications revolution: mobile phones. Spreadtrum's trial by fire and sustained performance as an originator and producer of some of the core technology that powers mobile devices came to show that China's industrial capabilities could reach deeper than ever before.

Spreadtrum's development as a company has both been influenced by and been an influencer on the Chinese wireless industry's technological capabilities. The chip maker offers Chinese handset manufacturers the processor technology that enables the distinctively Chinese "bells and whistles" of multiple SIM cards, cameras, video playback, and power management that distinguish whimsical *shanzhai*-inspired whitebox feature phones. Phones made by ZTE, Huawei, and Tianyu rank as the major drivers of Spreadtrum's revenues. Since its acquisition of Quorum, the company has been able to offer phone makers a "full system solution" that integrates baseband modems with RF transceivers. According to iSuppli, Spreadtrum expanded its share of China's 2G baseband market from 6.5 percent in 2008 to 18.6 percent in 2010. This growth came at the expense of established chipmakers MediaTek, Infineon, ST-Ericsson, and Texas Instruments, the latter finally deciding to abandon the 2G baseband market altogether. Spreadtrum's performance in these areas indicates how the firm has contributed to mobile phone sectors in China and throughout the world, supplying critical products and intensifying the competitiveness of the wireless chip market while also advancing—in impressive ways—the technological frontier of the global wireless industry.

As for future developments, the next-stage battlegrounds for wireless communications in China will take place in the 3G segment and beyond. When Spreadtrum listed in 2007, the PRC's wide-scale adoption of 3G was eagerly anticipated but repeatedly delayed. The company had already unveiled in April 2004 the inaugural product in its showcase SC8800 series of baseband chips, which Spreadtrum touts as the world's first single chip with dual-mode China Mobile 3G standard capabilities. Yet the firm had to wait another five years before the MIIT got around to awarding 3G licenses to mobile carriers. It waited another two years before China's 3G marketplace finally showed signs of taking off. Nevertheless, by 2010, Spreadtrum had emerged as one of only three semiconductor companies shipping China Mobile's 3G standard chips. In the subsegment of TD-SCDMA standard fixed-wireless 3G (which essentially constitutes Wi-Fi local area network infrastructure), it obtained a market share of over 70 percent.[25] Although fixed wireless is a niche market, the level of market dominance that Spreadtrum has obtained in that segment may well be a harbinger of just how large a company it eventually could become.

Shortsighted Shorting

In 2009, Spreadtrum had pulled back from the brink of corporate oblivion with an effective turnaround strategy. Its rebuilding of market share through investment and acquisitions was not a one-off tactical move, however, but central to its business model. Investment and acquisition costs would need to be maintained to fuel expansion based on this operating framework. In addition, to grow its customer base, management elected to assume higher inventory costs to facilitate and support market demand. All this entailed big risks, including what was probably the hard-to-fathom risk that, through these efforts, potential red flags might appear that could later serve as fodder for shorting the company's stock.

In terms of its ongoing technological advances, during the first half of 2011 (the months leading up to the short attack on its shares), Spreadtrum pulled off two major developments, one resulting from internal R&D investment and the other from corporate acquisition.

The company's internal development concerned creation of a chip processed at the scale of 40-nanometer (nm) circuitry intersections, or "nodes." Nanotechnology, based on objects constructed at the atomic level of one-billionth of a meter, represents the future direction of integrated circuitry. Chinese media heralded Spreadtrum's accomplishment as "a breakthrough in China's independent research and development of semiconductors," calling attention to how most of the world's wireless semi manufacturers produce at best at the scale of 65 nm and that Spreadtrum's 40-nm chip "indicated China's homegrown chip makers now are at the top of this field."[26] With a 40-nm node measuring about 1,750 times less than the thickness of a sheet of paper, such a development is an undeniably impressive accomplishment (although in the chip world generally, Intel's 45-nm semiconductors first appeared in 2007 and by 2011 the frontier of chip manufacturing processes had already evolved to a minimum size of 22 nm). For wireless baseband applications, Spreadtrum's innovation of a 40-nm semiconductor resulted in a device boasting higher performance, lower power consumption, and less cost. The company scheduled its first TD-SCDMA 3G chip based on 40-nm technology for release in 2011 with a full series of 40-nm chips planned for 2012.

Another major tech-related development came in June 2011, when Spreadtrum began a two-staged acquisition of MobilePeak, a designer of chips based on WCDMA (3G), HSPA (3.5G), and HSPA+ standards—global markets for which Spreadtrum lacked access prior to the acquisition. MobilePeak also operated a dual base in Shanghai and San Diego, which resembled the Sino-American structure of Spreadtrum's own R&D operations. Spreadtrum's 40-nm design capability combined with MobilePeak's WCDMA technology offered new enticing market possibilities. Analysts were estimating that the Spreadtrum–MobilePeak merger would provide a springboard for Spreadtrum to enter the 4G market by 2012. Samsung Securities conjectured, "If demand for dual mode 4G is strong, SPRD will join Qualcomm and MediaTek as one of few IC design companies capable of providing dual mode 4G handsets."[27]

As impressive as these developments were technologically, from an accounting standpoint, the company was also stressing its books. Part of Spreadtrum's turnaround strategy entailed offering extended product evaluation periods to customers in order to win their business. From 4Q 2009, the company began to offer a product quality inspection period of up to 90 days as an incentive to attract new accounts and lock in key customers. To an even greater degree, the company would stockpile inventory in anticipation of customer demand so as to ensure being able to deliver products on time and in sufficient quantity. All this led to increasingly high levels of unpurchased inventory. On the plus side, this type of policy supports an aggressive sales strategy to build revenues and market share. On the downside, it also raises

Table 4.1 Spreadtrum Product Inventory Levels ($ millions)

	As of December 31, 2010	As of March 31, 2011
Recorded as Deferred Cost (Sold and Waiting Inspection Approval)	$60	$83
Quarter-on-Quarter Increase: 38%		
Recorded as Other Inventory (Stockpiled Products)	$73	$115
Q-o-Q Increase: 58%		
TOTAL INVENTORY *Q-o-Q Increase: 49%*	$133	$198

Source: Spreadtrum Communications

the risk that the inventory might have to be written off if shipped products are rejected after inspection or stockpiled new products do not attract their anticipated sales (see Table 4.1).

Since the company's quarter-on-quarter revenue between the periods of Q4 2010 and Q1 2011 grew 8.3 percent (about one-sixth of the rate of increase in inventory), the disproportionate growth in inventory increased the company's financial risk. Drops in gross margin for Spreadtrum and its major competitor, MediaTek, as the two companies battled for market share during that time also suggested the possibility of continued margin compression. Market consensus seems to have accounted for these trends following Spreadtrum's Q1 2011 earnings announcement on May 5. The stock that day closed at $22.02 and then fairly consistently declined to $14.68 by June 10, the day after the company announced its 44 percent acquisition of MobilePeak.

Among Spreadtrum bulls, opinions may differ on whether the market's pricing of SPRD was accurate in light of all the sales growth and increased technological potential that the company was building up. As far as bearish sentiment is concerned, what is hard to argue is how, in characteristically short-biased fashion, the Muddy Waters open letter utterly ignored any aspect of Spreadtrum's technological advances or other accomplishments of its turnaround strategy. These aspects of the Spreadtrum story are in fact key to appreciating the nature of its business. Instead of looking at them for an understanding of the company's operations and prospects, alarms were sounded about inventory levels and the legitimacy of a two-stage acquisition for MobilePeak. The singular, tunnel-vision focus on only the downside risks of business model–based activities at a target company is a perennial weak spot in short attacks against anything other than manifestly fraudulent issuers.

Nearly six months after a halfhearted run at Spreadtrum, in November 2011, Muddy Waters broke a long silence and returned with an extensively detailed series of short reports on Chinese outdoor advertising company Focus Media (NASD:FMCN). Trading at around $25 before the attack, similar to the case with Spreadtrum, the stock plummeted immediately after Muddy Waters' initial posting and then recovered. FMCN's ADSs finished 2011 trading at about $20. Those results are perhaps not conclusive enough for that company's management to claim total vindication, but the extent of the rebound certainly defies the gist of the allegations thrown at them. FMCN's share price recovery also again points to how the China short bubble that started to swell in mid-2010 had essentially petered out by the second half of 2011.

As for Spreadtrum, its complete vindication is hard to dispute. A combination of well-reasoned explanations, proactive intervention by management, and solid company fundamentals convinced the market to drive SPRD shares to as high as $17.82 on July 5, a mere five trading days after the open letter surfaced. Within another three months, SPRD shares were trading above their pre-attack level of $20. During the severe general market turmoil of mid-August 2011, SPDR actually gained 12.1 percent, moving from $14.42 on August 10 to $16.17 on August 18. On the latter date, the company announced that the CEO, CFO, and new CTO (the founder of MobilePeak), had altogether purchased a total of 281,766 ADSs of Spreadtrum on the open market, at prices ranging from approximately $14 to $15.30 per ADS. Those purchases represented personal investments by those managers of between $3.9 million and $4.3 million, demonstrating a willingness to risk their own money on the company's future. That is exactly the kind of straight-talking information that can blunt bearish conjectures and move investors from misunderstanding, skepticism, or fence-sitting toward joining in on wagering for a company's success.

Shorts Caught Short

The difference between a horror story and a success story in the stock markets is profound, but the distinguishing underpinning factors are not always so readily identifiable. A change of senior management *might* represent a positive move to restructure operations with leaders better suited for the tasks at hand. *Or* it might serve as a warning sign that knowledgeable and more conscionable insiders are abandoning a sinking ship. In an industry where survivability, not to mention profitability, depends on being responsive to customers with fast delivery of reliable products, stockpiling inventory and accumulating deferred costs *perhaps* represents management's best efforts to serve investor interests even though it adds risk of inventory write-offs. To enhance a company's technology base and broaden its market access, acquisitions *might* conceivably provide effective means to increase shareholder value over the long term though the transaction may have complexities and depress the company's near-term stock price.

To get at the truth of a company's present operations and future prospects, a stock market must provide a kind of "transactional democracy" whereby freedom of inquiry and expression enhances information quality and flow beyond any regulatory requirements for corporate transparency. The questions and answers that are exchanged in the process of transacting shares provide a crucial mechanism in the *getting* of a company story that drives the capital that is *betting* on its future.

Yet for this freewheeling interaction to function as a social good instead of a medium for chaos, a sense of responsibility is necessary too. U.S. Supreme Court Justice Oliver Wendell Holmes Jr. famously ruled nearly a century ago: "The most stringent protection of free speech would not protect a man in falsely shouting fire in a theatre and causing a panic."[28] The high-strung sensitivity toward accusations of Chinese stock frauds that permeated U.S. equity markets around the middle of 2011 had put investors in a mind-set not unlike that of an audience packed into a theater glued to the images of a horror film, as if anxiously dreading the next murderous act of a crazed character played by Jack Nicholson. All that was required was for someone to shout out loud enough to stir pandemonium.

As Muddy Waters' allegations against Spreadtrum began to seem more like someone crying wolf, Carson Block described his actions in a generously favorable light, revealed in the following exchange between America's most famous China short seller and Bloomberg TV's Erik Schatzker:

> Schatzker: Carson, some people have criticized the approach you took with your latest short, Spreadtrum . . . Instead of publishing detailed research, you just wrote an open letter to the chairman saying that you had some concerns about financials and notifying him that you took a short position. Why not do your homework first?

> Block: Well . . . I'm getting uncomfortable actually with this idea that we're Ninja assassins that are going to take the stock price down a huge percentage within minutes or days. And so what I'd like to do to protect investors is I'd like to point out the issues and start a dialogue and get people thinking about these red flags before we come out with a report that sends the stock down 70−80 percent.[29]

When asked the logical follow-up question by Schatzker—"If you're not a Ninja assassin, how do you think of yourself?"—Block answered (with no discernible hint of irony): "I think of myself as somebody protecting investors."

If the overriding goal of the letter had not been to enrich those in a short position on SPRD (the sole group of people in the stock who would profit from a decline in share price), then a person of influence genuinely interested in the welfare of long-term investors would address concerns directly with management, not over the Internet. If management failed to demonstrate an ability or willingness to answer key questions, publicizing any perceived issues would remain an option. What is so offputting about remarks like Block's is not that the actions of shorts are so obviously self-serving but that short sellers have a habit of adopting sanctimonious attitudes and claiming that they are somehow altruistically motivated.

Shorts *do* deserve immense credit for times when they eschew unsubstantiated assumptions about a company and dig deep enough to expose issues that other observers have failed to uncover, even if the short sellers are simply driven by self-interest (enlightened or otherwise). Schatzker's point about doing homework to properly understand an investment target, whether one is short or long, is the enduring principle that applies. It lies at the root of why equity markets are such valuable tools for economic understanding, serving as information arenas that generate data whose meaning is served up for individual interpretation. A market's ongoing debates over the "fair value" for a given stock price are never definitively conclusive. But the contesting bull-against-bear, long-versus-short arguments in combination ultimately succeed as adversely paired drivers in the process of information verification.

While the activities of shorts can beneficially facilitate market corrections, short seller research is atypically biased since it invariably aims to incite massive share sell-offs. This is only logical from a short position; the more that a share price falls, the more that a short seller stands to profit. Sell-side research can in some ways suffer from a similar bias geared in the opposite direction; its ultimate goal *usually* (though not always) is to encourage purchasing of a stock to get the share price to a level higher than the prevailing market price. Since reforms implemented after the dot-com bubble of the late twentieth century, however, sell-side analysts generally operate in a manner that demands logically well-reasoned justification for their stock recommendations. They do not typically aim for extreme share valuations; nor are they fundamentally incentivized to focus on short-term, hit-and-run gains in the way that short sellers are.

A point of brand distinction for Muddy Waters Research is that it takes its name from a Chinese expression, "muddy the waters to catch the fish" (*hunshui moyu*, 浑水摸鱼). The phrase relates to use of deception to gain profit. Undeniably, a number of Chinese companies that have listed in the United States are guilty of employing underhanded methods to deceive investors. The next chapter looks at this issue in greater detail. Yet the phenomenon is not as pervasive among Chinese stocks as committed China bears would like to have the markets believe. The absence of debilitating short attacks on China concept stocks since mid-2011 testifies to as much.

Another idiomatic Chinese expression, from none other than China's most revered philosopher, Confucius, seems more apt here:

"To acknowledge what you know, and admit what you do not, that is true knowledge" (知之为知之、不知为不知、是知也).[30] Without carefully checking their facts, those who purport to unmask deception can themselves be deceiving. As Spreadtrum's "shining moment" illustrates, in an age where information can be easier to broadcast than it can be to accurately interpret, and unsubstantiated assumptions about Chinese companies can mislead more than enlighten, advantage will go to those who manage to separate out the known from the unknown, the content from the noise.

Chapter 5

Calling the Bluff

Truths, Fictions, and CRMs

Financial professionals are increasingly questioning the costs of the Sarbanes-Oxley Act of 2002 (SOX). Some have argued that SOX has had a chilling effect on the cross-listings of international companies in U.S. markets . . . foreign companies are a boon to U.S. institutional and individual investors because they allow them to take advantage of international diversification without having to trade in a foreign market. Maintaining foreign companies' presence in the U.S. market would benefit not only the cross-listed foreign companies, but U.S. investors as well.

The authors' analysis indicates that the passage of SOX has had a detrimental impact on international companies' decisions whether to cross-list in the United States. The authors find that new ADR cross-listings relative to new domestic listings are at their lowest level in 16 years. This finding, coupled with the fact that ADR delistings relative to domestic delistings are at their greatest level in the past 16 years, reinforces the belief that SOX has had a chilling effect on cross-listings in the United States.

—Hong Zhu and Ken Small, *CPA Journal*, March 2007[1]

Are U.S. equity markets too tough for foreign issuers to list their shares? The question would seem laughable in the wake of the Chinese stock scandals that kept popping up like so many whack-a-moles between the consecutive halves of 2010 and 2011. Before then, however, the question received serious attention. Concerns about a possible chilling effect from the requirements of Sarbanes-Oxley on foreign American Depositary Receipts (ADRs) as cited by Professors Zhu and Small convey a sense of these earlier sentiments. Apart from their own conclusions, the two academics had plenty of additional expert opinions to point to in arguing for more lenient treatment of overseas companies that wanted to list in the United States.

By 2007, the breakout year for Chinese IPOs, a body of scholarly literature had arisen that viewed foreign issuers who cross-listed (meaning they had already listed in a foreign market and were coming to U.S. exchanges for an additional listing) as obligated by something known as bonding. Bonding assumes that an implicit pledge is made by issuers to protect minority shareholders.[2] Arguments for the bonding motive hold that by virtue of foreign companies selecting the NYSE or NASDAQ to cross-list their shares, the firms willingly subject themselves to be held accountable to U.S. securities laws and a specific market's listing standards. If the companies were not prepared to comply with those requirements, the argument goes, they instead would choose to trade their shares on less demanding U.S. platforms like the Pink Sheets. Alternatively, they could go to less stringently administered overseas stock markets, such as London or Hong Kong. In other words, cross-listed companies on the NYSE or NASDAQ could be assumed to be fully up to the standards of whatever venue they had chosen for issuing their shares.

As subsequent events tellingly revealed, this sort of thinking was naive. The drumbeat of news about troubled Chinese companies that had listed on the NYSE and NASDAQ exposed firms that acted in ways that resembled nothing like bonding to minority shareholder interests. The alleged "chilling effect" of SOX regulations had not managed to keep these bad plays off the markets either.

Although no evidence ever showed that troubled issuances that had entered the U.S. markets via an IPO were ever more than a small portion of total Chinese listings, in another segment of the Chinese issuance space, a less encouraging picture emerged. For Chinese companies that had come to U.S. markets through a backdoor process known as the reverse merger, disturbing patterns—emanating from both Chinese and U.S. sources—surfaced. One study by Reuters estimated that a grouping of 122 Chinese reverse merger issuances experienced a loss of $18 billion in market capitalization from the peak of their stock prices up until July 2011.[3] Part of this loss in market value cannot be separated from market overreaction—à la "'Spreadtrum' was the mirror image of 'MURDER'"—left in the wake of the mass of short attacks that swarmed up until the middle of 2011. Nevertheless, more systemic issues were undeniably at work as well.

Initial Misgivings

Stipulations in SOX might not have been stringent enough to prevent all inappropriate Chinese stock issuers from arriving on U.S. markets, but elements of the legislation did prove effective in identifying problems that lurked beneath the surface of certain Chinese listings.

The Public Company Accounting Oversight Board (PCAOB), the "auditor of auditors" responsible for monitoring accounting compliance under Title I of SOX, issued a first and prophetic warning about the way some U.S. accounting firms were approving the financial records of Chinese companies in July 2010. The board found a disproportionately large number of small-scale American certified public accountants (CPAs) had been signing off on audits for China concept issuers. The small U.S. audit houses that the agency zeroed in on were run by fewer than five partners. The partners were, in turn, supported by fewer than ten accounting professionals. *How*, PCAOB officials came to wonder, *could such small CPA shops manage to examine the books of companies located all the way over in China?* For some, it turned out, not very well (if at all).

One case reviewed by the PCAOB entailed an auditor who, lacking Chinese-language capabilities, got around this limitation by engaging an outside consulting firm instead of, as would be expected, adding staff who were versed in Chinese. This meant that third-party consultants, whose greatest qualification, the PCAOB concluded, was merely ability to "read, write, and speak the language of the area," conducted all audit-related fieldwork. To make matters worse, rather than engaging the consultancy for interpretation services and business advice on how the CPA could implement the audit work that the CPA itself was supposed to conduct, the auditor effectively farmed out the entire audit process to the consulting firm. According to this arrangement, consultants reported back their observations to the auditor and translated financial statements that the issuer had prepared on its own. The auditor then approved these self-reported statements without performing any independent verifications. In other words, the company being audited effectively ran the audit process with the U.S. CPA rubber stamping the results.[4]

In a global economy where outsourcing has become a norm of international business operations, this degree of work dispersion by U.S. CPAs abuses the logic of the outsourcing concept. An enterprise can legitimately outsource functions that *support* its core competences (the unique strengths that underpin a company's competitiveness), but outsourcing does not apply to the *competences themselves*. In that auditors of public companies are entrusted for the benefit of all shareholders to provide highly qualified and independently objective assessments of a public company's financial records, that central obligation is grossly corrupted if audit responsibilities are abrogated by the CPA and in effect handed over to the company being audited.

The PCAOB encountered another case of a small CPA firm that went through more of the motions relating to its audit responsibilities but still ended up avoiding the all-important audit work itself. In this instance, the managing partner and engagement partner from the U.S. accountancy at least bothered to make a trip to China to meet with an issuer's board and management to get an elemental understanding of the company's business. The U.S. CPA then hired a China-based accounting firm to conduct all the on-the-ground auditing tasks. Certainly better than having nonaccountants merely report back observations and translate company-supplied financial documents, this arrangement hardly provided investors in a U.S.-listed company the level of review and approval of financial information that they expect and, in fact, U.S. law requires.

The agency discovered that the "U.S. firm's personnel did not travel to the China region during the audit" yet nevertheless issued "an audit report stating that it had audited the financial statements."[5] As much as this flies in the face of the very reason only authorized accountancies are permitted to conduct audits on U.S. public companies, the American CPA tried to justify its actions based on a part of the PCAOB code known as AU Section 543. Hardly a loophole, this area of the code provides for use of "other independent auditors" when a company of large enough scale—specifically, a firm with "subsidiaries, divisions, branches, components, or investments included in the financial statements"—is being audited and a third-party "other auditor" handles the audit of one or more of these component divisions. Nowhere does the section authorize a handover of the principal audit responsibilities to a third party, though that is how the U.S. CPA chose to interpret it.[6]

That less stringent interpretation is especially surprising in light of how, among the highly detailed PCAOB codes, an entire section, AU 316, on "Consideration of Fraud in a Financial Statement Audit," lists out a panoply of risk factors and clearly lays out the need for professional skepticism in conducting an audit. In that case and others, the arm's-length and basically disinterested approach a number of small-scale, U.S.-certified accounting firms applied to their audit work on Chinese companies violated central principles of the accounting audit function. These instances of auditor failure, though somewhat exceptional, at the same time illustrate the vital role that auditors play in ensuring the quality of foreign listings in U.S. markets. If the audit process does not function properly, the integrity of the China–U.S. equity exchange suffers in kind.

In Through the Back Door

Accompanying the wave of Chinese companies conducting IPOs in U.S. equity markets, Chinese issuers using a process known as the reverse merger (RM, also styled a "reverse takeover" or RTO) fueled a surge in micro- and small-cap listings.

Despite the sudden notoriety that RMs and RTOs from China acquired during the brief boom in Chinese stock shorts, the reverse merger has been a part of U.S. equity markets for a long time. No less than America's most revered investor, the "Sage of Omaha," Warren

Buffett, created his flagship funding platform, Berkshire Hathaway (NYSE:BRK.A; BRK.B), out of a reverse merger in 1964. Iconic, multibillion-dollar American firms like Texas Instruments (NYSE:TXN) and Occidental Petroleum (NYSE:OXY) emerged from RM transactions as well.[7]

RMs appeal because of the time and cost they save in bringing private companies public. Though not considered a typical means for listing shares, and not infrequently associated with shady dealings, RMs are not intrinsically problematic. Problems arise because these deals are not subject to the same due diligence, transactional scrutiny, regulatory oversight, and transparent listing processes that are required for an IPO. An RTO is more liable to abuse by unscrupulous issuers (who can mislead their servicing auditors, financial advisors, and lawyers so as to cheat investors) or dishonest or negligent service providers (especially stock promoters who can similarly mislead issuers and investors alike). The worst possible scenario is a combination of misbehaving issuers and service providers working in tandem to scam investors.

An RM occurs when a privately held company merges with a publicly traded entity in order to go public. The private company puts up the cash for the deal and swaps out its shares for controlling equity in the public vehicle. The public company often functions as a shell for the private company to enter into. Typically, the shells used for mergers are previously active enterprises that have since become dormant. There are also clean shells whose creation and Securities and Exchange Commission (SEC) paperwork maintenance is handled by financial advisors who keep them "on the shelf," as it were, saving to use them for when an RM opportunity arises. Most RM shells trade over the counter. Yet if the private company entering into the shell brings along enough of a financial track record with it, it can arrange to quickly up-list to NASDAQ or the NYSE. *Viola!*—the private company goes public on a major U.S. exchange without all the rigmarole of a conventional IPO.

The curious twist residing within the concept of an RM is that technically the acquiring party in the deal is the public company. Its shares are the ones that remain trading at the end of the transaction. Yet it is the private firm that drives the deal, pays the public company for consideration of the share swap, and handles the associated transaction fees. It is the private company's name (usually) that the newly merged entity adopts. It is also the private company's leadership that takes over management and majority ownership (frequently on the order of 80 to 90 percent) of the publicly traded firm.

Reverse takeovers came into vogue among small American firms, fast-growing technology enterprises in particular, after the popping of the dot-com bubble in 2000. Rather than struggle to find private equity financing during those bleak days for venture capital or have to pay for the fees that investment banks, law firms, and accounts charge for conventional IPO services, small-size American firms found that they could transact a backdoor IPO for far less time and money.

From a financial perspective, the only major drawback for going public in this fashion is that an RTO does not involve actually selling shares to raise any funds, which is, after all, the main purpose of a public stock issuance. RMs therefore frequently conduct what is known as a PIPE, shorthand for "private investment in public equity." In a typical PIPE, the newly public but undercapitalized company will give attractive terms to a purchaser, usually a hedge fund, to buy a large block of its shares.

Like their U.S. counterparts, small Chinese companies were drawn by the expediency and reduced costs of reverse mergers. A mini-industry of small-scale financial advisors, funders, stock promoters, lawyers, and accounting firms focused on Chinese clients rose up to serve the vast number of Chinese firms looking to raise between a few million to tens of millions of dollars through RMs. As problems with these backdoor-listed companies came to light, this ecosystem of Chinese RMs increasingly caught the eye of regulators, short sellers, and the media.

Following up from its July 2010 alert concerning irregularities with audits on certain Chinese firms, in March 2011, the PCAOB released a research note on Chinese RMs, considered by then so much in a class by themselves that the agency coined a "CRM" acronym to categorize them.[8] Though not condemning CRMs outright, the regulator reiterated its concern about substandard audit work. Through research covering more than a three-year period between FY 2007 and Q1 2010, the PCAOB counted a total of 159 RMs from China, making the number of backdoor IPOs larger by almost three times the 56 conventional IPOs by Chinese companies that took place over the same time frame.

At the end of the period studied, 87 percent of the Chinese firms that had listed via a traditional IPO had market capitalizations greater than $75 million. Nearly the reverse was true for CRMs, of which only 33 percent had capitalizations of at least that size—a relatively low threshold for a U.S. publicly listed company.

By Wall Street standards, most RMs from China were too puny to matter. That was the rub. Individually, the CRMs were small potatoes. In aggregate, however, their capitalization was $12.8 billion—still meager compared to the numerous multibillion-dollar mid- and large-cap companies that dominate the attention of equity markets, but sizable enough to do damage if there were problems with underlying quality. The smaller sizes of CRMs also made them that much more attractive to small funds and individual investors, who generally prefer lower-priced stocks and the potential for high returns that these small-cap plays offer.

Dawn of the CRM Dread

An investigation by the PCAOB discovered that 97 percent of CRM market capitalization ($12.4 billion of equity value in total) was being audited by "triennial" accounting firms (CPAs whose client base is so limited that the board only inspects these auditors once every three years).[9] That much equity being minded by tiny, infrequently inspected accountants that demonstrated questionable abilities to audit Chinese issuers posed a risk level that had not been seriously contemplated before.

Within a few weeks of the release of this PCAOB report, Luis Aguilar, the head of the SEC, addressed the Council of Institutional Investors ("the voice of corporate governance") at their annual Spring Meeting in Washington, D.C. Titling his speech "Facilitating Real Capital Formation," America's top securities regulator explained how he felt "concern that the U.S. capital markets are being exploited by certain foreign companies, not only harming U.S. investors, but also negatively effecting the environment for capital formation."[10] By that time in the spring of 2011, questions about the veracity of Chinese stocks trading in U.S. markets had become a searing-hot topic of American finance; little room was left for wondering to which "foreign companies" Aguilar was referring.

After explaining his views on what he called America's "real economy"—essentially, the nation's productive economic capacity—the commissioner spoke about the need for capital formation to support its functioning. He then launched into his description of the elephant in the room: CRMs.

> I am worried by the systematic concerns surrounding the quality of the financial reporting by these companies . . . U.S. auditing firms may be issuing audit opinions on the financials, but not engaging in any of their own work. Instead, the U.S. firm may be issuing an opinion based almost entirely on work performed by Chinese audit firms. If this is true, it could appear that the U.S. audit firms are simply selling their name and PCAOB-registered status because they are not engaging in independent activity to confirm that the work they are relying on is of high quality. This is significant for a lot of reasons, including that the PCAOB has been prevented from inspecting audit firms in China.[11]

Here, Aguilar's comments touched on two critical points. The first was that certain registered CPAs were effectively hawking their power of auditory authority to Chinese firms, thereby corroding the integrity of U.S. equity markets. The second, and more diplomatically touchy, issue was the inability of the PCAOB to directly verify how the CPAs that it regulates were performing audits in China. This latter point, fraught as it was with Chinese sensitivities regarding sovereign rights, would become the central friction point between U.S. and Chinese regulators over the supervision required to smoothly facilitate continued deal flow through the China–U.S. public equity pipeline.

China, whose world outlook is profoundly influenced by humiliating experiences it endured through encounters with Western powers during earlier periods of the last two centuries—is viscerally sensitive to perceived encroachments on its sovereignty. Of course, for their part, U.S. regulators also have plenty to be sensitive about regarding America's more recent experiences with failures in accounting oversight.

The PCAOB's very existence came about as a legislative reaction to the economic destruction wrought by accounting fraud that precipitated the failure of a major U.S. companies like Enron, a firm's whose mass-scale deceptions were aided by the complicity of its auditor, Arthur Andersen. The impact of Andersen's demise following the Enron debacle in 2002 has indelibly left its mark on the global accounting profession, cutting down what previously had been a cohort of the "Big Five" transnational accountancies to today's grouping of the "Big Four." The commissioner's speech—read from a manuscript extensively citing a variety of general, government, and academic sources—with its detailed rationale of how lack of government supervision for trillions of dollars in mortgage-backed securities and collateralized debt had contributed to a meltdown in the global financial system was itself another sign of how past lapses in oversight were influencing the SEC's thinking.

Wrapping up his remarks, America's chief financial markets regulator spoke about the ramifications for the PCAOB's review of Chinese RMs and their significance to the operations of the world's largest equities exchange marketplace:

> Finally, and to return to our earlier topic of capital formation, it's important to see the connection between capital formation and strong enforcement of securities laws. We have seen clearly that capital formation is improved with solid disclosures—but what happens when the disclosures are lies? That's when we need strong enforcement. Capital formation is strengthened when investors have confidence that the laws will be obeyed and that, when they're not, that the fraudsters will be made to pay.[12]

Although the commissioner probably had no inkling of it at the time, the challenges posed to auditors in verifying the accuracy of disclosures from Chinese companies—and the further challenges posed to U.S. regulators in assuring oversight for those verifications—had only been touched on with the scandals involving diminutive American CPAs and small-scale CRMs. As of April 2011, the highest profile failure of a

Chinese IPO issuance had yet to fully unravel. Yet when it finally did late the following month, accounting and disclosure issues with that company, NYSE-listed Longtop Financial Technologies (NYSE:LFT), would raise to a whole new level the stakes involved in effectively regulating U.S.-listed Chinese companies.

A Short Love Affair for CRMs

What stirred misgivings for U.S. regulators presented a rich vein of opportunity for some market players. Suspicion-arousing numbers in CRM financials touched off 2010's wave of short attacks on China concept stocks and bearish sentiments toward Chinese issuances generally.

Carson Block of Muddy Waters, who arose from obscurity to become America's most visible China short seller, first made a name for himself when posting in late June 2010, immediately prior to PCAOB's alert on CRMs, a short attack piece on the Chinese reverse takeover issuer, NYSE Amex Equities–listed Orient Paper (AMEX:ONP). The report relied principally on observations made during a site visit to ONP's manufacturing facilities along with referencing industry comparables to raise disquieting questions about the company's legitimacy. In terms of financial analysis, the number crunching was largely back-of-the-envelope and inferential in nature. The conclusions however, were—true to the short-seller oeuvre—characteristically bold. Muddy Waters claimed that Orient Paper had overstated revenues by "approximately 40 times," overvalued its assets "by at least 10 times," and inflated inventory values "by millions of dollars."[13] For a stock that was trading at $8.43 (providing ONP with a market cap of $154 million), the report set a price target of less than $1.

The short seller's coverage on Orient Paper extended to follow-on appeals for investors to dump the shares. Market reaction was not as a strong as would have been expected had the allegations really stuck. By the week of July 30, the price hit a low of $4.45 during a period of high-volume trading, with over 7 million shares exchanged. It then bounced back. By the end of the year, six months after the short report and well into a growing number of allegations against other CRMs, ONP shares finished 2010 trading at $6.36, about a 25 percent decline from the level immediately preceding the attack—hardly a slam dunk against the company considering the extent of the allegations lodged against it.

Although the report failed to move the market anywhere close to the targeted price drop, the concerns it and the PCAOB alert had triggered did not fade away. Soon the financial media was reporting back on investigations of its own.

A *Barron's* feature article that ran in late August profiled a number of the personalities in China and the United States who were active in pushing companies through the CRM pipeline. Readers got a chance to see up close how a cast of characters including stock promoters, accountants, bankers, hedge fund managers, and lawyers were actively bringing CRMs to market. Picking up on themes that had been touched on in Muddy Waters' inaugural report, the Orient Paper story was revisited. ONP was described as one of "China's most volatile reverse takeover stocks" along with Gulf Resources (NASDAQ:GURE), both companies that shared a connection to individuals with blemished backgrounds and shadowy operations, such as one Kit Tsui.

The *Barron's* piece noted that with his first U.S.-listed company, NASDAQ-traded Industries International, Tsui had been forced to step down after the company's auditor charged that management had misreported related-party deals and Chinese authorities forced its main business into insolvency. ONP representatives were said to blame Tsui for various irregularities called out by Muddy Waters. The *Barron's* reporters stated that they had left messages seeking comment at Tsui's offices in Beijing, Shenzhen, and Shanghai but "heard nothing back. We also visited the address of Tsui's firm, China Finance and China U.S. Strategy, in New York, near Rockefeller Center, but building attendants said the floor was vacant."[14] The image emerging of the central characters involved with RTOs from China was looking increasingly opaque.

One of the most revealing insights to come out of the *Barron's* reporting was the performance of Chinese RTOs versus a benchmark of the Halter USX China Index, a composite of NASDAQ- and NYSE-listed firms with a market capitalization of at least $50 million. Using robust statistical modeling to analyze longitudinal share data, the article's authors, Bill Alpert and Leslie Norton, examined 349 CRMs over the length of time that they had been listed, up to a maximum of 154

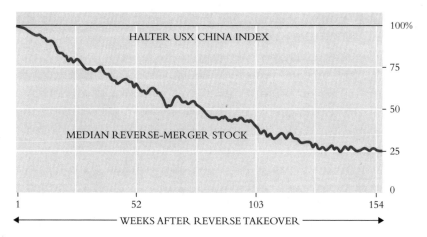

Figure 5.1 Way below Par: *Median Performance of Chinese Reverse Mergers versus the USX China Index*
SOURCE: Barron's

weeks. The median return for these stocks consistently underperformed the Halter USX, sinking to 75 percent below the index when stretched out to a terminal point of 154 weeks.

Apart from Orient Paper, other CRMs mentioned in the article were AgFeed Industries (NASDAQ:FEED), Deer Consumer Products (NASDAQ:DEER), CleanTech Innovations (PINK:CTEK), SkyPeople Fruit Juice (NASDAQ:SPU), China Natural Gas (NASDAQ:CHNG), and RINO International (the most notorious stock of the bunch, whose delisting from NASDAQ a few months later turned up the heat of discussion on Chinese issuances).

At the time of the *Barron's* report, FEED was trading at $2.35, but in August 2011 it fell to under $1. This occurred after the company announced earlier in the month an unexpected $17 million loss for the second quarter, which included over $9 million in collection expenses related to outstanding accounts receivable plus an additional $5 million in bad debts. CleanTech was trading on the Over-The-Counter Bulletin Board (OTCBB) in August 2010. It up-listed to NASDAQ in December that year only to be told days later by NASDAQ officials that it would be forced to down-list again because company management "intentionally failed" to adhere to its "obligations to timely disclose material information" concerning financing that occurred during the company's listing application process.[15]

The stock to emerge as the worst of the group was RINO, a producer of environmental protection equipment for use in China's iron and steel industries. RINO earned the ignominious distinction of becoming the second target of Muddy Waters with a short report issued on November 10, 2010. In its second research piece, the short seller had become noticeably more refined with its report analytics and tone, meticulously pulling apart RINO's corporate structure, customer channels, use of capital, and tax reporting. The report also connected the dots with RINO's auditor, Orange County, California–based Frazer Frost. Echoing the *Barron's* article, the short seller observed that Frazer Frost was the auditor of other worrisome CRMs as well.

In less than a week following allegations that the auditor had failed to scrutinize red flags at RINO, Frazer Frost confirmed in a telephone conversation with RINO's chief executive officer (CEO) that at least two of the company's purported six major sales contracts were fraudulent and that, with others, "there might be problems."[16] On November 17, NASDAQ suspended trading of RINO shares. With the company offering no exculpating evidence, on November 29 the exchange announced that it would delist RINO altogether. After Frazer Frost renounced all company financial reports starting from 2008 as invalid, RINO's board commissioned an outside law firm and forensic accountancy to investigate. By March 2011, both outside investigators had resigned, along with the head of the audit committee and every remaining independent director.[17] By September 2011, a stock that had been trading at its peak above $15 (providing RINO with a market cap of $444 million) was hovering just north of 10 cents.

With growing frequency throughout the second half of 2010, others piled in for a love fest for shorting Chinese stocks. In his Bronte Capital blog, Sydney, Australia–based John Hempton in September that year walked through inconsistencies in the website operations and financial statements of Chinese travel agent consolidator Universal Travel Group (NYSE:UTA). The company immediately issued a press release with boilerplate categorical denials and assertions that it was "aggressively pursuing all legal remedies against Bronte Capital and John Hempton for the damages caused to the Company and its shareholders."

The stock dropped from a previous level of above $5 and then rallied based on company reassurances—until, that is, it failed to file an annual report. Claiming that management and the audit committee were "unwilling to cooperate and help facilitate the audit process," the auditor resigned and the stock was halted in April 2011 at $3.96.[18]

Andrew Left, a short seller blogger of many years who operates Citron Research from his base in Beverly Hills, California, had been including Chinese stocks among his targets since 2006. Following on the heels of Muddy Waters in the summer of 2010, Citron posted a report on China Biotics that August. The stock plummeted over 90 percent before its auditor finally resigned in June 2011. The stock was delisted from NASDAQ the next month, just as the mass of short attacks on Chinese stocks noticeably dropped off.

Unaccountable Accounting

On December 20, 2010, the CPA Frazer Frost's predecessor partnership, Moore Stephens Wurth Frazer and Torbet (MSWFT), earned another unsought distinction as the first CRM audit firm to be sanctioned by the SEC. The penalties included a censure, cease-and-desist orders, fines, and, for the engagement partner who handled the failed CRM, a ban of no less than two years from practicing as an auditor of any publicly traded firm. This turn of events followed by barely one month the NASDAQ delisting of Frazer Frost client RINO International. That might at first blush seem like speedy justice, but in this case, the antecedents of the sanctions run farther back. The SEC's actions concerned work the auditor did on China Energy Savings Technology, Inc., another formerly NASDAQ-listed CRM, for accounting fraud that occurred during the fiscal years 2004 to 2005.

The systemic failures committed by MSWFT and the engagement partner, Kerry Dean Yamagata, as portrayed in the SEC findings detail a kind of revenue-reporting shell game carried out by the company, with the auditor playing along.[19] The way in which the audit work commenced but then failed to deliver much of any meaningful functions offers up a representative mini-drama from the annals of CRM implosions.

- In accordance with PCAOB requirements, at the outset of the assignment MSWFT ran an initial risk assessment of China Energy. The assessment identified that there was high opportunity for the company to exaggerate revenues, provide insufficient accounting controls, and overstate assets. The auditor further acknowledged that verification of revenue recognition would be "the key issue" in the engagement.
- Confirming an initial warning sign, in its first annual audit, the MSWFT engagement team determined that the company's "internal controls over sales and over cash receipts and disbursements . . . were not operating effectively and could not be relied upon."
- While trying to conduct fieldwork in China involving inventory inspections, bank account verifications, and customer confirmations, the auditors found it could not complete these basic tasks. When visiting a site in Shenzhen to inspect inventory that had been claimed in annual reports, the team discovered that the items did not exist. Company management explained that the materials were in fact in three other locations, two of which were hundreds of miles away.
- Instead of calling attention to these issues, MSWFT simply contracted out the fieldwork on the highly suspicious accounting to a Beijing-based CPA. The local contractor, which lacked registration for U.S.-listed company audits, then effectively controlled the audit work on China Energy for two fiscal years.
- Since China Energy itself lacked personnel trained in U.S. accounting standards, known as generally accepted accounting principles (GAAP), MSWFT ended up guiding and at times stepping in to perform internal accounting work on behalf China Energy to ensure GAAP compliance.
- Even when inappropriately fulfilling the company's internal accounting functions this way, the auditor committed major errors. When making the critical earnings per share (EPS) calculation for FY 2004, MSWFT factored in an incorrect number of shares and provided the company with an EPS figure that overstated results by about 41 percent.
- In the area of revenue recognition, the self-acknowledged "key issue" of MSWFT's engagement, in one year China Energy prematurely or improperly recognized over 50 percent of its revenue. Incredibly, MSWFT's engagement partner accepted the company's

defense of booking the revenue this way "even though," according to the SEC findings, "those explanations were inconsistent with the company's prior representations and with contracts and other company records."

Other transgressions as documented by the SEC in this case are similarly outlandish. The company's unjustified reclassification of sales contracts was particularly egregious. One classification allowed for immediate revenue recognition based on payment at shipment; another recognized payment only after the company's equipment was installed and operating. China Energy would arbitrarily alter contract types on already processed orders to argue for earlier revenue recognition (payment at shipment) rather than what the contract specified (payment upon operation). MSWFT accepted these changes without making any separate confirmations. It continued accepting the company's contract alterations even when documents later appeared that clearly contradicted the modifications. Contracts from previous quarters would reappear as part of current accounts and be reclassified under new contract types as well. Sales contracts were accepted as proof of revenue though they lacked corroborating evidence that payment was ever received.

The Din of CRM Noise

At the time of the SEC ruling against MSWFT, Congress was considering action of its own. Leaders of the House Financial Services Committee suggested holding hearings on accounting issues with Chinese companies at the start of 2011. Committee member and rising political star Representative Christopher Lee, expressed to the *Wall Street Journal* his concerns about financial reporting by Chinese issuers, seeing the possibility of wide-scale deception similar to the Ponzi scheme practiced against unsuspecting investors by the infamous Bernard Madoff. The recently elected congressman from New York claimed that "the integrity of the data could be flawed, and I don't want this to be a junior Madoff scandal. China is the [world's] second-largest economy, and it's growing at such a rapid pace there is an opportunity for exploitation and fraud."[20] Yet before any hearings could be held, Lee had resigned from Congress in February (this following news of a deception and disclosure scandal of another sort in which the married congressman tried to date a woman he met online by lying about his background and emailing a revealing photo of himself). Further legislative action on the matter petered out. Yet concern about Chinese stock issuances would not dissipate quite so quickly.

James Surowiecki, reprising his Cassandra's voice about Chinese stock listings after the 1997 IPO of CTHK/China Mobile, wrote a piece that appeared in the January 31, 2011, edition of *The New Yorker* titled "Don't Enter the Dragon." Now referring to China Mobile as one of China's "well-established giants" on U.S. equity markets, he warned readers against "more speculative 'small-cap' companies, hundreds of which now trade on U.S. stock exchanges."[21] Serving as something of midpoint marker in the uproar against Chinese listings, in the half-year periods immediately preceding and immediately following Surowiecki's article, short reports and media stories on troubled Chinese issuances successively followed one after another, stimulating market anticipation for a Chinese stock fraud *du jour*. Questions about the viability of the China–to–New York flow of public equity financings intensified. From the time of the RINO bombshell in November 2010, up to May 2011, Reuters tallied 21 Chinese issuances that had either been delisted from main board markets or had trading in their shares suspended.[22]

An editorial in the China Economic Review brought some worthwhile—and typically missing—perspective to the unraveling situation. Commenting on SEC Commissioner Aguilar's April 6 announcement about a formal investigation into Chinese firms listed on U.S. exchanges, the magazine's lead editorial for May 2011 advocated a more balanced reading of the situation:

> Although the mud appears to be sticking to Brand China, the SEC must proceed carefully in its investigation. Throwing an undignified tantrum will benefit no one. While it is obvious there were some very bad apples in the RTO barrel, there were also companies that listed through reverse mergers for the same reasons Western firms do: necessity, ignorance, and bad advice. Exonerating the innocent is just as important as castigating the guilty, and speculators should not be absolved of

their responsibility. Even given fraudulent statements by management, it could be argued that risk-averse investors had all the information they needed to stay away. A bit of digging into the history of many Chinese RTOs throws up a network of small foreign auditors, investment banks, consultants and PR firms. These financial service providers facilitated, even encouraged, unqualified Chinese companies to list. In RINO's case, a Western auditor appears to have helped Chinese managers defraud U.S. retail investors. But in other cases, particularly in the over-the-counter markets, Chinese firms were more the victims of fee-based scams than the perpetrators.[23]

This type of nuanced analysis unfortunately was drowned out amid the din of panicked shouting that dominated general discourse on the topic of CRMs. Apart from the obviously biased short reports and short-seller blogs, downbeat press reports tended to dwell on high-profile Chinese stock frauds. Not that frauds were not newsworthy topics; they were. But discussions on them typically lacked a sense of basic context. Especially within online media, what purported to pass for informed discussion on an important subject in global finance was often overshadowed by histrionics.

Josh Brown, notable for over-the-top blog ramblings, earned exclusive coverage for his extreme views via a webcast and an article posting by Yahoo! Finance's Daily Ticker host, Aaron Task. Task's article headline, "Invasion of the Chinese Reverse Mergers: 'We Are Under Attack,' Josh Brown Says," reflects the pervasive hyperbole.[24] Writing just two days after Commissioner Aguilar's speech, the more even-handed *Forbes* contributor Walter Pavlo posted a blog that opens with the statement: "For the life of me, I can't figure out why anyone would think a reverse merger into a shell company on an exchange (NASDAQ or NYSE) is a legitimate business transaction."[25] While Pavlo has a point insofar as shells are potentially subject to abuse, the tone of shock and dismay is rather ironic considering that the NYSE *itself* became a publicly traded company by virtue of an RM.

Yes, the most esteemed equity market on the planet and the greatest symbol of American capitalism, the New York Stock Exchange, is an RM enterprise.

On December 6, 2005, the 1,366-seat owners of what was then the clubby, privately held Big Board voted to go public via an RM with NYSE-listed Archipelago, the owner of Chicago's all-electronic stock and derivatives market ArcaEx. Although not involving a shell transaction, the deal still offered to the merging parties the distinctive advantages of an RM transaction with its lower costs and expediency of execution. The NYSE explained that its members "view the merger as a way to strengthen the Exchange's global competitiveness and as a big win overall, particularly for investors, who now have a chance to own a piece of a larger-than-life American icon."[26] *Institutional Investor* magazine dubbed John Thain, the NYSE CEO who had orchestrated the $10 billion deal, "Superthain." The publication, a leading voice for investment intelligence on U.S. capital markets, observed how the RM fit as part of a set of sweeping accomplishments by Thain, who had "restored the reputation of the scandal-tarnished NYSE and transformed it from a private club into a public company."[27] How times had changed from when an RM would be seen as a way to improve a company's reputation rather than to ruin it.

A Reversal for RM Overhype

The big unreported story of Chinese RMs concerns how out of hundreds of CRMs, the vast majority survived the incredibly intense scrutiny of Chinese issuances that began in mid-2010. The cases of those that made it through might not grab headlines, but they represent more of what the CRMs are actually about. As a group, they have not proven to be brilliant performers, but they are a far cry from having shown themselves to be essentially made up of fraudulent issuers either. And there are an unaccounted number of promising Chinese firms that suffer from undervaluation due to the lingering effects of bad advice received during their journey to the U.S. equity markets and the residual market bias that still tends to discount CRM issuers.

One maligned CRM that stands out for gaining at least partial attention as well as a degree of redemption is Yongye International (NASDAQ:YONG), a Beijing-headquartered organic fertilizer company with production operations in Inner Mongolia. YONG stock started trading on NASDAQ in 2009, following a 2008 RM. Throughout most of 2010, its shares fetched around $8, earning "buy" ratings from sell-side analysts at Oppenheimer and Brean Murray.

Around the height of the CRM panic in 2011, a number of shorts started attacking the company. YONG was trading at an even $5 on May 11 when OLP Global, a China-experienced research house that disseminates its reports only within the institutional investment community, issued the second of two negative write-ups on Yongye. One week later, Absaroka Capital Management, a Wyoming-based hedge fund with a penchant for bombastic commentary on Chinese stocks, publicly issued a report that began by characterizing Yongye as an outright fraud and claimed to have "irrefutable evidence" against the company. In large red capital letters, it screamed out its rating on the company as "CONVICTION SELL." The hedge fund, in characteristic fashion for these types of reports, estimated the fertilizer maker's fundamental share value to be just $1.

Despite claims to present "irrefutable evidence" at the beginning of its report, throughout the body of the document the short-selling fund phrased its statements much more tentatively. Allegations that management looted cash from the company, fraudulently manipulated earnings, and other instances of purported deception and malfeasance were consistently prefaced by phrasings along the lines of how something "appears" suspect or "raises doubts." According to the report's actual contents, the supposedly undeniable transgressions seemed merely suspiciously questionable. Despite the obvious leaps of logic and desperate-sounding tone of its sweeping conclusions, the report had a noticeable impact. Market jitters sent YONG shares plunging to an all-time low of $3.52 the day following the Absaroka piece.

The company responded with a spirited but rambling defense that did little to help its cause; the exasperated tone of the counterattack against its accusers merely heaped more muck on the controversy. The stock briefly rebounded to under $4 but then sank down again.

What put YONG shares back on track were much more resonant statements of action. One was by the CEO, who elected to invest up to $3 million of his own money in purchasing Yongye shares on the open market. The other was by Morgan Stanley, whose Asian private equity fund decided to put in $50 million for newly issued convertible preferred shares of YONG.

Evidently, others who knew the company rather well felt its fundamental share value greatly exceeded $1 and were willing to stake some hard cash on *that* conviction. In announcing the $50 million purchase, Homer Sun, managing director of Morgan Stanley Private Equity Asia (MSPEA), remarked, "After extensive due diligence, we believe Yongye to be an exceptional company that has built significant brand recognition in China's agriculture industry." He added, with words containing subtle poignancy, his fund's observation that Yongye's "core products address an important need for farmers to enhance yield for crops planted on soil that has become degraded by decades of over-fertilization."[28] The comment indirectly points to one of the under-appreciated travesties of how overhyped short attacks that are lacking in merit unjustly destroy not only economic value but also the social value provided by companies that meaningfully contribute to society.

Following the announced $53 million in combined investment, Yongye shares rocketed 42 percent in a single day. They closed out the month trading at $5.33. A core challenge for Yongye management was that they were organizing a sizable chunk of private equity investment as a publicly traded company while under attack in the U.S. marketplace and in U.S. courts (after the release of short reports, *de rigueur* class action lawsuits against the company followed). In light of these circumstances, an injection of private equity capital would almost assuredly be expected to have significant conditions attached. Yongye was no exception.

Details of the MSPEA deal came out in the Form S-3 prospectus that the company filed with the SEC after the highly publicized $50 million convertible preferred share purchase. Min Tang-Varner at Morningstar Equity Research interpreted the bottom-line impact to mean that the redemption clause for conversion of preferred into common shares posed risks for long-term shareholders. By the analyst's estimates, MSPEA would reap at least a 13.2 percent increase in its investment over five years if the company were to meet its net income targets. That windfall would not itself pose any issues. But if the company failed to meet its targets, then the fixed redemption price for the preferred shares would still guarantee MSPEA a minimum 20 percent internal rate of return. That locked-in IRR might mean that the company would have to issue more equity to cover its obligations. That in turn would dilute the value of stocks owned by other shareholders with MSPEA set to gain an even higher return because of antidilution clauses in its investment terms. Tang-Varner concluded that the deal as structured is "not in the best interests of existing institutional and retail investors. In our opinion, this investment vehicle is set up with an uncapped upside and heavily hedged downside for Morgan Stanley, which disproportionately shifts returns to this large shareholder at the expense of regular investors."[29]

In light of the deal's possible negative ramifications for the ordinary shareholder base, it is not surprising that YONG shares dropped from the level of $4.71 on August 3 (the day of the SEC filing) to $4.01 on August 8 (the day before the company announced its second-quarter earnings). It was not until the company reported a solid second quarter and raised its guidance on revenue and net income for the year that the share price started regaining some of the ground that it had lost since the short attacks.

Because of the "good news, bad news" elements of Yongye's private equity infusion, the company's future stock performance likely will be driven mainly by how the market interprets Yongye's progress in achieving net income targets. Expectations have been set high, adding to management's pressures. Nevertheless, Yongye can be considered one of the fortunate ones. The quality of its operations rated highly enough to still attract a big-name investor when market momentum was betting against the company. Other Chinese RM firms that might be operationally sound but have yet to devise a means to signal to the market their underlying value face much greater challenges in demonstrating their worth.

Chapter 6

Longtop Financial

The Costs of Dirty Dealing

China's Longtop Financial Technologies Ltd. . . . . shares soared in their U.S. stock market debut on Wednesday, the year's best by a Chinese company. Longtop's American Depository Shares closed up 85 percent, making it the latest in a string of hot Chinese IPOs that have posted double-digit percentage gains in first-day trading on the Nasdaq or the New York Stock Exchange.

—Reuters, October 25, 2007[1]

The Longtop Shocker

The flurry of accusations and short attacks against Chinese issuances that emerged, peaked, and then dropped off between mid-2010 and mid-2011 focused mainly on Chinese reverse mergers (CRMs). The prevailing assumption was that Chinese backdoor IPO issuers—audited by small, disinterested certified public accountant (CPA) firms—were the source of problems. A once-stellar IPO and NYSE-listed company, Longtop Financial Technologies Ltd. (NYSE:LFT), provided a shocking exception to this rule.

A software developer for banks and other financial services companies in China, Longtop listed on the New York Stock Exchange in late October 2007. The company raised $184 million in an IPO that saw the price for each of Longtop's 10.4 million American Depository Shares (ADSs) close at $32.40 on the first day of trading—an 85 percent pop. The offering as described in a Reuters article—noting that it was "the latest in a string of hot Chinese IPOs that have posted double-digit percentage gains in first-day trading"—captures the ebullient market mood.[2] The piece also pointed out that by that time in 2007, the value of Chinese IPOs on U.S. exchanges had exploded by more than 500 percent on a year-by-year basis. Longtop was an early leader in the wave of Chinese issuances that was sweeping Wall Street.

Goldman Sachs and Deutsche Bank, two of the world's most venerable bulge bracket investment banks, underwrote Longtop's share offering, signalling one of the best possible endorsements for the stock. The global investment community remained supportive enough of Longtop that two years later, in November 2009, the company was able to raise another $127 million in a secondary offering of about 4.3 million ADSs. Deutsche Bank and Morgan Stanley served as joint book runners for the follow-on sale, signaling a continuous vote of confidence for the company.

The high-end imprimatur conferred on Longtop by these top global financial institutions was also extended by the big-name law firms that worked on Longtop's IPO, Latham & Watkins and O'Melveny & Myers. Same for the company's Big Four auditor, Deloitte Touche Tohmatsu. Deloitte reviewed the company's books from before the share debut and throughout Longtop's life as an NYSE-listed firm. Further lending credibility to the stock, the company managed to attract a bevy of sell-side analysts from a host of global investment banks including BNP Paribas, CLSA, Deutsche Bank, Goldman Sachs, Janney Montgomery Scott, Jefferies, Kaufman Brothers, Macquarie, Morgan Stanley, Oppenheimer, and William Blair.

At the beginning of 2010, the year Chinese IPOs set a new record for offerings in the United States, Longtop's share price broke through $40. China's financial system had uniquely come out of the global financial crisis unscathed. Longtop was seen to provide investors access to the high-tech side of a Chinese financial industry that was leading the world and primed to expand to new heights. Reflecting pervasively bullish sentiments on the stock, when Morgan Stanley Research initiated coverage in July 2010, it made LFT its top pick among all the China software industry companies that it followed.[3]

By late 2010–early 2011, rising concern over reverse mergers (RMs) from China had stripped away the luster of most Chinese share offerings. Bears began to speculate that even a highly vouched for company like Longtop was boasting figures that were just too good to be true. For over a year, the company had been contending with rumors that the superior cost performance it reported was based on doctored figures; that the phenomenal numbers came from a murky human resources outsourcing model that hid actual expenses.

None of the accusations had much effect. The company's stock price set a new high of $42.73 in November 2010, just as market sentiment was turning decisively skeptical of Chinese offerings. Then on April 26, 2011, two influential Chinese short sellers located on opposite sides of the world and far away from China—Sydney-based John Hempton of Bronte Capital and Beverly Hills–based Andrew Left of Citron Research— posted blogs that questioned Longtop's industry-defying ability to generate outsize earnings. Now the accusations were starting to stick.

Citron's blog, the more detailed and pointedly critical of the two, began: "To think the fraud in the U.S.-listed Chinese stocks is limited to the RTO [reverse takeover] market is naive. Citron introduces a story that has all the markings of a complete stock fraud."[4] In this instance, the short seller had compelling facts to present, starting with Longtop's reported gross margins of nearly 70 percent and operating margins of about 50 percent. These were abnormally greater than the company's peers, whose gross margin (GM) and operating margin (OM) never exceeded 50 percent and 25 percent, respectively. These credulity-stretching profit margins were viewed by Citron as automatic red flags that had been insufficiently scrutinized by the company's auditor and covering analysts. Citron charged the company with fraudulently stating its earnings since as far back as the time of its IPO. It then reviewed three likely sources of the financial misreporting.

The first was what seemed to be the overly convenient and excessively used outsourcing arrangement, which allowed LFT to transfer its human resource (HR) costs, the bulk of the software firm's expenses, off its balance sheet. Citron noted that "extreme outsourcing" had been a telltale sign at recently halted or delisted RM-structured Chinese issuances. Another major cause for concern for the short seller was its discovery that the company, along with its chairman and the CEO, had been embroiled in litigation alleging misrepresentation and unfair competition around the start of Longtop's founding. This was a fact that had never made its way into the IPO prospectus, yet it was a significant enough legal imbroglio to make its way into a Chinese legal textbook published by the prestigious Tsinghua University Press.[5] The third area of concern was the chairman's gifting away of 70 percent of his stock holdings to employees and friends. Citron suspected that this likely served to help fund cover-ups of items that the company did not want disclosed.

Within 24 hours, the company had organized a conference call to rebut the Citron report and related allegations. The company's Canadian CFO, Derek Palaschuk (a former audit account manager at PricewaterhouseCoopers and previously experienced CFO at two highly regarded NASDAQ-listed Chinese Internet companies), served as point man to defend the beleaguered firm.

Palaschuk explained that Longtop's policy was not to respond to rumors, but because the Citron report seemed to have "caused unwarranted and disturbing turbulence in the trading market for our shares," the company felt compelled to address the charges.[6] Expanding on the company's categorical denials, the CFO took grave offense at Citron's accusations of fraud. Said Palaschuk, "We are deeply outraged that anyone purporting to conduct reputable market research would make such a statement without basis." Reassuring investors that all would be made clear when the company reported its upcoming quarterly and annual financial statements, the CFO further took umbrage at the way in which the company's CPA had been disparaged. "You can see from this report that it also attacks Deloitte, our auditors . . . . We have a very close dialogue with our auditors and we have been communicating with them regularly on market rumors of fraud since these attacks on Longtop surfaced well over a year ago."

Longtop justified its high margins as owing to the company's focus on standardized software sales, which the CFO claimed allowed the firm to generate margins in that category of around 90 percent. Competitors, he explained, sold lower-margin customized software.

The CFO defended lack of disclosure about the textbook court case called out by Citron as old and immaterial—it concerned events of a previous decade and resulted in only a minor conviction in Chinese court on unfair competition with the more serious charges of misrepresentation thrown out. Palaschuk also addressed the questionable share transfers from the chairman, characterizing these as arising from the generosity of a man said to be wealthy enough to no longer be "motivated by money."

One thing that left an uneasy feeling with even the company's most ardent outside supporters was Longtop's rather unconvincing claim that although it had recently announced a share repurchase program of up to $100 million, it was unable to implement the purchase of any shares. The reason? According to the CFO, "some potentially positive material information" had arisen shortly after the announcement that caused the company's lawyers to advise management against making any share purchases as such actions might be construed as insider trading. An update on the progress with the share buybacks was promised for the company's May 23 earnings call.

The bears continued to growl. The company's explanations were too evasive, they said. They openly challenged Deloitte to complete an audit of the financials in a way that fully addressed the accounting discrepancies that had been raised. In addition to the usual rumor mill and negative blogging, by early May, OLP Global had reproduced copies of internal company financial documents that further cast doubts on Longtop's suspect HR outsourcing practices. Citron came out with a follow-on blog the same day. The newly surfaced information cast more doubts on how Longtop accounted for labor-related payments and operating results that the company claimed to have achieved through a series of corporate acquisitions.

A Fallen Icon

Such dismantling of the respectable image of Longtop—and, by extension, potentially any Chinese company that went through a supposedly well-vetted IPO—was creating a deeper crisis of confidence for Chinese issuances. Shorts kept up the pressure. Believers in the Longtop story waivered. Then the implosion began.

On May 18, in a tersely written press release, the company announced that it would not in fact report earnings as previously scheduled on May 23. No further explanation was given. With that, Longtop management set in motion challenges that would confront the China–U.S. public equity relationship in a way that had never tested the dynamic before.

The NYSE responded by immediately halting trading in LFT shares. At the time of their closing price on May 16 (one day prior to the earnings call cancellation based on time zone differences), an ADS of Longtop sold for $18.93. That provided the company with a market cap of slightly over $1 billion. On May 19, Longtop's once ardently supportive CFO resigned. Within another three days, its Big Four CPA, Deloitte, joined him in heading for the exit. Apart from information that detailed these occurrences as contained in the company's subsequent Securities and Exchange Commission (SEC) filings, the company effectively went dark following the departures.

Deloitte's resignation letter dated May 22 described issues involved with getting to the bottom of Longtop's financial situation. The firm's purported transgressions were, for a well-reputed company once regarded at the top of its industry, so brazen and unprecedented that even the most caustic of the company's short sellers had failed to foresee them.

Apparently in response to pressure from short sellers, Deloitte related in its letter that it had decided to make follow-up visits to "certain banks." The auditor had discovered that when double-checking Longtop's financials, proper documentation turned out to be seriously lacking. The laundry list of disconcerting items entailed:

> statements by bank staff that their bank had no record of certain transactions; confirmation replies previously received were said to be false; significant differences in deposit balances reported by the bank staff compared with the amounts identified in previously received confirmations (and in the books and records of the Group); and significant bank borrowings reported by bank staff not identified in previously received confirmations (and not recorded in the books and records of the Group).[7]

Because things were essentially worse than anyone had imagined, the auditor commenced a second round of formal on-site confirmations at banks on May 17. Then matters turned almost surreal, according to the verbatim description of events in the letter.

> Within hours however, as a result of intervention by the Company's officials including the Chief Operating Officer, the confirmation process was stopped amid serious and troubling new developments including: calls to banks by the Company asserting that Deloitte was not their auditor; seizure by the Company's staff of second round bank confirmation documentation on bank premises; threats to stop our staff leaving the Company premises unless they allowed the Company to retain our audit files then on the premises; and then seizure by the Company of certain of our working papers.[8]

Following this physical showdown between company executives and the company's auditor, the CFO who had been so outraged by short seller accusations tendered his resignation. Longtop's chairman, Jia Xiaogong (whom the recently resigned CFO had less than a month earlier described as motivated by altruistic values), made a call to a managing partner at Deloitte. If that effort at outreach was meant to help alleviate the severity of the situation, it seems to have produced the opposite effect. According to Deloitte, the chairman frankly admitted:

> "[T]here were [sic] fake revenue in the past so there were fake cash recorded on the books." Mr. Jia did not answer when questioned as to the extent and duration of the discrepancies. When asked who was involved, Mr. Jia answered: "senior management."[9]

Deception's Depths

Deloitte's jaw-dropping descriptions of the obstacles and harassment it claims to have encountered while attempting its last audit of Longtop—capped off by the seeming nonchalance with which the company's chairman allegedly acknowledged his firm's history of perpetuating fraud—was dutifully filed by Longtop with the SEC. If anything, that last act of perfunctory compliance and the information it revealed once again testify to how the U.S. equity market system retains a remarkable capacity to draw out insightful details on a listed issuer, even when that company is facing the end of its existence on a major exchange.

From the time of Deloitte's reported transgressions to the company's forced delisting from the NYSE in mid-August 2011 and in the months beyond, the auditor's letter in Longtop's 6-K effectively served as the last official word of any substance from the company. The day after Deloitte resigned, the company announced that the audit committee was going through the motions of retaining legal counsel and authorizing the use of forensic accountants to conduct an independent investigation.[10] In the same breath, Longtop also stated that it had appointed a new chief operating officer, apparently a tacit acknowledgment of Deloitte's allegation of audit interference by the previous COO.

Following these key announcements, the company lapsed into silence. Developments were left to speak for themselves. Within a month of Longtop's Big Board delisting, the stock, now trading over the counter with the ticker symbol LGFTY, commanded prices ranging from about 15 to 25 cents per ADS. That is close to 200 times less than what the shares traded for at their height of over $42 less than a year earlier. From a previous market capitalization exceeding $2 billion, at 20 cents a share, Longtop's capitalization fell just short of $10 million.

In the months after its stock suspension and delisting, the company's Chinese- and English-version websites remained strangely unchanged. The unadjusted language in the company's "About Longtop" description provided a lingering image of faded glory and once-enticing prospects:

> Longtop Inc. [sic] (NYSE:LFT), the first Chinese software company listed on the New York Stock Exchange, is a leading software development and solutions provider targeting the rapidly growing financial services industry in China. . . .
>
> Longtop's market leadership has received wide recognition. The American Banker newspaper and Financial Insights, an IDC [International Data Corporation] company, have named

Longtop the highest ranked Chinese financial technology provider in the worldwide 2009 and 2010 Fintech 100 lists. Furthermore, independent research firm IDC has named Longtop the No. 1 market share leader in China's Banking IT solution market and the No. 2 market share leader in China's Insurance IT solution market in calendar years 2008 and 2009. These No. 1 and No. 2 rankings are a strong endorsement of our winning track record in delivering high quality IT solutions to our customers, and our success in diversifying our business model as we are the only IT service provider in China that is in the top ten for both banking and insurance verticals.[11]

The company's superior industry rankings show that it had succeeded not only in deluding its auditor, equity analysts, and long-position investors, but independent market observers as well. Given that industry rankings are usually based on reported sales figures, this "collateral misinformation" is not necessarily surprising. Yet the comprehensiveness of the deception that Longtop managed to pull off is still extraordinary.

In the investment thesis that Longtop sold to those who bid LFT shares up to a market value of billions of dollars, the company had provided certain warnings. From the particularly American legal habit of extensively cautionary preconditions attached to any sales transaction, there were oddly prescient risk statements contained in the company's SEC annual report filings, laid out, no less, in bold italics.

If we fail to establish or maintain an effective system of internal controls, we may be unable to accurately report our financial results or prevent fraud, and investor confidence and the market price of our shares may, therefore, be adversely impacted.[12]

The consequences of such an eventuality were also spelled out:

Our shareholders may face difficulties in protecting their interests, and their ability to protect their rights through the U.S. federal courts may be limited, because we are incorporated under Cayman Islands law, conduct substantially all of our operations in China and all of our officers reside outside the United States.[13]

Of course, legalistic caveats by no stretch of the imagination provide any company with an excuse to defraud investors. But these clearly stated stipulations (which were followed by elaborating text) show how for an equity stake in a foreign company, even one listed on a major U.S. exchange, the same protections afforded by an investment in a U.S.-based company are unlikely to apply.

A China Problem?

Longtop could never justifiably have been mistaken for a "widows and orphans" kind of safe-haven stock. Lessons about extra degrees of *caveat emptor* required for equity bets on a Chinese issuance—or, for that matter, any foreign issuance—aside, farther reaching implications from this instance of fraud, especially as the deception was perpetuated by a well-capitalized firm and presumed leader in its industry, give plenty of reasons for pause.

When billions of dollars are wiped out of a stock market because of intentionally deceptive financial reporting, that moves the issue from the realm of individual investment concerns to the need for systemic protection of capital markets. When not only equity analysts but also industry experts are fooled by the misreporting of data from a supposedly category-leading company, that becomes a problem for the industry that the company represents. In a broader sense, whenever data is distorted by publicly listed companies (which are assumed to be basically transparent and to report only carefully scrutinized figures), those distortions poison the well of economic information that circulates regarding corporate performance and trends in a nation's economy. These are some of the deeper significances at stake with a failure such as Longtop's.

Foreign commentators, especially China pessimists and shorts, were quick to seize upon the case of Longtop and other failed Chinese listings as de facto evidence of much more serious issues with China Inc. Commenting on Longtop and other Chinese stock scandals, *New York Times* columnist Floyd Norris, a veteran Wall Street observer, conceded, "Frauds and audit failures can, and do, happen in many countries, including in the United States." He was quick to add: "But the audacity of these [Chinese] frauds, as well as the efforts to intimidate auditors, stand out."[14] That statement expresses well the sense of alarm and indignation about problematic Chinese stock issuances in the wake of Longtop.

As with the bewildered anger over RMs that caused CRMs to be chastised as categorically bad transactions, emotionally charged assessments of the presumably unprecedented nature and severity of Chinese stock frauds are best considered in broader context. Otherwise, American commentators risk appearing like the emblematic film character Captain Louis Renault, the charming but corrupt police chief in the film classic, *Casablanca*, who professes (immediately before collecting his card game winnings at a gambling den) to be "shocked—*shocked*—to find that gambling is going on in here!"[15]

Take—as just a larger but by no means singular example—the fallout from the demise of the formerly NYSE-listed energy trading company Enron. Instead of intimidating its auditor, company management found means to co-opt the engagement team at its CPA, Arthur Andersen. Managers and the audit team working together then facilitated an outright fraud never seen before in its scale and depth of deception. Misleading accounting practices fueled a stellar stock market capitalization for the company that peaked at nearly $80 billion in August 2000. That made the firm the seventh largest in the United States based on market value.

Enron's subsequent bankruptcy in December 2001 not only wiped out all that investment value but also catapulted the company to a new distinction as the largest bankruptcy in U.S. history. *Businessweek* observed that the actual economic damage caused by the company's implosion was difficult to estimate precisely because of the complex web of deceit that it had practiced with its auditor's participation: "Enron's bankruptcy filings show $13.1 billion in debt for the parent company and an additional $18.1 billion for affiliates. But that doesn't include at least $20 billion more estimated to exist off the balance sheet."[16] The tens of billions lost from vaporized market capitalization and unrecoverable items off and on the balance sheet merely serve to approximate the direct financial costs incurred by Enron's demise. There is still untallied economic destruction that Enron visited upon a patchwork of local energy systems and ordinary consumers in America

while it relied on accounting fraud to perpetuate its own energy trading scams as a regular part of its ongoing business operations.

Moreover, just as with Longtop, corporate governance issues
relating to Enron did not represent an isolated problem. Barely half
a year had passed before Enron's record-setting U.S. bankruptcy was
eclipsed by that of the NASDAQ-traded telecommunications firm,
WorldCom, which was valued at around $120 billion at its peak in
1999. There were clearly signs of more pervasive problems. As a team
of Brookings Institute researchers observed immediately following
Enron's demise:

> Several months down the road, Enron symbolizes the open-
> ing of a deep and dark Pandora's box, the end of which seems
> nowhere in sight. Since then, a surprising number of blue chip
> companies, including WorldCom, Xerox, and Bristol-Myers
> Squibb, which for years were part and parcel of all that sym-
> bolized the seemingly endless expansion of the U.S. econ-
> omy, have joined the unenviable ranks of those with scandals
> based in fraudulent corporate management and accounting
> practices.[17]

Barely seven years after the collapse of WorldCom and vows to
"never again" allow a repeat of such corporate abuses, a new spate of
governance and financial management issues felled an icon of U.S.
investment banking, NYSE-listed Lehman Brothers. Lehman claimed
a gargantuan $691 billion in assets when it filed for bankruptcy in
September 2008. Its failure, of course, was not a stand-alone incident,
either. A parade of failed or severely damaged financial institutions and
debilitated corporations filed by in its wake, all owing to similar problems
of greed, gross mismanagement, and insufficient regulatory oversight.

It goes without saying that vastly more egregious listed company
scandals carried out on U.S. soil by leading American corporations in
no way excuses relatively modest-scale failures in corporate governance
and financial reporting at U.S.-listed Chinese small- and mid-cap
companies. By the same token, failures like Longtop's do not indict
the entire system in China (or America) but do bring to light fundamental weaknesses that deserve remedy.

Whatever the smaller troubled Chinese issuances might lack in absolute value destruction, there are sufficient grounds for real concern based on the proliferation in recent years of Chinese listings, the rapid pace (and seeming ease) by which accounting problems have been exposed, and lack of a means for direct redress by U.S. market investors and regulators. The gradual buildup of these conditions has upped the stakes in the China–U.S. equity exchange dynamic to a new level. The wager is no longer about whether a Chinese stock is fairly valued and if risks are appropriately recognized. It is about whether this form of trade, the most mutually rewarding and strategically meaningful body of financial flows between the world's two greatest economic powers, can sufficiently realize its potential and avoid becoming representative of regrettably missed chances rather than seized opportunities.

New Stakes in the Game

By the close of 2011, new short attacks with any devastating impact on Chinese issuances had disappeared. That counts as no assurance that more high-profile scandals might not occur later, but the time when investors could expect another "Chinese stock fraud *du jour*" in U.S. equity markets has passed.

The years 2007 to 2010 had seen a continuous buildup of Chinese IPOs and RMs followed by a market correction that exposed problems with a number of listings. From the second half of 2011, the air had been let out of the bubble. If market participants and regulators can learn from past periods and get beyond the excesses of exuberance and panic, then the trading of Chinese equities in the United States will become more rewarding for investors, issuers, and the innumerable others who reap ancillary benefits.

Whatever the weaknesses of China's economy, the bears have yet to make a persuasive case that the People's Republic (PRC) will not continue to grow at relatively high rates for the foreseeable future. Investors from around the world who invest in Chinese equities through U.S. stock markets will be better off in proportion to how well the issuances they can select from represent the full range of growth sectors in the Chinese economy. Chinese companies and the industries in which they operate will, in turn, benefit in proportion to the degree that they can access high-quality global equity capital and gain exposure and experience in foreign markets, especially the United States, if they have aspirations to become true global leaders. To maintain and, ideally, expand upon the dynamism of this relationship will require commitment to resolving key issues that arise.

Going into 2012, the Sino-American public equity dynamic has been pushed to the edge, making the prospects for its continuation as a vibrant contributor to the global economy the biggest gamble to have emerged from its universe of interactions. By the time a reader is consuming these words, authorities in the United States and the PRC will have already found productive means to resolve a regulatory stalemate that has emerged, *or* they will have left matters in some state of limbo, *or* they will have allowed regulatory facilitation to retreat to the point where new (and possibly some preexisting) Chinese issuances in U.S. markets are imperiled or already a thing of the past. Whatever the final resolution, it is sure to have consequences of corresponding significance for the world economy.

In the wake of financial market catastrophes in America, the U.S. government has a habit of stepping in with corrective, often groundbreaking, legislation. Adaptability in the U.S. financial system is—like the progressively adaptive nature of the nation itself—one of its enduring strengths. From the Securities Exchange Act of 1934 (which gave birth to the SEC) up to two well-known acts of recent years (Sarbanes-Oxley of 2002 and Dodd-Frank of 2010), a pattern of responsively evolutionary regulation has guided development of America's equity markets. The trend with new regulations has largely been to strengthen the comprehensive reach and standards for compliance regarding two distinguishing elements that underpin U.S. stock market quality: transparency and accountability.

If audit inspection issues with Chinese companies listed in the United States had been limited to CRMs, the matter might have been sidelined to be addressed gradually over time. Then Longtop failed, and failed spectacularly. For American regulators, the incident wiped out any residual faith that might have been placed in abiding by the pace of the status quo. Revelations contained in Deloitte's resignation letter combined with the absence of any further rebuttals from the company seemed like an affront to the entire U.S. listing process. The failure of Longtop appeared not merely as a single corporate failure. It crystallized fundamental failures in oversight that allowed such a fraud to be perpetuated.

Since 2007, the year of Longtop's excitedly received IPO, the SEC had been requesting that the Chinese government permit inspectors from the Public Company Accounting Oversight Board (PCAOB) to review the work of board-registered accountancies based in China. Among those CPAs that the PCAOB wanted to inspect were the Chinese practices of Big Four auditors, such as Shanghai-based Deloitte Touche Tohmatsu Certified Public Accountants Ltd. and Beijing-based PricewaterhouseCoopers Zhong Tian CPAs Limited Company.

On the basis of rights of sovereignty, Chinese officials refused these requests. In the meantime, between 2007 and the middle of 2011, about 150 Chinese companies listed on U.S. equity markets via CRMs (approximately 25 percent of all RMs in the United States during that time). Nearly another 100 Chinese companies listed via the traditional IPO route.[18]

China, it warrants noting, is not the only country that has refused permission for PCAOB inspections of domestically certified accountancies. As of June 30, 2011, the PCAOB's list of board-registered foreign CPAs that had not been inspected in over four years contained small accountancies along with Big Four firms operating in major European economies such as the United Kingdom, Germany, Spain, Italy, and France.[19] Sensitivities regarding sovereign rights in accountancy inspection are by no means limited to the PRC.

At the same time, one can easily point out that there has not been a wave of companies from those European countries going to list on U.S. stock markets. Nor has there been a failure in foreign issuances of recent memory that grabbed so much attention and produced so many deeply embedded concerns as Longtop and the failed CRMs that preceded it.

In responding to the Longtop collapse, America's well-honed regulatory response mechanisms kicked in. The timeline and nature of the ensuing U.S. and Chinese regulatory dialogue highlights the urgency of resolution for the U.S. side. It also demonstrates how, in the rush for redress, the bilateral dialogue has stalled, with potentially severely negative consequences.

The SEC's Big Bet

Longtop filed a Form 6-K with the SEC on Thursday, May 23, 2011, in which it matter-of-factly attached the inculpatory Deloitte resignation letter. The SEC issued a subpoena on the following Monday, May 27, demanding that Deloitte in Shanghai submit documents relating to its audits of Longtop by Friday, July 8.

While pursuing Deloitte for documentation, SEC and PCAOB officials arranged to meet with their Chinese counterparts in Beijing, an event they scheduled to kick off just two working days after the subpoena deadline: Monday, July 11. "The Sino-U.S. Symposium on Audit Oversight," as it was dubbed, brought together American regulatory officials and their equivalents from China's Ministry of Finance (MOF) and the China Securities Regulatory Commission (CSRC).

The official joint press release that followed the meetings, which curiously was not issued until the month after discussions took place, proclaimed that the talks "represented an important step toward Sino-U.S. cooperation on audit oversight of public companies."[20] Although there is no reason to suspect that both sides did not genuinely share that sentiment, later developments indicate that American and Chinese officials interpreted the meaning and implications of that event very differently.

Less than two weeks following the joint press release, the SEC sent Longtop what is known as a Wells Notice, a warning that regulators feel they have accumulated enough evidence of a securities law violation to recommend that the commission take legal action against a company. The notice provides a targeted company with time to challenge the instigation of legal proceedings, which SEC filings show that the company did not do.

On August 18, just one day before the SEC issued its Wells Notice to Longtop, an article ran in the *Wall Street Journal* announcing "Chinese Audit Regulators to Visit U.S."[21] In it, PCAOB chairman James Doty confirmed that Chinese officials would come to Washington by October in order to progress discussions on the board's inspection of Chinese auditors serving U.S.-listed firms. This all followed from the positive outlook U.S. regulators had adopted since announcing the results of the July symposium.

Inspection of the 53 China-based audit firms that were registered with the PCAOB had become a high priority for Doty, who had previously gone on record as describing lack of inspection to be "a gaping hole in investor protection."[22] The board was aiming for an agreement to be concluded with Chinese authorities by the end of 2011 on a mutually acceptable means for conducting auditor audits. A reciprocal visit to Washington by Chinese officials in the fall of that year would be necessary for the schedule to stay on track.

The SEC's issuance of a Wells Notice to Longtop in mid-August underscored the eagerness of U.S. regulators to seek restitution in that watershed case. The Commission, which oversees the PCAOB, evidently was separately proceeding on a time scale more accelerated than the pace of the diplomatic negotiations that the PCAOB was spearheading.

Then on September 8, the SEC went a step further and commenced litigation, not against Longtop—which had proven utterly unresponsive and over which U.S. regulators wielded no real legal leverage, anyway—but against Deloitte in Shanghai. Technically speaking, Deloitte in China is as removed from U.S. legal jurisdiction as is Longtop. Yet the global accountancy has a significant U.S. presence and is well known to American regulators. Moreover, scrutiny of auditor activities lay at the heart of what U.S. officials had come to recognize as the chief contributor to problems with Chinese stock issuances.

In the announcement of its subpoena filed in U.S. District Court in Washington, D.C., the SEC explained, "Although [Deloitte] Shanghai is in possession of vast amounts of documents responsive to the subpoena, it has not produced any documents to the SEC to date. As a result, the Commission is unable to gain access to information that is critical to an investigation that has been authorized for the protection of public investors."[23]

In its "Memorandum of Points and Authorities" to support its subpoena application, the SEC adopted several positions that were certain to annoy Chinese authorities. Whether U.S. officials fully appreciated how much of an impact their actions would have has not been publicly disclosed. Yet at least two elements of the case that the SEC crafted had all the markings of hitting directly upon already known sensitivities among PRC officials, not to mention the very

letter of certain key articles in modern PRC law. The SEC's big bet on
the efficacy of a lawsuit against a China-based CPA was upped by an
even larger bet on the wisdom of the strategy and tactics it employed
in arguments contesting the legitimacy of China's own regulatory
privileges.

Upping the Ante

In its case against Deloitte Shanghai, the SEC's primary bet was
the that a U.S. district court would accept the suggestion that the
American judiciary has authority over a subpoena served against a
China-registered CPA (which would also imply that a U.S. court has
jurisdiction over the CPA itself).[24] Regardless of whatever the U.S.
federal courts would have to say about such a suggestion, in the context of ongoing negotiations with Chinese government officials over a
U.S. agency's inspection rights of China-based CPAs, those were fairly
controversial positions to be formally presenting in a court of law.

Although a subpoena submitted in this way was sure to hit a raw
nerve with Chinese authorities, the document on its own would be
unlikely to derail ongoing negotiations outright. Far more alarming
from a Chinese perspective were the SEC's elaborate arguments against
the rationale of Deloitte's legal defense, which relies on Chinese law as
justification to refuse handing over Longtop audit documents to U.S.
regulators.

The most contentious planks of the SEC document represent the
equivalent of four cards played in a diplomatic game of high-stakes
poker. Adjusting for more common terminology and removing legal
case references, the first card played by the SEC contended:

> Deloitte Shanghai has represented that it has reached out to
> the China Securities Regulatory Commission, which declined
> to consent to the production of materials and directed Deloitte
> Shanghai to consult three different Chinese Agencies (the
> Ministry of Finance, the States Secrets Bureau and the States
> Archives Bureau). It appears that these agencies have not yet
> authorized disclosure, nor have they explicitly instructed
> Deloitte Shanghai not to produce the documents (let alone

explained their reasoning). Even if these agencies explicitly direct Deloitte Shanghai not to produce the subpoenaed documents, it is hard to conceive of what legitimate Chinese interests such action would protect.[25]

According to this card's "face value," Deloitte had attempted to comply with the SEC's request to release its audit paperwork on Longtop. Indeed, why should it not? The Longtop fiasco only added to the number of troubled U.S.-listed Chinese companies that Deloitte operations in China had audited. The smart move would be for the CPA's management to show U.S. securities regulators that it was committed to getting to the bottom of the problem and setting things right.

That the CSRC would defer Deloitte's request for permission to MOF, its overseeing authority, is entirely consistent with PRC government protocol. This would especially apply in as high a profile matter as what Longtop represented. Moreover, the SEC and PCAOB had already interfaced with the CSRC and MOF in the highly touted Sino-U.S. Symposium on Audit Oversight that occurred in the wake of Longtop. It is hard to imagine that the CSRC would not want MOF approval for anything related to subjects covered by this ongoing dialogue.

Why the States Secrets Bureau and the States Archives Bureau were included as necessary sources of approval is not immediately discernible. Some observers have surmised that because the Longtop audit involved verifications of accounts at state-owned banks, which count prominently among Longtop's client base, audit material could potentially touch on privileged government information. Less charitable explanations, such as bank branch involvement in a cover-up, have also been suggested. But all theories are mere speculation, which gets to the bigger point.

Based on the dialogue that was progressing between the SEC/PCAOB and MOF/CSRC, a far more important question is *why did the SEC not reach out to its counterparts in China and simply ask what was going on with permitting Deloitte to release the requested documents?* Instead, the burden of explaining China's regulatory objectives in this case was put on the auditor even though U.S. government agencies appear to have much more direct channels available to them.

The Sino–U.S. Symposium on Audit Oversight, it is worth noting, although timed to coincide with pursuit of redress on Longtop, in fact was originally conceived during an earlier round of the even higher-level U.S.-China Strategic and Economic Dialogue (S&ED). Held in early May 2011, the third S&ED was officiated over by Secretary of State Hillary Rodham Clinton, Treasury Secretary Tim Geithner, and their Chinese counterparts, Chinese State Councilor Dai Bingguo and Chinese Vice Premier Wang Qishan. If either the Symposium on Audit Oversight or the S&ED had accomplished anything, it should have at least improved government agency counterpart communications between the United States and the PRC. Precisely such communication between the SEC/PCAOB and MOF/CSRC would have been put to good use to develop an understanding of the CSRC's rationale in referring approvals regarding Longtop upward to other authorities.

With no official confirmation on why the CSRC requested Deloitte to check with other national bureaucracies, the SEC's case pivoted on the auditor being made to justify how it came to be caught up in the nuances of China's bureaucratic machinations.

The second card played by the SEC stated:

> Deloitte Shanghai's counsel has argued that foreign secrecy laws *may* prohibit it from disclosing responsive documents to the Commission. More specifically, Deloitte Shanghai's counsel has claimed that without prior authorization from several different Chinese regulatory agencies (including the Ministry of Finance, the State Secrets Bureau, and the State Archives Bureau), which have thus far apparently not consented to Deloitte Shanghai's production of the subpoenaed documents, it would be a potential violation of Chinese law for Deloitte Shanghai to produce the responsive documents. These vague assertions of possible conflicts with a foreign law provide no justification for Deloitte Shanghai's continued noncompliance with the Subpoena.[26]

On behalf of defrauded Longtop investors and for the sake of protecting the integrity of the securities listed on U.S. equity markets, the

SEC is fully justified in its desire to obtain the Longtop audit records as a matter of urgency. But characterizations of "vague assertions of possible conflicts with a foreign law" seem to ignore the reality of the situation.

Deloitte Shanghai, although part of a multinational accountancy group, is still a China-based CPA subject to the laws of the PRC. It is required to follow the CSRC's directives, just as Deloitte operations in the United States are required to comply with SEC directives. The SEC's original brief (reproduced in full in the appendix of this book) provides ample citations of previous U.S. case law that rationalize its subpoena even when a respondent claims that secrecy laws of other countries prohibit such disclosure. Those precedents might well support the SEC's arguments in a U.S. court, but they are irrelevant (and arguably detrimental) to the ultimate goal of allowing PCAOB inspections in China. As with Deloitte, PCAOB officials will need to find ways to accommodate PRC law if they are to have any hope of conducting in-country inspections. Protesting the need for compliance with domestic Chinese laws works contrary to the larger goal of reaching a bilateral solution for authorization of PCAOB inspections in China.

The third card played in the SEC's court memorandum takes things even further. The document proffers that U.S. objectives in this case take precedence over whatever Chinese government interests might exist. That assertion is made all the more difficult to defend since at the time of the subpoena U.S. authorities had yet to verify how China actually defined its own interests. Nevertheless, the SEC argued:

> Most importantly, the United States' interest in obtaining the subpoenaed documents, which are necessary to an ongoing investigation into an apparently massive fraud on the domestic securities markets, far outweigh China's secrecy interests.[27]

Defrauded investors undeniably deserve justice. But does that necessitate denial of yet-undetermined Chinese government interests? If U.S. officials plan to deal with China by insisting that U.S. law unconditionally takes precedence over Chinese law, then the prospects for meaningful dialogue between the two governments seems rather bleak.

With the SEC's fourth card, which stands out as the most sweeping critique of the system that has held back Deloitte's release of subpoenaed documents, the U.S. securities regulator appears to insist that China has no basis for its own national regulations. Toward a country that has repeatedly argued its concerns about sovereignty in denying U.S. inspectors access to Chinese-licensed audit firms, this is—to say the least—an unorthodox move. The SEC insisted that

> the secrecy interests of China here are impossibly vague. According to Deloitte Shanghai, Chinese law prohibits the production of audit working papers to people or entities outside of China without express approvals from Chinese authorities. Similarly, according to Deloitte Shanghai, China's "States Secrets" laws preclude the production of information and documents "relating to the national economy" without prior approvals. However, it is entirely unclear what national interests of China are truly at stake. If the documents reveal large-scale fraud at Longtop, *a Cayman Islands company* with significant operations in China, one might naturally conclude that it is in China's interest to have documents produced so that the truth behind any fraud could be uncovered. Deloitte Shanghai has not asserted any way in which China's secrecy interests would actually be implicated, let alone compromised, by production of the responsive documents.[28]

The most persuasive element in this part of the SEC's case is that, indeed, "one might naturally conclude that it is in China's interest to have documents produced so that the truth behind any fraud could be uncovered." So why not engage the Chinese authorities on that basis? The second round of the Sino-U.S. Symposium on Audit Oversight (originally intended to be held in Washington, D.C., in October 2011) presumably would have been an ideal venue to address exactly that topic. Instead, just one month prior to the planned discussions, the U.S. government body slated to host the symposium filed documents that seem to preclude the concept of dialogue and unravel what progress had been made up to that point. Items for negotiation were turned into grist for litigation.

Beyond the Brink?

After the SEC's legal action against Deloitte, officials from China's MOF and the CSRC indefinitely postponed their reciprocal visit to Washington for phase two of bilateral discussions on audit oversight. No public statements explained the reasons for the delay.

Michael Rapaport, the *Wall Street Journal* reporter who had been covering developments with ongoing negotiations, broke the story about the postponement, observing: "In April, the SEC acknowledged China's sovereignty concerns . . . The SEC's action against Deloitte doesn't seem to be following that policy, though it isn't known if the commission tried working through the Chinese regulators before filing its lawsuit."[29]

Even if the SEC did try working through Chinese officials prior to beginning litigation against Deloitte, the court papers it filed could not have been viewed by the Chinese side as conducive to further discussions. Adding to already high tensions, on September 27, Robert Khuzami, director of enforcement at the SEC, revealed in an interview with Reuters that the U.S. Department of Justice (DOJ), along with the Federal Bureau of Investigation, had also gotten involved. A number of federal prosecutors around the United States were said to be taking part in the investigation. The director stated flatly: "Not having proper accounting and reliable audit review for publicly traded companies with operations in China is just not acceptable. We have to find a path to resolution of this issue." He further speculated that there will be "greater [DOJ] involvement as time goes on."[30]

Through these comments, it became publicly known that, along with at least four Chinese bureaucracies that were involved with the Longtop fiasco, the United States now had the DOJ and FBI joining in with the SEC and PCAOB. The situation was resembling a nuclear arms race in the form of stockpiling bureaucratic firepower. How, exactly, increasing government organizational involvement, especially agencies focused on crime and litigation instead of diplomacy, was expected to resolve a situation known to have origins in national sovereignty is unclear.

Ironically, the SEC has precedent cases that would have pointed toward the merits of using negotiation rather than court action to resolve similar impasses.

No less an intimately close ally of the United States than the United Kingdom—which, among many obvious commonalities, significantly shares with America the same legal heritage and equity capitalist culture—had initially prevented PCAOB inspections from taking place on British soil. Britain maintained its bar on inspections despite the urgency for U.S. authorities to get to the bottom of an unprecedented financial disaster: the collapse of Lehman Brothers. Not until the signing of an agreement between the UK's Professional Oversight Board (POB) and the PCAOB in January 2011 did American inspectors finally win permission to examine Ernst & Young's London operations to determine how that firm had audited Lehman Brothers' notorious off–balance sheet toxic assets known as Repo 105.

The UK–U.S. standoff was no minor spat. America had strong interest in conducting on-site inspections as quickly as possible. Verifying the Repo 105 arrangement was crucial to understanding what a U.S. bankruptcy court examiner determined were Lehman's attempts to portray a "materially misleading picture of the firm's financial condition."[31] This was in regard to the *largest bankruptcy in U.S. history.* Even with the gravity of the situation and the extremely high priority placed on its resolution, it took *three years* for the PCAOB to finally negotiate a satisfactory arrangement with Britain's POB. The two sides solved the impasse through an agreement that allowed for joint inspections to be conducted by officials from the PCAOB and the POB working together. The idea of joint inspections was also the type of solution that the PCAOB was hoping could be achieved by the end of 2011 for audit oversight in China.

In addition, the point hammered home in the SEC subpoena memorandum about Longtop being "*a Cayman Islands company* with significant operations in China" struck a nerve of another sort in Beijing. For some time, a number of Chinese government officials and advisors had been expressing concerns about unwelcome outside influence coming through foreign investment in strategic Chinese industries. The Internet sector is the most talked about example. The highly publicized showdown between Google and Chinese regulators in February 2010 over Google's disagreements with Chinese censorship policies, which resulted in Google losing its license to operate on the Chinese mainland, is one memorable symbol of the friction. Clashes arising from Google's presence in China related to that company's foreign direct investment in the PRC. Elements of the Chinese government have also grown concerned about indirect foreign investment through China-operating Internet companies that list in the United States.

Following the basic pattern originally established by CTHK/China Mobile's global listing, equity for Chinese companies operating in sectors that prohibit or restrict foreign ownership such as telecommunications, the Internet, education, and natural resources have for years been organized according to a structure known as the variable interest entity (VIE). Through multitiered contracts, VIEs allow for a foreign-listed holding company—typically located in a venue such as Hong Kong, the Cayman Islands, or the British Virgin Islands—to manage operations and expatriate profits from domestic Chinese enterprises. Though not the simplest way to do things, the arrangement has for many years accommodated Chinese and foreign interests in granting Chinese companies access to foreign capital and foreign investors access to some of China's most promising high-growth sectors.

Within ten days of the SEC filing its subpoena against Deloitte, Reuters ran a story headlined "China Company Structure Under Threat."[32] It started off by stating that the CSRC "is asking the government to clamp down on the controversial corporate structure used by companies such as Sina (NASDAQ:SINA) and Baidu (NASDAQ:BIDU) to list overseas." The spokesman for China's Ministry of Commerce (MOFCOM) acknowledged at the ministry's September monthly news briefing that within Chinese government, VIE structures lack "any laws to control, or any regulations and policies to regulate." The spokesman added that the MOFCOM "and other departments" will be investigating ways to regulate "investment by way of VIE."[33]

The *Wall Street Journal* promptly ran a detailed review of how changes to the VIE structure might impact U.S.-listed Chinese firms that had conducted IPOs on NASDAQ and the NYSE. The article remarked how increased attention on the VIE investment platform "comes amid broad efforts by Chinese officials this year to step up already extensive controls on the Internet."[34] It added that in September, MOFCOM had issued new rules covering how foreign investment channeled through the VIEs might in the future be included in national security reviews on mergers.

A Deutsche Bank analysis of the VIE controversy published in early October quoted the CSRC as having declared in its report on VIEs that the structure represents a "major threat to China's national security." The bank deduced that part of the motivation for China's securities regulator to describe the situation in such dire terms was, at least in part, to shield that agency from pressure exerted by the SEC and other overseas regulators.[35] If true, this would point to yet another instance of how the SEC's litigation tactics would advance neither the U.S. government's immediate goal of restitution in the Longtop case nor the larger goal of gaining access for PCAOB officials to inspect China-based auditors. Suffice it to say, such tactics also do not serve the U.S. government's overriding foreign policy objective to encourage China to further open up key markets to foreign participation.

As the U.S. Justice Department and SEC's enforcement division sought solutions to fraudulent Chinese stock issuances in American courts and the CSRC and MOFCOM looked to increase Chinese control over the corporate structures that make many of those issuances possible, the two sides were essentially recalibrating the regulatory equilibrium that allows for the interactive dance of the U.S.–China public equity exchange to function. For the sake of all market participants and the wider circle of beneficiaries, hopefully they will find productive means to resolve their disagreements. To do so will require greater creativity and commitment to dialogue than the two sides were exhibiting in late 2011.

A worst-case scenario would entail China shutting down the flow of new listings in the United States. Worse still, it could rescind the rights of VIEs to continue operating in China. This sort of nuclear option would wipe out vast amounts of existing market value and future wealth-creating opportunities, damaging public equity relations between the world's two largest economies beyond the point of recognition. Hopefully, such an eventuality will remain the stuff of speculation only.

Even with the Sino-American economic détente at an awkward and precarious juncture, the linked interests of the two sides remain unchanged. The reasons for continuing to bet on a thriving equity market dynamic between China and the United States have not diminished but increased. More than ever, investors in the United States and around the globe are compelled to tap into the unique growth opportunities that China offers in the face of less robust economic performance in the developed world. China, if it is to continue on the path of industrial upgrading and globalization of its companies, will lose out much more than mere foreign investment dollars if it turns its back on the capital quality and valuable foreign market experience provided by U.S. stock exchanges.

Although their tactics at times work at cross purposes, U.S. and Chinese regulators have never stopped sharing the goal of preventing abuses to their respective financial systems as part of continuing efforts to strengthen the economic welfare and development potential of their respective nations. Over time, the stakes have risen in the U.S.–China equity exchange dynamic, but so has the mutuality of objectives. Provided that the powers which allow the dynamic to take place can focus on fundamental common ground and get beyond their differences, investors need not cash in their chips just yet.

Chapter 7

Continuing the Bet

Accountability and Adaptability

The Tartar conquerors did not change the manners of the conquered nation; on the other hand, they protected and encouraged all the arts established in China, and adopted their laws: an extraordinary instance of the natural superiority which reason and genius have over blind force and barbarism.

—Voltaire[1]

Evolving Accountability

The situation of the United States pressing its case to allow for auditor inspections in foreign territories is not without historical irony. Nor is, more broadly, Chinese resistance to foreign pressure to conform with Western norms.

The United States once was—like China today—a high-growth, developing economy. From the late nineteenth to early twentieth century, low-paid, hardworking American laborers helped the United States build up a world-leading manufacturing base. America accomplished this largely at the expense of the industrial power of the world's dominant economy of the era, the United Kingdom. By 1914, American factories were cranking out 36 percent of global manufacturing output, roughly the same share that the United Kingdom had occupied in the 1870s. Over those years that United States ascended, the UK's industrial output shrank to less than half its previous level.[2]

As the UK's industrial base eroded, the country increased its capacity for more advanced economic activities such as financial services—a situation roughly analogous to the United States of 100 years later. Going into the twentieth century, Britain led the world in the export of capital, sending nearly one-fourth of its national wealth overseas. Within that large chunk of overseas bound investment, approximately another one-fourth went to the United States.

Here, the Brits got nervous. British investment in the United States "triggered the need for public accountancy services to protect individual investors residing in the UK from fraudulent or incompetent management in the US," notes accounting sciences scholar Thomas Lee.[3] Through an influx of British public accountants sent over for "conducting audits or investigations on behalf of British shareholders," America's businesses were monitored, and U.S. accounting practices were gradually brought up to prevailing global standards.

However offensive it might have seemed to some in the United States to witness the British—who, after all, had previously ruled over America as colonial masters—returning to positions of economic authority due to perceived deficiencies in America's own financial monitoring abilities, the importation of accounting expertise undeniably served to positively stimulate development of the U.S. economy.

By accepting the demands of British investors, the quality of U.S. corporate equity issuances improved. None other than the doyen of modern American finance, John Pierpont "J. P." Morgan, proactively embraced as far back as 1898 the distinctly "British practice" of engaging "independent, 'chartered' accountants to audit the corporation's accounts" of his Federal Steel Company.[4] Federal Steel constituted the first step in Morgan's eventually successful effort to create through corporate mergers a manufacturing giant that acted as a catalyst for advancing America's fledgling industrial might: United States Steel Corporation.

Upon its founding in 1901, U.S. Steel became the first company in the world with a capitalization in excess of $1 billion. Among its long-term economic contributions, the company served as a spring-board for America's global manufacturing leadership. Its success also added to the quality and liquidity of America's financial markets, help-ing set the stage for Wall Street to grow into the global powerhouse that it later became.

So a century ago the United States was on the receiving end of pressure to improve its own accounting standards. Now it is the one setting higher standards and pushing for improvements elsewhere. Times *do* change.

Herein lies a singular but highly relevant reference point for China if it truly is committed to building world-class companies. The U.S. Steel example provides a reminder about how a willingness to adapt, irrespective of any sensitivities, can serve to promote the quality of a nation's investment environment. U.S. Steel is far from the only instance of this. China can easily draw from its own pool of emblem-atic Chinese companies for inspiration.

China's breakout mega-IPO, CTHK/China Mobile—the "first course" in a banquet of massive Chinese global listings—shares similarities with U.S. Steel in terms of the forces underpinning both corporations' birth by industry consolidation and adoption of precedent-setting standards of transparency. Each company also gen-erated far-ranging spillover effects for their respective national econ-omies and the world at large. Their roles in stimulating worldwide interest for marketed public equities from their home countries, their contributions to fostering consumption and production of the advanced technology products associated with them, their diverse influences over vast swaths of business and society—all this resulted from a willingness to embrace uncharted risks, including compliance with new expectations for accountability in order to access global equity capital investors.

The Adaptability Challenge

For the United States to stay at the forefront of global capital mar-kets evolution, U.S. securities regulators will need to find ways to constructively respond to interests from outside America's borders as well as within. This represents a new challenge for a bureaucratic system that has traditionally operated with its gaze fixed on accommodating U.S. domestic interests and without incentives to consider foreign perspectives in its strategic outlook and tactical actions. America's past dominance in global finance is no guarantee that it can continue to dominate in the future. Adaption will be crucial to its maintaining a competitive edge.

China likewise, though in a much longer and broader historical context, has long been challenged not to be bound by the trappings of its own success. China's difficulty in looking past its own grandeur to recognize and respond to the realities of a world beyond has been a key feature in its encounters with more economically advanced countries of the modern age.

Voltaire, a contemporary of Adam Smith and fellow leading voice of the European Enlightenment, was along with the father of modern economic science a fan of China. France's towering figure of eighteenth-century letters had a tendency to overromanticize his views of Chinese civilization, but he could also be highly perceptive.

Commenting on the enduring quality of China's cultural achievements, for example, Voltaire correctly observed that foreign conquerors generally felt compelled to conform to Chinese cultural and legal institutions, and not the other way around. In Voltaire's words, China's invaders "did not change the manners of the conquered nation; on the other hand, they protected and encouraged all the arts established in China, and adopted their laws."[5]

The foreign-ruled Chinese dynasties of the Liao (established in the tenth century), Jin (twelfth century), Yuan (thirteenth century), and Qing (seventeenth century) empires all followed this basic pattern of conquering China by force and then succumbing to its civilizing allure. The nation's material and cultural wealth was what drew the rulers from bordering societies to seize China; they desired to absorb the nation's civilizing influences in order to fully partake of that bounty.

As long as the rest of the world remained decidedly precapitalist and less economically developed than it, China could count on the foreign barbarians who crossed through its borders to treat the Central Nation with deference and respect. The thinking of early capitalist-era intellectuals such as Smith and Voltaire reflected some of the Western mind's residual sense of awe for the magnificence of Chinese civilization. Industrializing Western governments and men of commerce, however, were more apt to recognize the sheer power that the scientific and industrial revolutions had provided them for forcing open access to China's riches.

China's emperor Qianlong, who dismissively waved away gifts representing modern science and industry brought to him by a visiting British trade delegation in 1793, emphatically reinforced an age-old position of Chinese resistance to foreign cultural encroachment that in various guises continues to this day. For more than two centuries since that fateful, initial interaction with the forces of Western industrial capitalism, China has been searching for ways that allow it both to preserve its self-identity while effectively responding to the threats and opportunities presented by a modern and increasingly integrated world system.

China, too, will need to discover means of adaptability if it wants to realize the range of benefits available to it in the global economy of the twenty-first century. Since beginning market reforms in 1979, the country has economically progressed through a process of playing catch-up with Western levels of development. Now ranking as the world's number-two economy, China will find that catching up becomes less and less viable an end game the higher it ascends to the top of the economic ladder. The PRC will need to increasingly operate according to international standards if it is to effectively compete with other major economic powers. For a country that throughout most of its history has felt reassured by others repeatedly conforming to Chinese ways, finding culturally acceptable means to learn from and integrate foreign best practices is perhaps the greatest hurdle it faces.

The bets riding on Chinese issuances in American stock markets extend well beyond the transactions that drive individual issuer share prices. The forces that underpin China concept stocks trading in the United States connect into wide-ranging aspects of history, society, business, and economics in both countries. That makes maintaining the Sino-American public equity dynamic exceptionally complex. It also makes far more significant the transformations that it facilitates for the relationship's two principal actors. The origins of impasses in the relationship can be profound. The potential rewards for "gung ho" efforts to resolve issues as they emerge are greater still.

Appendix

Securities and Exchange Commission Memorandum in Support of its Subpoena to Deloitte Touche Tohmatsu CPA Ltd. of Shanghai

UNITED STATES DISTRICT COURT FOR THE DISTRICT OF COLUMBIA **U.S. Securities and Exchange Commission** 100 F Street, N.E. Washington, DC 20549 Movant, v. **Deloitte Touche Tohmatsu CPA Ltd.** 30/F Bund Center 222 Yan An Road East Shanghai 200002, PRC Respondent.	MISC. No. _____

SECURITIES AND EXCHANGE COMMISSION'S MEMO-
RANDUM OF POINTS AND AUTHORITIES IN SUPPORT OF
APPLICATION FOR ORDER TO SHOW CAUSE AND ORDER
REQUIRING COMPLIANCE WITH A SUBPOENA

This action seeks enforcement of an administrative subpoena (the
"Subpoena") issued by the Securities and Exchange Commission
("SEC" or "Commission") to Deloitte Touche Tohmatsu CPA Ltd.
("D&T Shanghai" or the "Respondent") as part of an investigation
(*In the Matter of Longtop Financial Technologies Limited*, SEC File No.
HO-11698) into possible violations of the federal securities laws.

I. Summary

Pursuant to the Commission's statutory authority to investigate possible violations of the federal securities laws, the staff of the SEC's
Division of Enforcement (the "Staff") is conducting an investigation
into possible fraud and other violations concerning the securities of
Longtop Financial Technologies Limited ("Longtop"), a foreign private issuer the securities of which are registered with the Commission
and traded on U.S. markets. D&T Shanghai audited Longtop's financial statements for several years, both before and after Longtop's 2007
initial public offering in the United States. D&T Shanghai resigned
as auditor for Longtop on May 22, 2011, after discovering numerous
financial improprieties while conducting its audit of Longtop for the
year ended March 31, 2011.

On May 27, 2011, the SEC staff served the Subpoena on D&T
Shanghai's prior United States counsel, who represented that he had
authority to accept service of the Subpoena. Notwithstanding the
fact that it has acknowledged possessing vast amounts of responsive
documents, D&T Shanghai has refused to produce any documents to
the SEC.

A district court is bound to enforce an administrative subpoena
if the information sought "is within the authority of the agency, the
demand is not too indefinite and the information sought is reasonably
relevant." *United States* v. *Morton Salt Co.,* 338 U.S. 632, 652 (1950).
Because the Commission has fulfilled these limited requirements,

and because D&T Shanghai has not raised any valid challenge to the Subpoena, this Court should enter a show cause order against D&T Shanghai and require compliance with the Subpoena.

II. Statement of Facts

A. Deloitte Touche Tohmatsu CPA LTD ("D &T Shanghai")

D&T Shanghai is an accounting firm based in the People's Republic of China and registered in the United States as a public accounting firm with the Public Company Accounting Oversight Board (the "PCAOB"). Deitch Decl. ¶ 6. D&T Shanghai is a Chinese member firm of Deloitte Touche Tohmatsu Limited, a UK private company. *Id.*

B. The Longtop Investigation

Longtop is a Cayman Islands corporation with principal offices in Hong Kong and Xiamen, China. Deitch Decl. ¶ 5. Longtop is a foreign private issuer the securities of which are registered with the Commission pursuant to Section 12 of the Exchange Act [15 U.S.C. § 78 (1)]. *Id.* Longtop's American depositary shares ("ADSs") have been listed on the New York Stock Exchange ("NYSE") under the symbol LFT. *Id.* Longtop files annual reports on Form 20-F and furnishes reports on Form 6-K with the Commission pursuant to Section 13(a) of the Exchange Act and related rules thereunder. *Id.* Longtop also filed registration statements with the Commission to raise hundreds of millions of dollars from investors, including on Forms F1 and Form F-3. *Id.* at ¶ 7.

D&T Shanghai was Longtop's auditor from at least 2007 until D&T Shanghai resigned on May 22, 2011. Deitch Decl. ¶ 6. In that capacity, D&T Shanghai prepared and issued audit reports filed by Longtop with the Commission. *Id.* at ¶ 8. For example, for the fiscal year ended March 31, 2010, Longtop reported total revenue of $169 million and net income of $59 million, and D&T Shanghai issued an audit report dated July 16, 2010, expressing an unqualified opinion on Longtop's consolidated financial statements. *Id.* at ¶ 9. In addition, in connection with Longtop's raising hundreds of millions of dollars through securities offerings, D&T Shanghai consented to the use of its audit reports in Longtop's registration statements filed with the Commission. *Id.* at ¶ 7.

On May 17, 2011, trading in Longtop's ADSs was halted by the NYSE. Deitch Decl. ¶ 10. At the time trading was halted, Longtop's ADSs were priced at $18.93 per share with 57 million shares outstanding, resulting in a market capitalization of approximately $1.08 billion. *Id.*

On May 23, 2011, Longtop furnished a report on Form 6-K announcing that D&T Shanghai had resigned as its auditor and attaching D&T Shanghai's letter of resignation. Deitch Decl. ¶ 11. In the same Form 6-K, Longtop announced that Derek Palaschuk, Longtop's Chief Financial Officer, tendered his resignation by letter, dated May 19, 2011. *Id.* As discussed further in the accompanying declaration of Lisa Deitch, D&T Shanghai indicated in its letter of resignation that it was resigning because it had identified numerous indicia of financial fraud at Longtop and it further indicated that D&T Shanghai's prior year audit reports for Longtop could no longer be relied upon by investors. *Id.* at ¶¶ 12–13.

On May 25, 2011, the Commission issued an Order Directing Private Investigation and Designating Officers to Take Testimony in a matter entitled *In the Matter of Longtop Financial Technologies Limited,* SEC File No. HO-11698 (the "Formal Order"). Deitch Decl. ¶ 3, Ex. A. The Formal Order authorizes members of the SEC Staff to investigate whether antifraud and/or reporting provisions of the federal securities laws have been or are being violated by any persons or entities in connection with the offer, sale and/or purchase of securities in Longtop. *Id.* The Formal Order also authorized the staff to determine whether any person or entity involved in the matter has engaged "in any acts or practices of similar purport or object." *Id.*

C. The Subpoena

As part of the *Longtop* investigation, the SEC Staff served an administrative subpoena (the "Subpoena") on D&T Shanghai's prior United States counsel, Douglas Cox, of Gibson Dunn & Crutcher LLP, on May 27, 2011. Deitch Decl. ¶ 17. On May 23, 2011, Mr. Cox had confirmed to the Staff that he was authorized and willing to accept service of the Subpoena on D&T Shanghai's behalf. *Id*. D&T Shanghai has not contested the service or the validity of the Subpoena. *Id*. Accordingly, this constituted proper and valid service of process on D&T Shanghai.

In the Subpoena, the SEC Staff requested that D&T Shanghai, through its custodian of records, produce documents, from between January 1, 2007, and the date of the Subpoena, related to D&T Shanghai's business and, in particular, its activities as Longtop's auditor. *See* Deitch Decl. Exhibit C. The Subpoena required responsive documents to be produced to the Staff in Washington, D.C. by June 10, 2011. *Id*. On June 9, 2011, the Staff granted D&T Shanghai a one-week extension, until June 17, 2011, to respond to the Subpoena. *Id*. at ¶ 19. The Staff was subsequently contacted by new legal counsel for D&T Shanghai, Michael Warden of Sidley Austin LLP, who requested that the Staff further extend the return date of the Subpoena. *Id*. at ¶ 19–20. The Staff agreed to extend further the return date of the Subpoena until July 8, 2011. *Id*.

To date, D&T Shanghai has failed to comply with the Subpoena in every respect. Deitch Decl. ¶ 21. Instead, as described more fully in the accompanying Deitch declaration, on July 8, 2011, in lieu of producing the required documents, counsel for D&T Shanghai submitted a letter to the Staff indicating that it was refusing to comply with the Subpoena because, among other things, it believed that (i) it could not be compelled to produce documents predating July 21, 2010, the effective date of the Dodd-Frank Wall Street Reform and Consumer Protection Act (the "Dodd-Frank Act"), P.L. 111-2003 (July 21, 2010), and (ii) it believed producing *any* of the responsive documents may subject it to sanctions under Chinese law. *Id*. at ¶¶ 22–24.

III. Argument

A. This Court Has Jurisdiction Over This Action and Over the Respondent.

This Court has subject matter jurisdiction to enforce the Subpoena in aid of the Commission's investigation. Congress has authorized the Commission to seek, and the federal courts to issue, an order compelling compliance with its subpoenas upon application by the Commission. Section 21(c) of the Securities Exchange Act of 1934 (the "Exchange Act") [15 U.S.C. § 78u(c)]; Section 22(b) of the Securities Act of 1933 (the "Securities Act") [15 U.S.C. § 77v(b)][1]; Section 21(c) of the Exchange Act provides that the Commission may make application in any jurisdiction where its investigation is being carried on or where a person to whom the subpoena is issued resides or does business. Here, not only is the investigation being carried on in Washington, D.C., the Subpoena requires that documents and other information be produced here. Deitch Dec. Ex C.

This Court also has personal jurisdiction over D&T Shanghai. It is well recognized that "[t]he Securities Exchange Act permits the exercise of personal jurisdiction to the limits of the Due Process Clause of the Fifth Amendment." *SEC* v. *Knowles,* 87 F.3d 413, 417 (10th Cir. 1996); *SEC* v. *Unifund SAL,* 910 F.2d 1028, 1033 (2d Cir. 1990); *accord Busch* v. *Buchman, Buchman & O'Brien,* 11 F.3d 1255, 1258 (5th Cir. 1994); *SEC* v. *Compania Internacional Financiera S.A.,* No. 11 Civ. 4904, 2011 WL 3251813, at *4 (S.D.N.Y. July 29, 2011); *SEC* v. *Lines Overseas Mgt., Ltd,* No. 04-302, 2007 WL 581909, at *2 (D.D.C. Feb. 21, 2007). Under the Due Process Clause of the Fifth Amendment, personal jurisdiction over a party exists as long as that party has sufficient "minimum contacts" with the jurisdiction. *International Shoe Co.* v. *Washington,* 326 U.S. 310, 316 (1945). The exercise of jurisdiction must not "offend 'traditional notions off air play and substantial justice.'" *Id.* (quoting *Milliken* v. *Meyer, 311* U.S. 457, 463 (1940)). Put differently, the party's activities within the jurisdiction must render it foreseeable that the party should reasonably anticipate being hailed into the forum court. *World-Wide Volkswagen Corp.* v. *Woodson,* 444 U.S. 286,297 (1980).

Here, the mandates of the Fifth Amendment's Due Process Clause have been satisfied. As reflected in the accompanying declaration, the Subpoena is directly related to the numerous purposeful contacts D&T Shanghai has and currently maintains with the United States securities markets, including the fact that D&T Shanghai consented that its audit reports for Longtop could be filed annually with the Commission knowing full well that they would be relied upon by U.S. investors. *See, e.g.,* Deitch Dec. ¶¶ 7–9 (discussing D&T Shanghai's involvement in auditing Longtop's financial statements and filing reports with the Commission). That is more than sufficient to constitute "minimum contacts." *See Knowles,* 87 F.3d at 417 (former president of Bahamian companies had sufficient minimum contacts with United States to support district court's exercise of personal jurisdiction enforcing administrative subpoena, based on his trading activities directed toward United States and relating to matters underlying the SEC investigation); *Unifund SAL,* 910 F.2d at 1033 (upholding personal jurisdiction over foreign investors alleged to have conducted insider trading in securities of a United States corporation traded on a United States exchange); *PerezRubio* v. *Wyckoff,* 718 F. Supp. 217, 229-31 (S.D.N.Y. 1989) (upholding personal jurisdiction over a foreign investment house and its individual officers because the purpose of the corporation was to purchase United States securities on United States exchanges, in part for United States citizens), *overruled on other grounds by PT United Can Co., Ltd* v. *Crown Cork & Seal Co., Inc.,* 138 F.3d 65 (2d Cir. 1998); *SEC* v. *Gilbert,* 82 F.R.D. 723, 725-26 (S.D.N.Y. 1979) (holding that exercise of personal jurisdiction over a Swiss bank whose only contacts with the United States were four brokerage accounts maintained at three U.S. securities dealers would satisfy due process). Indeed, in correspondence to date, D&T Shanghai has not in any way challenged the service of the Subpoena or its validity.

B. The Commission Has Met Its Burden for Enforcement of the Subpoena.

A district court is bound to enforce an administrative subpoena "if the inquiry 'is within the authority of the agency, the demand is not too indefinite and the information sought is reasonably relevant.'" *Morton Salt,* 338 U.S. at 652; *see also SEC* v. *Arthur Young & Co., 584* F.2d 1018, 1023–24 (D.C. Cir. 1978); *In re Administrative Subpoena John Doe* v. *United States,* 253 F.3d 256, 262 (6th Cir. 2001). Because the Commission has met these criteria in this case, the Court should enforce the Subpoena.

First, the Commission has authority to conduct the investigation authorized by the Formal Order. Congress gave the Commission broad authority to conduct investigations into possible violations of the federal securities laws and to demand production of evidence germane to such investigations. The investigative powers of the Commission are statutory and are analogous to those of a grand jury. *Morton Salt,* 338 U.S. at 642–43. Like a grand jury, an agency "can investigate merely on suspicion that the law is being violated, or just because it wants assurance that it is not." *Id.* Thus, courts have recognized that the SEC is acting within the scope of its Congressionally granted authority even where its investigation is based on nothing more than "official curiosity." *See, e.g., Arthur Young & Co.,* 584 F.2d at 1023–24 & n. 45. Furthermore, Section 21(b) of the Exchange Act empowers the Commission, or its designated officers, to subpoena witnesses, compel their attendance, take evidence, and "require the production of *any* books, papers, correspondence, memoranda, or other records which the Commission deems relevant or material to the inquiry." 15 U.S.C. § 78u(b) (emphasis added). Section 19(c) of the Securities Act vests the Commission and its designated officers with essentially the same power. *See* 15 U.S.C. § 77s. In light of this statutory language, courts have consistently recognized the SEC's broad authority to issue administrative subpoenas. *See SEC v. Jerry T. O'Brien, Inc.,* 467 U.S. 735, 743 (1984) ("The provisions vesting the SEC with the power to issue and seek enforcement of subpoenas are expansive."); *SEC v. Dresser Indus.,* 628 F.2d 1368, 1379-80 (D.C. Cif.) *(en banc)* ("Given this broad statutory mandate, there is virtually no possibility that in issuing this subpoena, the SEC was acting ultra vires."); *Arthur Young & Co.,* 584 F.2d at 1023–24.

Here, the Commission has exercised its statutory authority and authorized the SEC Staff to investigate whether, among other things, antifraud and/or other provisions of the federal securities laws have been or are being violated by any persons or entities in connection with the offer, sale and/or purchase of securities in Longtop. The Staff, consistent with the Formal Order, seeks to obtain documents from D&T Shanghai related to its audits of Longtop, which may provide evidence of potential violations of U.S. law. The SEC's investigation and the Subpoena issued to D&T Shanghai in connection therewith are unquestionably within the scope of the Formal Orders and the SEC's authorized law-enforcement powers.

Second, the Staff that issued the Subpoena has met the only administrative prerequisites to issuing the Subpoena: the Commission's issuance of a formal order of investigation designating its officers to, among other things, issue subpoenas on its behalf. *SEC* v. *Blackfoot Bituminous, Inc.,* 622 F.2d 512,514 (10th Cir. 1980) (citing the Rules of Practice Relating to Investigations, 17 C.F.R. §§ 203.1 *et seq.* (1979). Here, the Commission issued its Formal Order in the *Longtop* investigation prior to issuing the Subpoena. The Subpoena was issued pursuant to this Formal Order and was signed by an officer designated in the Formal Order as required by SEC Rules. Deitch Decl. ¶ 4. *See* SEC Rules Relating to Investigations. 17 C.F.R. § 203.8 (referencing 17 C.F.R. § 201.232(c) and 201.150(c)(l)). Accordingly, the Subpoena is valid and proper.

Finally, the documents being sought by the Subpoena are not indefinite and are reasonably relevant to, and within the scope of, the Commission's investigation. Information is reasonably relevant to an investigation when it is "not plainly incompetent or irrelevant to any legal purpose." *Endicott Johnson* v. *Perkins,* 317 U.S. 501, 509 (1943). The scope of the Staff's subpoena power is "co-extensive" with its investigative power, and the Staff is given the sole discretion to determine what is relevant to an investigation. *Arthur Young & Co.,* 584 F.2d at 1031.

In the present case, the Staff has determined that the information and documents sought from D&T Shanghai are relevant to the Commission's investigation. For example, the Staff believes the documents sought by the Commission from D&T Shanghai relating to its incomplete audit of Longtop for the year ended March 31, 2011, may reveal information as to D&T Shanghai's discovery of false financial records at Longtop. Deitch Decl. ¶ 26. Similarly, documents related to prior year audits that D&T Shanghai completed of Longtop may reveal how any fraud schemes at Longtop were able to continue for years undetected. *Id.* In short, the Subpoena seeks the basic information necessary to ferret out whether there was a fraud and, if there was, who was behind it, how significant it was, and how it was conducted. Thus, the Commission has met its threshold requirements for enforcement of the subpoena issued to D&T Shanghai.

C. *This Court Should Order D&T Shanghai to Produce All Documents Responsive to the Subpoena.*

In correspondence with the Commission, D&T Shanghai has asserted that even though the Subpoena calls for the production of documents from January 1, 2007, through the date of the Subpoena, D&T Shanghai objects to the production of any documents that predate July 21, 2010, the effective date of the Dodd-Frank Act. This objection is entirely without merit, and the Commission respectfully requests that this Court order D&T Shanghai to produce *all* documents that are responsive to the Subpoena, irrespective of their date.

Respondent's argument is apparently based on a misunderstanding of the legal basis for the Subpoena. As set forth above, the Commission's subpoena is a proper administrative subpoena, and the documents it seeks are well within its mandate. *See* Section 21(b) of the Exchange Act [15 U.S.C. § 78u(b)] (empowering the Commission, or its designated officers, to subpoena witnesses, compel their attendance, take evidence, and require the production of books, papers, correspondence, memoranda, or other records which the Commission deems relevant or material to the inquiry); Section 19(c) of the Securities Act [15 U.S.C. § 77s]; *SEC v. Jerry T. O'Brien, Inc.,* 467 U.S. 735, 743 (1984) ("The provisions vesting the SEC with the power to issue and seek enforcement of subpoenas are expansive."); *SEC v. Dresser Indus.,* 628 F.2d 1368, 1379 (D.C. Cir.) *(en banc)* ("Given this broad statutory mandate, there is virtually no possibility that in issuing this subpoena, the SEC was acting ultra vires."); *Arthur Young & Co.,* 584 F.2d at 1023–24. This administrative subpoena power has been in place for decades prior to the enactment of the Dodd-Frank Act.

D&T Shanghai, however, has suggested that the Subpoena's scope is necessarily constrained by Section 106 of the Sarbanes-Oxley Act, 15 U.S.C. § 7216 ("Section 106"), as amended by § 929J of the Dodd-Frank Act. Section 106 provides, in relevant part, that:

> If a foreign public accounting firm performs material services upon which a registered public accounting firm relies in the conduct of an audit or interim review, issues an audit report,

performs audit work, or conducts interim reviews, the foreign public accounting firm shall --

(A) produce the audit work papers of the foreign public accounting firm and all other documents of the firm related to any such audit work or interim review to the Commission or the [PCAOB], upon request of the Commission or the [PCAOB]; and

(B) be subject to the jurisdiction of the courts of the United States for purposes of enforcement of any request for such documents.[2]

D&T Shanghai apparently claims that Section 106 provides the *sole* means by which the Commission can request or obtain its audit work papers.[3] Simply put, there is no basis for such a claim. Nothing in either the text or the legislative history of Section 106 can be read to suggest that, either before or after its enactment, let alone its amendment by the Dodd-Frank Act in 2010, the SEC lacked the authority to subpoena audit work papers or any other documents from foreign public accounting firms. Indeed, it has always been the law that foreign public accounting firms—just like any other accounting firm, person or other entity—can be subject to properly issued subpoenas. *See, e.g., First American Corp. v. Price Waterhouse LLP,* 988 F.Supp. 353 (S.D.N.Y. 1997) (ordering United Kingdom accounting partnership to comply with subpoena for audit work papers in private securities fraud litigation). As long as the subpoenaed documents are properly within the scope of the SEC's broad investigative authority, the subpoena is valid. *See SEC v. Dresser Indus.,* 628 Fold at 1379. ("Given this broad statutory mandate, there is virtually no possibility that in issuing this subpoena, the SEC was acting ultra vires.") Section 106 merely provides an additional mechanism for the SEC to request audit work papers and related documents from foreign accounting firms, which firms may at times be difficult to serve with a subpoena.[4]

In sum, D&T Shanghai's claim that it should not be required to produce documents that were created prior to July 21, 2010, notwithstanding the fact that such documents are plainly responsive to the Subpoena, is entirely without merit.

D. Chinese Law Provides No Justification for the Respondent's Non-Compliance with the Commission's Subpoena.

D&T Shanghai's alternative basis for not complying with the Subpoena—namely, that it is precluded from doing so by Chinese law—is equally unavailing. D&T Shanghai's counsel has argued that foreign secrecy laws *may* prohibit it from disclosing responsive documents to the Commission. *See* Deitch Decl. ¶¶ 22–23. More specifically, D&T Shanghai's counsel has claimed that without prior authorization from several different Chinese regulatory agencies (including the Ministry of Finance, the State Secrets Bureau, and the State Archives Bureau),[5] which have thus far apparently not consented to D&T Shanghai's production of the subpoenaed documents, it would be a potential violation of Chinese law for D&T Shanghai to produce the responsive documents. *See id.* These vague assertions of possible conflicts with a foreign law provide no justification for D&T Shanghai's continued non-compliance with the Subpoena. *See SEC* v. *Euro Security Fund,* Case No. 98 CIV. 7347 (DLC), 1999 WL 182598, ★3 (S.D.N.Y. April 2, 1999) (noting that the party opposing discovery bears the burden of proving the existence of an actual conflict between the foreign law and U.S. discovery obligations; "[i]llusory references to foreign secrecy without any specifics are insufficient to create a conflict").

Assuming (without conceding) that Chinese laws may prohibit the disclosure of certain responsive documents, this Court should nevertheless order D&T Shanghai to comply with the Subpoena. In *Societe Internationale Pour Participations Industrielles et Commerciales, S.A.* v. *Rogers,* 357 U.S. 197 (1958), the Supreme Court rejected an argument that the existence of foreign secrecy laws precluded a U.S. court from ordering a foreign party under its jurisdiction to disclose information in a U.S. judicial proceeding. *Id.* at 204–05. In rejecting this argument, the Supreme Court reasoned that adoption of such a broad rule would thwart an important public policy interest in enforcing federal statutes. *Id.; see also Societi Nationale Industrielle Airospatiale* v. *United States District Court for the Southern District of Iowa, 482 U.S.* 522, 544 n.29 (1987) (observing that blocking statutes do not "deprive an American court of the power to order a party subject to its jurisdiction to produce evidence even though the act of production may violate [those] statute[s]." (citing *Societe Internationale*, 357 U.S. at 204206)).

Following *Societe Internationale*, where subpoena recipients cite foreign laws as a defense to compliance with a subpoena, courts consider the recipient's good faith along with a series of factors drawn from the Restatement on Foreign Relations Law, including: (a) the competing interests of the nations whose laws are in conflict; (b) the extent and nature of hardship of compliance for the party or witness from whom discovery is sought; (c) the extent to which the required conduct is to take place in the territory of the other state; (d) the nationality of the person; (e) the importance to the litigation of the information and documents requested; and (f) the ability to obtain the subpoenaed information through alternative means. *See, e.g., Societi Nationale Industrielle Aerospatiale*, 482 U.S. at 544 n.28 (endorsing Restatement factors as relevant to comity analysis); *SEC v. Banca Della Svizzera Italiana*, 92 F.R.D. 111, 116–17 (S.D.N.Y. 1981) (collecting cases); *Minpeco v. Conticommodity Services, Inc.*, 116 F.R.D. 517, 523 (S.D.N.Y. 1987); *Euro Security Fund*, 1999 WL 182598, at *3; *cf United States v. Bank of Nova Scotia*, 691 F.2d 1384, 1389–91 (11th Cir. 1982) (applying similar balancing test in the context of grand jury subpoena).

Even assuming (without conceding) that D&T Shanghai is acting in good faith by refusing to comply with the Subpoena in any respect, a review of these various factors makes plain that this Court should enforce the Subpoena and require D&T Shanghai to produce the requested documents directly to the Commission and without further delay. (a) *Competing National Interests.* Most importantly, the United States' interest in obtaining the subpoenaed documents, which are necessary to an ongoing investigation into an apparently massive fraud on the domestic securities markets, far outweigh China's secrecy interests. Prior courts have reached a similar conclusion when considering whether foreign states' secrecy laws preclude compliance with SEC subpoenas, *see, e.g., Euro Security Fund*, 1999 WL 182598, at *4; *Banca Della*, 92 F.R.D. at 117, and the United States' interests are particularly strong here. There are already indications that Longtop may have perpetrated an extensive fraud during and after seeking out and obtaining hundreds of millions of dollars in financing through the United States securities markets. *See* Deitch Decl. ¶¶ 7–15. D&T Shanghai, wittingly or unwittingly, audited Longtop's financial statements throughout this period, and consented to the inclusion of its audit reports in Longtop's registration statements and other filings, knowing full well that these audit opinions would be relied upon by U.S. investors. *See id.* The pending Subpoena is narrowly tailored to obtain precisely the documents and information that D&T Shanghai has that can help the Commission ferret out any fraud involving Longtop.

The national interest in obtaining compliance with the Subpoena is underscored by the fact that Congress enacted Section 106 of the Sarbanes-Oxley Act, in responding to concern over precisely this issue—that U.S. investors may be harmed by the lack of transparency in foreign auditing firms. As explained in Part C above, Section 106 created an additional mechanism for the Commission to seek out and obtain audit work papers and related documents from foreign public accounting firms when those firms were conducting audits. Here, while the Commission was able to serve the Subpoena on D&T Shanghai successfully, that does not diminish the strong national interest in obtaining foreign audit work papers that is exemplified in Section 106.

By contrast, the secrecy interests of China here are impossibly vague. According to D&T Shanghai, Chinese law prohibits the production of audit working papers to people or entities outside of China without express approvals from Chinese authorities. *See* Deitch Decl. ¶¶ 22–23. Similarly, according to D&T Shanghai, China's "States Secrets" laws preclude the production of information and documents "relating to the national economy" without prior approvals. *Id.* However, it is entirely unclear what national interests of China are truly at stake. If the documents reveal large-scale fraud at Longtop, *a Cayman Islands company* with significant operations in China, one might naturally conclude that it is in China's interest to have documents produced so that the truth behind any fraud could be uncovered. D&T Shanghai has not asserted any way in which China's secrecy interests would actually be implicated, let alone compromised, by production of the responsive documents.

As set forth above and in the accompanying declaration, D&T Shanghai has represented that it has reached out to the CSRC, which declined to consent to the production of materials and directed D&T

Shanghai to consult three different Chinese Agencies (the Ministry of Finance, the States Secrets Bureau and the States Archives Bureau). Deitch Decl. ¶ 23. It appears that these agencies have not yet authorized disclosure, nor have they explicitly instructed D&T Shanghai not to produce the documents (let alone explained their reasoning). Even if these agencies explicitly direct D&T Shanghai not to produce the subpoenaed documents, it is hard to conceive of what legitimate Chinese interests such action would protect. *See Richmark Corp.* v. *Timber Falling Consultants,* 959 F.2d 1468 (9th Cir. 1992) (upholding contempt sanctions against corporation that refused to produce discovery by citing Chinese blocking statutes, and noting that neither the defendant nor China had "identified any way in which disclosure of the information requested here will significantly affect the PRC's interests in confidentiality"); *Euro Security Fund,* 1999 WL 182598, at ★1 0 (dismissing respondent's claim that Swiss secrecy laws precluded production of materials, in part, because respondents "provided no evidence of Swiss interests besides a generic appeal to 'Swiss secrecy'"); *Compagnie Francaise d'Assurance Pour Ie Commerce Exterieur* v. *Phillips Petroleum Co.,* 105 F.R.D. 19 (S.D.N.Y. 1984) (ordering discovery notwithstanding presence of French blocking statute, in part because "the legislative history of the [French] statute gives strong indications that it was never expected nor intended to be enforced against French subjects but was intended rather to provide them with tactical weapons and bargaining chips in foreign courts" (citation omitted).[6] Accordingly, the Commission respectfully submits that this factor weighs heavily in favor of enforcing the Subpoena.

(b) *Hardship to D&T Shanghai.* While D&T Shanghai has claimed that it would be subject to potential civil and criminal sanctions if required to comply with the Subpoena, those claims appear entirely speculative. Admittedly, a genuine risk of imprisonment "constitutes a weighty excuse for nonproduction." *Societe Internationale Pour Participations Industrielles et Commerciales,* 357 U.S. at 211. But here, not only does that risk appear illusory, it is a risk D&T Shanghai knowingly accepted by availing itself of the U.S. securities markets. D&T Shanghai should not be permitted to willfully avail itself of the benefits of auditing financial statements of issuers with securities registered with the Commission and then claim hardship to avoid the U.S. legal requirements that come along with those benefits. *See Richmark,* 959 F.2d at 1477 ("[I]f the hardship is self-imposed, or if [the defendant] could have avoided it, the fact that it finds itself in an undesirable position will not work against disclosure of the requested information."); *Banca Della,* 92 F.R.D. at 117 (rejecting defendant's request to preclude discovery based on Swiss secrecy laws and observing that "[the defendant] invaded American securities markets and profited in some measure thereby. It cannot rely on Swiss nondisclosure law to shield this activity").

As explained in the accompanying declaration, D&T Shanghai received over $4 million for audit-related services it provided to Longtop since 2006. Deitch Decl. ¶ 27. It performed these services and accepted these fees knowing full well that it could be subject to subpoenas and all other forms of U.S. legal process. It should not now be surprised by the consequences of its own choices. *See Banca Della,* 92 F.R.D. at 119. ("It would be a travesty of justice to permit a foreign company to invade American markets, violate American laws if they were indeed violated, withdraw profits and resist accountability for itself and its principals for the illegality by claiming their anonymity under foreign law.") Accordingly, the Commission respectfully submits that this factor is at least neutral.

(c) *Location of compliance.* It is the Staff's understanding that the bulk of the responsive files were generated in and are currently located in China. However, D&T Shanghai has also represented that the vast bulk of the responsive materials are maintained in electronic form, which minimizes any hardship of actual physical production, and limits the amount of material that has to be gathered from a foreign jurisdiction. Moreover, the actual production would take place here in the United States. *See Banca Della,* 92 F.R.D. at 119. ("Performance may be said to occur here as well as in Switzerland since the actual answering of the interrogatories will presumably take place in the United States, where [the respondent]'s lawyers are.") Accordingly, the Commission respectfully submits that this factor is at least neutral.

(d) *The Nationality of the Respondent.* As noted above, D&T Shanghai is a Chinese member finn of Deloitte Touche Tohmatsu Limited, a UK private company. In addition, D&T Shanghai has made millions of dollars from auditing foreign issuers seeking capital from the U.S. securities markets. Thus, while D&T Shanghai is formally a Chinese entity, it has also long benefited from its international connections, minimizing any protection it should get for being foreign. *See Banca Della,* 92 F.R.D. at 119 (noting, in deciding to enforce subpoena, that "it is true that [respondent] is a Swiss corporation. However, its transnational character, as evidenced by its large number of foreign affiliates, and its New York 'subsidiary' (so styled by it), render this Court less reluctant to order [the respondent] to conform to our laws even where such an order may cause conflict with Swiss law"). Accordingly, the Commission respectfully submits that this factor is at least neutral.

(e) *Importance of Information.* The importance to the investigation of the information under Subpoena, like the importance of the U.S. interests at stake more generally, is significant. *See In re Air Crash at Taipei, Taiwan on October* 31, *2000,* 211 F.R.D. 374, 37778 (C.D. Cal. 2002) (ordering compliance with discovery over foreign law objections and noting that "this information is crucial to plaintiffs' ability to prosecute their claims; therefore, this factor weighs in favor of disclosure"). As set forth above and in the accompanying declaration of Lisa Deitch, the Subpoenaed documents are critical to the ongoing investigation of Longtop, particularly because of the inability of the Commission to obtain documents or information from certain other parties about Longtop. *See* Deitch Decl. ¶ 26. Even if the Commission is able to take testimony from or obtain documents from Longtop or third parties, there is simply no substitute for D&T Shanghai's audit work papers and related files. These documents are unquestionably necessary to complete the picture of any fraud at Longtop and identify who was involved. Accordingly, the Commission respectfully submits that this factor weighs heavily in favor of enforcing the Subpoena.

(f) *Alternative Means.* Finally, there do not appear to be any alternative means of obtaining the subpoenaed information. It is beyond serious dispute that there is no third party from which the Commission could obtain the requested information—D&T Shanghai is the sole entity that possesses its audit work papers and related information. Nevertheless, in correspondence prior to the commencement of this enforcement action, D&T Shanghai has claimed that it is willing to provide a subset of the documents under Subpoena to the CSRC, and suggested that the SEC can and should seek to obtain the requested information from that foreign regulator. Indeed, D&T Shanghai has claimed that this is an "alternative means" that is expressly contemplated in Section 106 of the Sarbanes-Oxley Act.[7] In fact, the Commission respectfully submits that this is not an acceptable alternative means of production.

First, there is no assurance that D&T Shanghai were to produce documents to Chinese regulators, those regulators would provide them to the SEC. Indeed, based upon D&T Shanghai's representations, it appears that such regulators would *not* produce the subpoenaed documents on to the SEC. Second, any interim production of the documents to Chinese regulators would necessarily result in significant delay. While such delays may be tolerable in the context of routine reviews of foreign auditing practices, in the context of an active investigation into a possible billion-dollar fraud scheme—where Longtop remains a going concern with countless investors—such a delay is simply untenable.

IV. Conclusion

The Commission is unable to gain access to relevant information and documents in an investigation that has been authorized for the protection of public investors, notwithstanding the fact that it has properly served an administrative Subpoena on the Respondent and the Respondent has acknowledged that it is in possession of vast numbers of responsive documents. Accordingly, the Commission requests that the Court act expeditiously to grant this application and issue: (i) an order, in the form submitted, requiring the Respondent to show cause why it should not be ordered to comply with the Subpoena; (ii) if the Respondent fails to show adequate cause as to its refusal to comply with the Subpoena, an order requiring it to comply with the Subpoena by immediately producing all responsive documents; and (iii) such other and further relief as may be necessary and appropriate to achieve compliance with the Subpoena directed to the Respondent.

Dated: September 8, 2011

> Respectfully submitted,
> Mark Lanpher
>
> Attorney for Plaintiff
> SECURITIES AND EXCHANGE COMMISSION
> 100 F Street, NE
> Washington, DC 20549
> (202) 551-4879 (Lanpher)
> Fax: (202) 772-9228
> E-mail: lanpherm@sec.gov

Of Counsel:
ANTONIA CHION
New York Bar Attorney Registration No. 1873405
LISA WEINSTEIN DEITCH
California Bar No. 137492
HELAINE SCHWARTZ
New York Bar Attorney Registration No. 1917046

Notes

Preface

1. 桓寬 [Huan Kuan], 《鹽鐵論》 [*Discourses on Salt and Iron*], "錯幣第四" [Part 4, The Minting of Coin].

Chapter 1

1. Jim Rogers, *A Bull in China: Investing Profitably in the World's Greatest Market* (New York: Random House, 2007), Kindle edition locations 85–87.

2. Data taken from International Monetary Fund (IMF), World Economic Outlook Database, April 2011, www.imf.org.

3. Xinhua, "China's Annual FDI Hits Record 105 bln USD," January 18, 2011.

4. American Chamber of Commerce in the People's Republic of China, *American Business in China, 2011 White Paper* (Beijing, 2011), 16, 14.

5. For details on the ill-fated Huawei investment, see Shayndi Raice and Andrew Dowell, "Huawei Drops U.S. Deal Amid Opposition," *Wall Street Journal*, February 21, 2011.

6. China Venture, *Annual Statistics & Analysis of China's VC/PE Investments* (2010), March 8, 2011, http://en.chinaventure.com.cn/Report/321.html.

7. Reuters reported in July 2007 that the $254 billion market cap of the ICBC had exceeded the $251 billion valuation of Citigroup, which previously

held the title of world's largest bank. See Lu Jianxin, "China ICBC Tops Citigroup as World's Biggest Bank," Reuters, July 23, 2007.

Chapter 2

1. Renaissance Capital, *2009 Global IPO Market Review and 2010 Outlook* (Renaissance Capital, 2010), 7.

2. Mao Zedong, "On Contradiction," *Selected Works of Mao Tse-tung,* available at www.marxists.org/reference/archive/mao/selected-works/volume-1/mswv1_17 .htm.

3. Renaissance Capital, *2010 Global IPO Market Review and 2011 Outlook* (Renaissance Capital, 2011), 3. Note that the Renaissance data only counts IPOs with a minimum $50 million market capitalization and excludes warrants and Special Purpose Acquisition Companies (SPACs).

4. Renaissance Capital, *2007 Annual IPO Review,* http://www.ipohome.com/ marketwatch/review/ 2007review.asp.

5. Ernst & Young, *Global IPO Trends Report 2009* (Ernst & Young, 2010), 4: "Global IPO activity fell by 61% in deal numbers and 67% in funds raised."

6. IMF, World Economic Database, April 2011.

7. PricewaterhouseCoopers, *2009 US IPO Watch* (PricewaterhouseCoopers, 2010), 4.

8. IDC, *China Gaming End-User Survey 2008 and China Gaming 2008–2012 Forecast and Analysis,* quoted in ChangYou.com Limited, *Prospectus* (2009), 90.

9. Laura Mandaro, "Changyou.com Climbs 25% in IPO Debut," MarketWatch.com, April 2, 2009.

10. Dan Gallagher and Steve Gelsi, "Shanda Games' Shares Fall on Initial Public Offering," MarketWatch.com, September 25, 2009.

11. See, for example, Chris Isidore, "The Great Recession," CNNMoney.com, March 25, 2009, for a sense of how negative sentiment had become about the U.S. economy just prior to the ChangYou.com IPO.

12. Renaissance Capital, *2009 Global IPO Market Review and 2010 Outlook,* 2.

13. David Barboza, "Sparse U.S. Listings Prompt Rush on China I.P.O.s," *New York Times,* February 11, 2010.

14. PricewaterhouseCoopers, *2009 US IPO Watch,* 7, 14.

15. Scott Gehsmann, *PwC 2010 US IPO Watch* (PricewaterhouseCoopers, 2011), passim.

16. Ibid.

17. 王海涛 [Wang Haitao], "纳斯达克比深圳还要近吗" [Is NASDAQ Closer Than Shenzhen?], 《新京报》 [*Beijing News*], 2010年11月23日 [November 23, 2010], B02.

18. Lulu Chen, "Massive Stock Scheme Revealed," *South China Morning Post*, December 12, 2011.

19. Steve Gelsi, "China Cache Skyrockets on Wall Street," MarketWatch.com, October 1, 2010.

20. Renaissance Capital, *2010 Global IPO Market Review and 2011 Outlook*, 11–12.

21. IMF, World Economic Outlook Database, April 2011.

22. World Federation of Exchanges website: Statistics, Monthly Reports, www .world-exchanges.org/statistics/monthly-reports.

23. Amar Gill, Jamie Allen, and Simon Powell, *CG Watch 2010: Corporate Governance in Asia*, (CLSA Asia-Pacific Markets, 2010), 3.

24. 宋晓军、王小东、黄纪苏、宋强、刘仰 [Song Xiaojun et al.], 《中国不高兴：大时代、大目标及我们的内忧外患》 [*Unhappy China: A Major Era, a Grand Vision, and Our Internal Weaknesses and External Threats*], (南京：江苏人民出版社 [Nanjing: Jiangsu People's Publishing], 2009), 97.

25. Ibid., 110.

26. Niall Ferguson and Moritz Schularick, "'Chimerica' and the Global Asset Market Boom," *International Finance* 10 (3) (Winter 2007), 215–239.

27. Michael Lind, "The Failure of Shareholder Capitalism," Salon.com, March 29, 2011.

28. Adam Smith, *An Inquiry into the Nature and Causes of the Wealth of Nations* (1776), Book I, Chapter 8, Paragraph 24. The text here and throughout is based on the online edition of the book, provided courtesy of the Library of Economics and Liberty. See www.econlib.org/library/Smith/smWN.html.

29. Ibid., I, 11, Paragraph 129.

30. Ibid., I, 8, 39.

31. Ibid., I, 3, 7.

32. Smith went so far to state, in I, 9, 15: "China seems to have been long stationary, and had probably long ago acquired that full complement of riches which is consistent with the nature of its laws and institutions. But this complement may be much inferior to what, with other laws and institutions, the nature of its soil, climate, and situation might admit of. A country which neglects or despises foreign commerce, and which admits the vessels of foreign nations into one or two of its ports only, cannot transact the same quantity of business which it might do with different laws and institutions. In a country too, where, though the rich or the owners of large capitals enjoy a good deal of security, the poor or the owners of small capitals enjoy scarce any, but are liable, under the pretence of justice, to be pillaged and plundered at any time by the inferior mandarines, the quantity of stock employed in all the different branches of business transacted within it, can never be equal to what the nature and extent of that business might admit."

He expanded on this theme in IV, 9, 40: "The Chinese have little respect for foreign trade. 'Your beggarly commerce!' was the language in which the Mandarins of Pekin used to talk to Mr. de Lange, the Russian envoy, concerning it. Except with Japan, the Chinese carry on, themselves, and in their own bottoms, little or no foreign trade; and it is only into one or two ports of their kingdom that they even admit the ships of foreign nations. Foreign trade therefore is, in China, every way confined within a much narrower circle than that to which it would naturally extend itself, if more freedom was allowed to it, either in their own ships, or in those of foreign nations."

Smith rounds off by noting that whatever opulence China had already attained, it could only benefit further by foreign commerce. "A more extensive foreign trade, however, which to this great home market added the foreign market of all the rest of the world; especially if any considerable part of this trade was carried on in Chinese ships; could scarce fail to increase very much the manufactures of China, and to improve very much the productive powers of its manufacturing industry. By a more extensive navigation, the Chinese would naturally learn the art of using and constructing themselves all the different machines made use of in other countries, as well as the other improvements of art and industry which are practised in all the different parts of the world. Upon their present plan they have little opportunity except that of the Japanese" (IV, 9, 41).

33. Ibid., I, 5, 4.

34. Eugene Fama, "Efficient Capital Markets: A Review of Theory and Empirical Work," *Journal of Finance* 25 (2) (May 1970), 383.

35. Fischer Black, "Noise," *Journal of Finance* 41 (3) (July 1986), 529.

36. John M Keynes, *The General Theory of Employment, Interest and Money* (London/Cambridge: Macmillan/Cambridge University Press, 1936; reprinted 1973), 161.

37. Charles Kindleberger, *Manias, Panics, and Crashes: A History of Financial Crises* (New York: John Wiley & Sons, 1996), 23.

38. Merriam-Webster, www.merriam-webster.com.

39. Oxford University Press, *The Oxford Essential Dictionary of the U.S. Military,* available at www.answers.com/library/US%20Military%20Dictionary.

Chapter 3

1. Wang Xiangwei, "Push For China Telecom Float," *South China Morning Post*, October 16, 1997.

2. Unless otherwise noted, the exchange rate for conversions is Chinese ¥6.46 per US$.

3. Ding Lu, "China's Telecommunications Infrastructure Buildup: On Its Own Way," in *Deregulation and Interdependence in the Asia-Pacific Region*, NBER-EASE Vol. 8 (Chicago: University of Chicago Press, 2000), 374.

4. Peter Lovelock, *The China Telecom (Hong Kong) IPO: Money for Nothing?* (Hong Kong: University of Hong Kong Center for Asian Business Cases), 2.

5. Andrew Chetham, "Mainland Aims to Meet Own Funding Needs," *South China Morning Post*, June 10, 1997.

6. Erik Guyot and Shanthi Kalathil, "Tapping Chinese Phone Issue Carries Risk," *The Globe and Mail* (reprinting the *Wall Street Journal*), October 6, 1997.

7. Lovelock, *The China Telecom (Hong Kong) IPO*, 5.

8. Wang Xiangwei, "Push for China Telecom Float," *South China Morning Post*, October 16, 1997.

9. Edward Gargan, "The Asian Crisis: The Currency Battle," *New York Times*, October 24, 1997.

10. *The Economist*, "Safe Harbour No More," October 23, 1997.

11. Agency France Presse, "Hong Kong's Biggest Share Offer Closes Amid Fears of Falling Bourse," October 16, 1997.

12. Agency France Presse, "Hong Kong Shares Plunge Again as Afternoon Session Opens," October 23, 1997; *Euroweek*, "CNAC Deal Postponed as China Telecom Follows Markets Down," October 24, 1997.

13. Shanthi Kalathil, "China Telecom Faces Bad Start in Hong Kong," *The Globe and Mail*, October 22, 1997.

14. *Financial Post Daily*, "China Telecom IPO Only 30 Times Oversubscribed," October 17, 1997.

15. Agency France Presse, "China Telecom to List Below Offer Price Despite 35.2 Times Subscribed," October 22, 1997.

16. Kate Linebaugh, "Hong Kong Elite Score on IPOs," *Wall Street Journal*, June 2, 2006.

17. Guyot and Kalathil, "Tapping Chinese Phone Issue Carries Risk."

18. *Euroweek*, "CICC/Goldman Sachs May Revise China Telecom Price Range Upwards as All Signs Indicate Massive Oversubscription," October 10, 1997.

19. ITU World Telecommunication, ICT Indicators Database, www.itu.int/ict/statistics.

20. *Euroweek*, "CNAC Deal Postponed," October 24, 1997.

21. James Surowiecki, "Is There Anything U.S. Investors Won't Buy?" *Slate*, November 14, 1997, http://www.slate.com/id/2628/.

22. Peter Bernstein, *Against the Gods: The Remarkable Story of Risk* (New York: John Wiley, 1996), 68.

23. Jason Dean, "U.S. Financier Helps a Chairman Shake China Inc.," *Wall Street Journal*, September 28, 2006.

24. Regina Abrami, William Kirby, Warren McFarlan, Ning Xiangdong, and Tracy Yuen Manty, *China Netcom: Corporate Governance in China (A)* (Boston: Harvard Business School Publishing), 2008.

25. Patti Waldmeier, "China Mobile Vice-president Sacked," *Financial Times*, December 31, 2009; 李微敖、慈冰 [Li Weiao, Ci Bing], "张春江落'网' [Zhang Chunjiang Caught in 'Net']," 《财经》[*Caijing Magazine*], 2010, 年01月04日 [January 4, 2010], http://magazine.caijing.com.cn.

26. 李微敖、慈冰[Li Weiao, Ci Bing], "张春江落'网' [Zhang Chunjiang Caught in 'Net']."

27. *China Daily*, "SOE Execs Under Graft Scanner," January 8, 2010, china-daily.com.cn.

28. Jerry Solomon, "From Bogus Foreign Offerings," *Congressional Press Releases*, October 30, 1997.

29. *GoldenEye*, United Artists, 1995.

30. Cheng Li, "China's Telecom Industry on the Move: Domestic Competition, Global Ambition, and Leadership Transistion," *China Leadership Monitor*, Fall 2006 (19), 5, www.hoover.org/publications/china-leadership-monitor.

31. Business Monitor International, *China Telecommunications Report, Q2 2011*, 36–37, 62.

32. International Data Corporation, *Worldwide Quarterly Mobile Phone Tracker*, January 28, 2011, www.idc.com.

33. Business Monitor International, *China Telecommunications Report*, 18.

34. BRICI data from Marcos Aguiar, Vlasislav Boutenko, David Michael, Vaishali Rastogi, Arvind Subramanian, and Yvonne Zhou, *The Internet's New Billion: Digital Consumers in Brazil, Russia, India, China, and Indonesia* (Boston Consulting Group, 2009).

35. Jin-Li Hu, Hsiang-Tzu Wan, and Hang Zhu, "The Business Model of a Shanzhai Mobile Firm in China," *Australian Journal of Business and Management Research* 1 (3), June 2011, 55.

36. Sherman So, "MediaTek Rides High In Bandit Territory," *Asia Times*, May 26, 2010.

37. Yongjiang Shi, "Shan-Zhai: Alternative Manufacturing—Making the Unaffordable Affordable," University of Cambridge, Centre for International Manufacturing, *CIM Briefing*, 2009, www.ifm.eng.cam.ac.uk/free/.

38. Makiko Taniguchi and Eddie Wu, "Shanzhai: Copycat Designs as an Open Platform for Innovation," *Patterns*, 2009, patterns.ideo.com.

39. David Barboza, "In China, Knockoff Cellphones Are a Hit," *New York Times*, April 27, 2009.

40. 工业和信息化部　[Ministry of Industry and Information Technology], "2009 年我国3G和TD发展总体情况" ["The General Condition of Our Nation's 3G and TD Development"], January 14, 2010, www.miit.gov.cn. At the end of 2009, the ¥/$ exchange rate was ¥6.83/$.

41. Luis Enriquez, Stefan Schmitgen, and George Sun, "The True Value of Mobile Phones to Developing Markets," *The McKinsey Quarterly*, Web Exclusive, February 2007, www.mckinseyquarterly.com.

42. 工信部 [MIIT],　"2009年我国3G和TD发展总体情况" ["The General Condition of Our Nation's 3G and TD Development"].

43. 工信部　[MIIT],　"工业和信息化部通告2011年第二季度电信服务有关情况" ["MIIT Announcement on Conditions Relating to 2011 Second Quarter Telecommunications Services "], July 25, 2011, www.miit.gov.cn. Yu Tianyu, "3G User Numbers Not So Hot," *China Daily*, July 30, 2011; Business Monitor International, ibid.

44. Leping Huang, *Smartphones China* (Nomura International, 2011).

45. International Monetary Fund, World Economic Outlook Database, April 2011, www.imf.org.

46. Lee Chyen Yee and Huang Yuntao, "Analysis: Apple Juggernaut to See More China Gains," Reuters, July 25, 2011.

47. Loretta Chao and Yukari Iwatani Kane, "Apple Eyes Bigger Slice of Chinese Market," *Wall Street Journal*, July 19, 2011.

48. Colin McCallum, *Sector Review: China Telecoms Sector* (Credit Suisse, 2011), 13.

49. Carl Walter and Fraser Howie, *Red Capitalism: The Fragile Foundation of China's Extraordinary Rise* (Singapore: John Wiley & Sons, 2011), 162.

50. Lovelock, *The China Telecom (Hong Kong) IPO*, 7.

51. Richard McGregor, *The Party: The Secret World of China's Communist Rulers* (London: Penguin Books, 2011), 89.

Chapter 4

1. Mark Gongloff, "Spreadtrum Mounts Its Defense," *Wall Street Journal*, June 29, 2011.

2. Carson Block and Sean Regan, *Orient Paper Inc.* (Muddy Waters Research, 2010), 1, www.muddywatersresearch.com

3. Carson Block, "Open Letter to SPRD Chairman re Muddy Waters' Concerns," June 28, 2011, 6.

4. Block and Regan, *Orient Paper Inc.*

5. Block, "Open Letter."

6. Lynn Cowan, "Chinese IPOs No Longer Sizzling," *Wall Street Journal*, May 17, 2011.

7. Ryan Vlastelica and Daniel Bases, "Chinese Stock Scams are the Latest U.S. Import," Reuters, May 11, 2011.

8. Floyd Norris, "The Audacity of Chinese Frauds," *New York Times*, May 26, 2011.

9. Tim Hanson, "Is China a Complete Joke?" *Motley Fool*, June 1, 2011.

10. Stefan Chang, *Spreadtrum, No Panic Here* (Samsung Securities, 2011), 1.

11. Bill Lu, *Spreadtrum Communications Inc., Quick Comment: Concerns Look Overdone* (Morgan Stanley Research Asia/Pacific, 2011), 1.

12. Carson Block, *Sino-Forest Corporation* (Muddy Waters Research, 2011), 1.

13. Charles Stein, "Paulson Not Alone as 'Mistake' on Sino-Forest Hurts Davis Funds," Bloomberg, June 22, 2011.

14. Christopher Donville and Sungwoo Park, "Billionaire Chandler Lifts Sino-Forest Stake as Block Prompts Paulson Exit," Bloomberg, July 21, 2011.

15. Stein, "Paulson Not Alone."

16. Davis New York Venture Fund, www.davisfunds.com/funds/nyventure_fund.

17. Sakthi Prasad, "Greenberg's Starr Investments sues China MediaExpress," Reuters, March 22, 2011.

18. Ryan Vlastelica, "Analysis: Muddy Waters is 5-for-5 on China Short Calls," Reuters, June 6, 2011.

19. Reuters, "Spreadtrum Communications IPO Prices above Range," June 26, 2007.

20. Block, "Open Letter," 3.

21. Spreadtrum Communications Inc., *2008 Annual Report* (Form 20-F), 28.

22. Global Semiconductor Alliance, Semiconductor & Fabless Facts, www .gsaglobal.org/resources/ industrydata/facts.asp.

23. Vincent Gu, "China Fabless Market to Double in Size by 2015," iSuppli press release, May 30, 2011, www.isuppli.com.

24. Spreadtrum Communications Inc., "Spreadtrum Conference Call Presentation," June 29, 2011, 5.

25. Alex Gauna, *Spreadtrum Communications* (JMP Securities, 2010), 4.

26. Bi Mingxin, "Chinese Company Launches 40nm Chip," Xinhua News, January 20, 2011.

27. Stefan Chang and Emerson Chan, *Spreadtrum, A Positive Move* (Samsung Securities, 2011), 1.

28. *Schenck v. United States,* 249 U.S. 47 (1919), www.law.cornell.edu.

29. Bloomberg Television interview, June 30, 2011.

30. 《論語》[*The Analects of Confucius*], "為政第二" [Book 2], 17 [Passage 17].

Chapter 5

1. Hong Zhu and Ken Small, "Has Sarbanes-Oxley Led to a Chilling in the U.S. Cross-Listing Market?" *CPA Journal* (March 2007), www.cpajournal.com.

2. Professors Zhu and Small specifically cite William Reese, Jr., and Michael Weisbach, "Protection of Minority Shareholder Interest, Cross-Listings in the United States, and Subsequent Equity Offerings," *Journal of Financial Economics* 66 (1) (October 2002). Reese and Weisbach draw notably from Rafael La Porta, Florencio Lopez-de-Silanes, Andrei Shleifer, and Robert Vishny (a provocative economics research team that has written extensive about differing national legal traditions and equity market performance) and their "Legal Determinants of External Finance," *Journal of Finance* 52 (3) (July 1997) along with "Law and Finance," *Journal of Political Economy* 106 (6) (December 1998). From the realm of legal scholarship, the paper draws from arguments made by Columbia University Law School's John Coffee in his encyclopedic "The Future as History: The Prospects for Global Convergence in Corporate Governance and Its Implications," *Northwestern University Law Review* 93 (3) (Spring 1999).

3. Lilla Zuill, "Longtop Soars in US Debut, Year's Best from China," Reuters, October 24, 2007.

4. Public Company Accounting Oversight Board, *Auditor Considerations Regarding Using the Work of Other Auditors and Engaging Assistants from Outside the Firm*, Staff Audit Practice Alert No. 6 (July 12, 2010), 7.

5. Ibid., 3.

6. AU Section 543, "Part of Audit Performed by Other Independent Auditors," §.01, http://pcaobus.org/Standards/Auditing/Pages/default.aspx.

7. David Feldman and Steven Dresner, *Reverse Mergers: And Other Alternatives to Traditional IPOs*, 2nd ed. (New York: Bloomberg Press, 2009), 1.

8. Public Company Accounting Oversight Board, *Activity Summary and Audit Implications for Reverse Mergers Involving Companies from the China Region: January 1, 2007 through March 31, 2010*, Research Note 2011-P1, March 14, 2011.

9. Ibid., 3–6.

10. Luis Aguilar, "Facilitating Real Capital Formation," speech delivered to the Council of Institutional Investors Spring Meeting, April 4, 2011, www.sec.gov.

11. Ibid.

12. Ibid.

13. Block and Regan, *Orient Paper Inc.,* 1.

14. Bill Alpert and Leslie Norton, "Beware This Chinese Export," *Barron's*, August 28, 2010.

15. Cleantech Innovations, Inc., *Form 8-K*, filed January 20, 2011.

16. RINO International Corporation, *Form 8-KA*, filed November 29, 2010.

17. Joshua Gallu, "SEC Suspends Trades in Rino International Amid Fraud Allegations," Bloomberg, April 11, 2011.

18. Universal Travel Group, *Form 8-K*, filed April 14, 2011.

19. United States Securities and Exchange Commission, *Administrative Proceeding File No. 3–14167*, December 20, 2010.

20. Dennis Berman, "Congress and the SEC Hit Stocks Made in China," *Wall Street Journal*, December 20, 2010.

21. James Surowiecki, "Don't Enter the Dragon," *The New Yorker*, January 31, 2011.

22. Ryan Vlastelica and Daniel Bases, "Chinese Stock Scams are the Latest U.S. Import," Reuters, May 11, 2011.

23. The House View (Editorial), "Wheat from Chaff," *China Economic Review*, May 2011.

24. Aaron Task, "Invasion of the Chinese Reverse Mergers: 'We Are Under Attack' Josh Brown Says," *Daily Ticker*, May 20, 2011, http://finance.yahoo.com/blogs/daily-ticker

25. Walter Pavlo, "Fraud in Chinese Reverse Mergers on American Exchanges— And We're Surprised?" April 8, 2011, http://forbes.com/sites/walterpavlo

26. "NYSE–Archipelago Merger Goes to a Vote," *The Exchange* 12 (11) (November 2005), www.nyse.com/about/publication/1131536261135.html.

27. *Institutional Investor*, "The Adventures of Sperthain" (June 2006).

28. Yongye International, Inc., "Yongye International Announces Agreement Regarding $50 Million Equity Investment by Morgan Stanley Private Equity Asia," May 31, 2011.

29. Min Tang-Varner, *Yongye Reports Strong Second-Quarter Results, But Concerns About Morgan Stanley's Investment Linger*, Morningstar Equity Research, August 9, 2011.

Chapter 6

1. Lilla Zuill, "Longtop Soars in U.S. Debut, Year's Best from China," Reuters, October 24, 2007.

2. Ibid.

3. Carol Wang, *Longtop Financial Technologies Ltd.*, Morgan Stanley Research, July 30, 2010.

4. Andrew Left, *Citron Reports on Longtop Financial*, April 26, 2011, www.citronresearch.com.

5. 孔祥俊, 刘泽宇, 武建英 [Kong Xiangjun, Liu Zeyu, and Wu Jian Ying], 《反不正当竞争法: 原理规则案例》 [*Anti-Unfair Competition Law: Principle Rules Case Studies*], (北京: 清华大学出版社, 2006年 [Beijing: Tsinghua University Press, 2006]).

6. Longtop Financial Technologies Ltd., conference call, April 28, 2011.

7. Deloitte Touche Tohmatsu CPA Ltd., Longtop Financial Technologies independent auditor resignation letter, May 22, 2011 (per Longtop's Form 6-K filed with the SEC on May 23, 2011).

8. Ibid.

9. Ibid.

10. Longtop Financial Technologies Ltd., "Longtop Financial Technologies Limited Announces Resignation of Independent Auditor and Chief Financial Officer, Initiation of Independent Investigation, SEC Inquiry and COO Appointment," May 23, 2011.

11. Company website, About Longtop, "Introduction," http://en.longtop.com/news_info.aspx?cid=753.

12. Longtop Financial Technologies Limited, *Form 20-F* (annual report for the fiscal year ending March 31, 2010), July 15, 2010, 15.

13. Ibid., 24.

14. Floyd Norris, "The Audacity of Chinese Frauds," *New York Times*, May 26, 2011.

15. *Casablanca*, Warner Bros., 1942.

16. Wendy Zellner, Stephanie Anderson Forest, Emily Thornton, Peter Coy, Heather Timmons, Louis Lavelle, and David Henry, "The Fall of Enron," *Businessweek*, December 17, 2001.

17. Carol Graham, Robert Litan, and Sandip Sukhtankar, *The Bigger They Are, the Harder They Fall: An Estimate of the Costs of the Crisis in Corporate Governance*, Brookings Institute Working Paper, July 31, 2002, 2.

18. CRM data based on SEC figures and quoted in Jessica Holzer, "U.S. to Restart Talks on Inspecting Chinese Auditors," *Wall Street Journal*, July 7, 2011. IPO data compiled by Renaissance Capital.

19. U.S. Public Company Accounting Oversight Board, "Registered Firms Not Yet Inspected Even Though Four Years Have Passed Since Issuance of an Audit Report While Registered as of June 30, 2011."

20. U.S. Public Company Accounting Oversight Board, U.S. Securities and Exchange Commission, China Securities Regulatory Commission, and Chinese Ministry of Finance, "Chinese and U.S. Regulators Held Meeting in Beijing on Audit Oversight Cooperation," August 8, 2011.

21. Michael Rapoport, "Chinese Audit Regulators to Visit U.S.," *Wall Street Journal*, August 18, 2011.

22. Michael Rapoport, "Progress Cited on Audits in China," *Wall Street Journal*, August 9, 2011.

23. U.S. Securities & Exchange Commission, "SEC Files Subpoena Enforcement Action Against Deloitte & Touche in Shanghai," Litigation Release No. 22088, September 8, 2011.

24. Ibid., 5.

25. Ibid., 17–18.

26. Ibid., 14.

27. Ibid.

28. Ibid., 16.

29. Michael Rapaport, "U.S.-Chinese Progress on Accounting Is Dealt Setback," *Wall Street Journal*, October 4, 2011.

30. Andrea Shalal-Esa and Sarah N. Lynch, "Justice Department Probing Chinese Accounting," Reuters, September 29, 2011.

31. Anton Valukas, *Report of the Examiner in the Chapter 11 Proceedings of Lehman Brothers Holdings Inc.* (Chicago: Jenner & Block, 2010), 732.

32. Stephen Aldred and Don Durfee, "China Company Structure Under Threat," Reuters, September 18, 2011.

33. Shen Danyang, Ministry of Commerce Monthly News Briefing, September 20, 2011.

34. Dinny McMahon and Owen Fletcher, "China Studies Foreign IPOs," *Wall Street Journal*, September 21, 2011.

35. Alan Hellawell, Alex Yao, and Eva Leung, *The VIE: An Analysis of Motivations*, (Deutsche Bank, 2011), 2–3.

Chapter 7

1. Voltaire (François-Marie Arouet), *The Works of Voltaire: A Contemporary Version*, trans. William F. Fleming, critique and biography by John Morley (New York: E.R. DuMont, 1901), 176.

2. Mira Wilkins, *The History of Foreign Investment in the United States to 1914* (Cambridge, Mass.: Harvard University Press, 1989), 142.

3. Thomas Lee, *The Development of the American Public Accounting Profession: Scottish Chartered Accountants and the Early American Public Accountancy Profession* (Abingdon, UK: Routledge, 2006), 4.

4. Nathan Rosenberg and L. E. Birdzell Jr., *How the West Grew Rich: The Economic Transformation of the Industrial World* (New York: Basic Books, 1986), 226.

5. Voltaire, *Works*.

About the Author

Rob Koepp is an American writer, consultant, and business executive with an eclectic background in finance, economics, technology, and the liberal arts. Dividing his time among the United States, Europe, and Asia throughout his education and career, Rob began full-time work after college as an itinerant researcher on a Watson Fellowship where he studied the evolution of Chinese-based calligraphies in countries throughout East Asia.

Fluent in Chinese and Japanese (and sometimes known to be in possession of a passing command of English), Rob began regularly working in mainland China as a World Bank–sponsored researcher advising the Chinese government on technology-based regional development. He stayed on in the PRC to serve as the managing director at a Sino-foreign joint venture of the CITIC Group, China's largest financial conglomerate, and later as an advisor to foreign-based funds and corporations on their investment strategies in China. A graduate of Pomona College and Cambridge University, he currently resides in Beijing, where he works in financial and communications consulting.

Index